Tending the Garden:
A biography of Emeric & Rosemary Sala

Tending the Garden

A Biography of Emeric & Rosemary Sala

New Edition

Ilona Weinstein

ONE VOICE PRESS • ESSEX, MARYLAND

Tending the Garden: A Biography of Emeric and Rosemary Sala.
New Edition
Ilona Weinstein.

Copyright © 2016 by Ilona Weinstein.

All rights reserved. Except as permitted under U.S. Copyright Act of 1976, no part of this publication may be reproduced, distributed, or transmitted in any form or by any means, or stored in a database or retrieval system, without the prior written permission of the publisher.

All photographs courtesy of Ilona Weinstein.

The Bahá'í Writings copyright © Bahá'í International Community, various dates.

A Ten Year Crusade Diary for Southern Africa, edited by Lowell Johnson and Edith Johnson © The National Spiritual Assembly of the Bahá'ís of South Africa. Excerpts reproduced by kind permission of The National Spiritual Assembly of the Bahá'ís of South Africa.

Title page photograph © Revensis|Dreamstime.com

Published by One Voice Press, LLC
Essex, Maryland
www.onevoicepress.com

ISBN-13: 978-1-940135-46-5

Printed in Canada.

First Edition: July 2016
10 9 8 7 6 5 4 3 2 1

Table of Contents

Foreword — vii

Introduction — ix

From Old World to New — 15

Montreal — 24

The Maxwell Family — 56

St. Lambert—1930's, 1940's, & 1950's — 79

Africa and the Ten Year Crusade — 146

Africa—Shifting of Gears — 195

Montreal—Guadalajara — 216

The Beautiful Process of Detaching — 253

Final Journeys — 262

Endnotes — 269

Appendix A — 289

Appendix B — 291

Glossary — 311

FOREWORD

Many religious communities undergo transformative moments in their collective life. The Bahá'í community of Canada is no exception. *Tending the Garden* exemplifies through letters, papers, and archival documents the story of Rosemary and Emeric Sala. Their love for the Bahá'í Faith has transmuted their personal interests and temperaments into a long life of service to their fellow human beings and to the Bahá'í Faith itself.

What the editor-and-writer Ms. Ilona Weinstein presents us is a tale mostly adorned by the Salas' own words that inform us of both the mundane and the dramatic aspects of their lives. There is nothing that can distract the reader from anything that does not touch those transformative moments. The book has a collection of remembrances about the historic visit of 'Abdu'l-Bahá to America in 1912, and we hear about the "Montreal Youth Group" of the 1930s whose members were among the first to grasp the significance of the World Order of Bahá'u'lláh as a leaven for the world to cherish and develop.

Sometimes in greater or lesser detail, we follow the impact of the Bahá'í summer schools as they provide the spiritual, social, and educational nutrients of the Bahá'í community. *Tending the Garden* encompasses the broad sweep of the Ten-Year Crusade of the Guardian of the Bahá'í Faith which stimulated the Canadian Bahá'ís to set their vision to territories beyond their familiar ones. Like a pulsating vein, the Crusade allowed the Salas to match their love and dedication for the new religion to the requirements of an age that was beginning to be unmoored from its traditional anchors. Whether in South America or Africa, the Salas bent their will to the needs of the new age: forsaking nationalism, and embracing the vision of a unified humanity.

The Salas recount their personal victories as evidence of the guiding power of Shoghi Effendi, the Guardian of the Bahá'í Faith; their occasional misfortune in the field of service as yet another way a new door has been opened for them to render another moment of service. A blockage over here merely serves to divert one's energies to a higher goal over there. Their letters, papers, and archival documents move the reader between the routine facets of their lives to momentous ones. Surely, contemporary Bahá'ís will long to learn more of the heroism of the Salas.

—WILL C. VAN DEN HOONAARD

INTRODUCTION TO THE NEW EDITION

"To every generation of young believers comes an opportunity to make a contribution to the fortunes of humanity, unique to their time of life."[1]

One day in the spring of 1926, a youth noticed an ad in a newspaper. A few months later, a young woman saw a sign on a downtown building. Thus began the adventures of Emeric Sala, of Jewish background, born in the Austro-Hungarian Empire, and Rosemary Gillies, of Scots-Presbyterian heritage. Both were attracted by words to a new faith which they investigated and soon joined. This book attempts to show how these two members of an earlier generation, during the days of the Great Depression, and during the turmoil of World War II, took every possible opportunity to contribute to the fortunes of humanity. And how they would continue to do so for the rest of their lives.

The Bahá'í Faith, when this chronicle begins, was barely known in Canada with some 60 Bahá'ís[2] scattered between Montreal, Toronto and Vancouver. This newest of world religions had been founded by Bahá'u'lláh in Persia in the middle of the 19th century. He brought new teachings all revolving around the essential principle of the oneness of humanity. (At the end of the book you will find an appendix which outlines some specific teachings and a glossary of Bahá'í terms.)

In this new faith there is no clergy. All Bahá'ís are "teachers", sharing their beliefs with anyone who is interested, in a spirit that encourages questions and independent search. Bahá'ís in the 20th century struggled to inform people of the Faith's existence and, through a unique administrative system, to put its principles into practice. These were the dramatic days of the first Bahá'í speaker in province or state, the first Bahá'í to settle in a country or territory. Emeric and Rosemary tore up roots, traveled and moved to what seemed outlandish places.

My father Paul was Emeric's younger brother. As a child I saw my aunt and uncle often, especially during summers when they spent time at their cottage adjoining our farm in Rivière Beaudette, not far from Montreal. Rosemary would sit with me under a willow tree by the lake, as she told stories of 'Abdu'l-Bahá. Once, she copied some of these stories into a small red notebook which she gave me as a birthday present. When they moved to Africa, letters between us began to cross oceans, and this correspondence would continue until their deaths. In spite of my own moves and dislocations, I managed to keep most of their letters.

Words had led both Rosemary and Emeric to the Faith. Letters, articles, notes, a book, provided channels of expression throughout their lives. One day I found myself in their last home in Mexico, surrounded by boxes overflowing with letters and notebooks. Rosemary had recently died and Emeric urged me: "Go through the boxes and take what you want." I found copies of letters from Shoghi Effendi, others from Rúhíyyih Khánum, and the Maxwells; notebooks filled with stories of early believers and correspondence with Bahá'í friends.

Emeric died ten years later. Again there were boxes to go through. I found another treasure trove of articles, reports, letters and a book manuscript. As I pored through these fascinating documents, the desire grew to share their words.

In their marriage, Rosemary and Emeric brought two strong personalities and very different backgrounds together with a pair of distinct literary "voices". Yet the words of one seemed to complement the words of the other. Always they were a team. In *Tending the Garden*, I have "teamed" their words, using extracts and linking them together with short, explanatory notes. Emeric's writing has an analytic tone, tempered with humour. His informal autobiography provides much information, especially at the beginning of the book. In succeeding chapters, their experiences and impressions are woven together through selections from letters, reports, interviews and articles. Rosemary's "storyteller voice" comes from the notebooks of stories she used for her talks and from passages of many letters. I used their original words, unedited, sometimes with minor corrections of grammar and spelling to ease the flow.

Omissions are indicated by ellipses ... and explanatory additions by square brackets [ ]. It should be noted that the primary source material, currently in my personal collection, will be donated to the Canadian National Archives.

Among their contributions these are highlights: While World War II raged, Emeric wrote about the unifying vision of Bahá'u'lláh. The resulting book, *This Earth One Country,* served for many years as an introduction to the Faith. Later in South Africa, Rosemary set up a project that would closely link her with many African people; this, during the time when the country was shrouded by the racist system of apartheid.

Tending the Garden was first published in 1998. Even before that time, my daughter Elin kept saying, "You must cite your sources!" As a result, a few years ago I began going over the book and my files with a fine-tooth comb hunting for references. In the process, I found precious material to add. In this edition there are nine excerpts of letters from the Guardian, five from Rúhíyyih Khánum, five from May Maxwell, and three from Sutherland Maxwell. Furthermore, since the first edition the age of the internet has arrived, with emails rapidly replacing letter-writing. There were now emails to include, such as those from Robert Mazibuko. Robert was working on his own book and generously shared stories of his experiences with the Salas in South Africa. Two additional sources of new material were Will van den Hoonaard's *Origins of the Bahá'í Community of Canada, 1898-1948,* published in 1996, and *A Ten Year Crusade Diary for Southern Africa,* issued in 2002.

Years have passed since an ad in a newspaper and a sign on a door drew Emeric and Rosemary to the Bahá'í Faith. This newest of world faiths has grown to become the second most-widespread religion and among the fastest growing, with members found in every country and territory on earth. Activities to which all are welcome, center now in neighborhoods all over the world. Just as Rosemary and Emeric did years ago, young men and women are breaking new ground, nurturing sapling souls. Taking what opportunities they can to "make a contribution to the fortunes of humanity, unique to their time of life."

1

FROM OLD WORLD TO NEW

Emeric and Rosemary were born at the beginning of the twentieth century in two very different places: Rosemary in a town in Scotland, part of the British Empire, and Emeric in a small hamlet in the Austro-Hungarian Empire. Unfortunately, there is little information about Rosemary's childhood and youth. Emeric however, wrote an autobiography for the family, thus many details are available about his early years and his struggles to leave Europe.

I was born in 1906—the year of the great earthquake of San Francisco—in Dombrovitza, Hungary, then part of the Austro-Hungarian Empire. My father supervised a large forest exploitation. We were living at the head of a small specially built narrow-gauge railway line. My younger sister, Blanca, and brother Paul were also born there. My youngest brother Ernest was born in Herrmanstadt [now Sibiu, Romania, but at that time, Hungary].

When I was eight years old, we saw from our window a regiment of Hungarian Hussars riding to the railway station and from there to the Serbian front. They were dressed in red and blue uniforms, garlanded with flowers, accompanied by music and the cheers of hundreds of onlookers. When the gaiety of this spectacle had passed, I asked my mother with tears in my eyes why can't I go with them to war to defend my beloved fatherland. Up to the age of 13, I was a well-indoctrinated Hungarian patriot, convinced that there was no better country to live in than Hungary.

Then my father placed me in a German Gymnasium (high school), as German was the language of Central Europe, to broaden my education. Here I learned to my great surprise that German literature, art and science were superior to that of Hungary. In fact I came to believe that it was superior to that of any other country in the world.

When I was fifteen, [after the end of World War I] our part of Hungary became part of Romania and I had to enroll in a Romanian high school, without knowing the language. I was the only foreigner in a class of 18 Romanians. I had to get up at five in the morning and study until late at night to master the language and the subjects without losing a year. After three years among the Romanians I discovered that they sincerely believed that their literature, history and art are among the most outstanding in the world, and were willing to fight, and if necessary die, for their country.

By now I had enough of nationalism. I could feel and see the hatred between nations ... This deep-rooted separation I found not only among nations and ethnic groups, but also among religions. In my town there were Lutherans, Catholics and [Romanian] Orthodox, who disliked each other, and all three hated the Jews. I was a young idealist with great dreams for the future of mankind. Most idealistic Jews of my generation became Zionists. I could not share their feelings since I believed that the time for nation-building is over.

The future in my view belonged to an international community in which ethnic, national and religious loyalties are subordinated to a greater loyalty, including all mankind. I wanted to get out of Europe where the atmosphere was choking me. I wanted to go to the new world, America, the dream of my generation.

Leaving Home

My father had a very good position with an Austro-Hungarian corporation...until the collapse of the Empire, when he lost not only his livelihood but through devaluation his lifesavings; life insurance and other investments were not worth the paper they were written on. Unemployment insurance or social security of any kind did not exist then. In desperation my mother had to appeal to her oldest sister Ilka, whose husband, Armin Valko, was the only wealthy member in our family. This was the bitterest pill for my father to take.[2]·

Knowing that American immigration restrictions at this time were severe, and rejecting the next possibility, Canada, as too cold, Emeric decided on Australia as his goal. But how was he to get there?

He found a job as German-Romanian correspondent for a shipping company in Constanza on the Black Sea and spent his free time at the harbour seeking work on ships bound for Australia. He had no luck. He was competing with too many experienced sailors. At the British Consulate, the secretary suggested he go to Hamburg in Germany. From there he would have a better chance to attain his goal of Australia.

> I went back to Sibiu and applied for a passport. Since I was approaching the age of compulsory military service, I got one for six months only. My mother, to whom I felt very close, tried to persuade me to give up this reckless idea of going into the strange wide world without money, proper papers or friends. With my education, she said, I could make a comfortable living in Romania, and we would all remain together. I was however, determined to get out, and was willing to risk my life in the attempt. I was driven by an irresistible urge I could not and would not suppress.
>
> When I was about seventeen, I had read a book in Hungarian by a vegetarian who became healthy and strong by living on raw food. I was impressed and wanted to experiment on myself. ...While following this diet as closely as possible [in Constanza] I could save enough money to pay for my fare to Hamburg and room and board for a few months.
>
> I packed a small suitcase and said goodbye without knowing if and when I would see my family again. My mother could not come to the station. When the train pulled out only my father, with tears in his eyes, and Paul who was then sixteen, waved their hands and then their handkerchiefs.[3]

En route to Hamburg, Emeric visited relatives.

> It was fall. The train was winding its way through the foothills of the Carpathians, the leaves turning in the sunshine. I stopped in Bolesov, Czechoslovakia, where my maternal grandfather, Marcus Adler, lived with the Steiner family.
>
> The last time I had seen them was ten years before, when my grandmother [Johanna] was also alive. At that time, in 1916, we came as refugees to stay one year, as our part of Transylvania was being invaded ... and my father was in the Austro-Hungarian army. My grandparents had a country store, two cows and a few acres of land. They had no electricity. The streets were muddy and unpaved. I helped my grandfather gather walnuts from under a tree. Now, ten years later, he looked to me much older and weak,

while I must have appeared to him grown up and strong. When I left for the unknown, he blessed me and gave me a slice of bread with salt, in conformity with custom. I was not religious but was touched by the gesture.

My next stop was Berlin, where my mother had arranged that I visit her second cousin, Mr. Kutchera, the owner of the famous Kaffee WIEN on Kurfuerstendamm Strasse. He welcomed me in his luxurious office, arranged for a sumptuous meal, and then told me that in his youth he went to New York to find gold on the streets - just as I want to do now. But since he did not know English, all he could get was a job as dishwasher. When he got tired of it, he came back to Germany. "Now," he said, "look at me; I am living comfortable and prosperous." He was very skeptical about the outcome of my adventure. Nevertheless, he gave me three English pounds in gold coins for good luck.[4]

Hamburg

Arriving in the port city of Hamburg, Emeric rented a small room in a boarding house. When Mrs. Schroeder, his landlady, learned why he had come to Hamburg, she was not encouraging. There were many unemployed in Germany, including thousands of sailors also looking for work. The only chance, she told him, would be to find work on foreign ships.

There was a mustering place, run by a Herr Kraemer, to fill occasional vacancies on foreign ships. I came to the yard in front of his office where about 100 sailors, mostly German, were loitering from morning until evening, day after day, week after week, waiting for a vacancy. ... Since my decision, about a year before to emigrate to an English-speaking country, I studied English almost every day. In school, I had had to study [several] languages, but not English. My English was, therefore, self-taught. I could read and spell, but could not communicate. Nobody understood my pronunciation, nor could I understand others. For instance, I asked for breed, meaning bread. I knew that in heat 'ea' was pronounced as 'e'. I therefore assumed that in bread 'ea' is pronounced the same way. When I said labor, I pronounced 'a' the same as in harbor. I could not believe that the English could be that inconsistent and illogical. Later, I had to unlearn my English and learn to speak it again. Why did the English not choose another phonetic language as their own?

I presented myself with trepidation before Mr. Kraemer, a retired sailor with a limp in his walk. To register me he wanted to see my passport. He then asked me a few questions in English. The examination was passable but not satisfactory. Besides I was never on a ship before. Nevertheless, he registered me as a deck hand. ... And then I started to wait in that yard, mostly wet and damp like Hamburg in late fall, from morning to sunset, day after day, week after week and month after month. I wrote home every week. My mother suggested I come home. ... I would now take any ship, anywhere. Australia seemed far away.

I discovered the brand of cigar Mr. Kraemer was smoking. I found an opportunity to give him about two dozen. It was not his fault that nobody wanted a deck hand. Foreign ships hired their crew in their home port. Only occasionally a seaman got sick or was discharged, and needed replacement. My chances were slim. Mrs. Schroeder guessed from my hands and word structure that I was not a laborer or a sailor. She knew I wanted to get out of Europe, and sympathized with my hardships. Occasionally, she gave me a hot soup. My money and also my passport were inexorably running out.

And then after three months of hopeless but persistent waiting, a friend told me to be there next Sunday as there might be a vacancy for a deckhand. ... Mr. Kraemer came out of his office and was asking us this Sunday afternoon (there were only about two dozen present) for a deckhand. He asked me to come in. The officer looked at me and asked if I spoke English. I answered yes Sir, I do speak English. When Mr. Kraemer confirmed this I was hired at fifteen dollars per month on the SS BURUTU of the Ellster Dempster Line, sailing next day for West Africa which was malaria country.[5]

Hazardous Journey

I felt like [I was] in heaven, for I was on the way. The BURUTU was a 10,000 ton freighter, registered in Liverpool, carrying a mixed cargo and was to return with peanuts for the manufacture of margarine. My roommate in a small cabin was another deckhand, a Berliner, who had sailed before. We had no bed-linen. For three months I slept on a thin straw mattress, and covered myself with a cheap grey horsehair blanket, made of waste cotton, which I had bought in a store. ... My duties alternated with the other deckhand.

One week I had to bring our meals from the galley to the mess hall, wash all the dishes, scrub the floor and the table ... and wash the bathrooms. The next week I worked on deck with the bosun and three seamen, washing the decks, painting, greasing steel cables, delivering messages.

My plan now was to catch malaria while in Africa, get hospitalized and when recovered, sign on a ship headed for Australia, or at least in that direction.

Leaving the Elbe we entered a very rough North Sea and I was wretchedly seasick. Being on kitchen duty I had to serve the meals three times a day, sickness or no sickness. To make matters worse as we sailed west we entered a storm and we had to circle three nights and days before we could enter the port of Antwerp. I was so miserable that I would have welcomed falling overboard. For me life was not worth living. Finally after an eternity of suffering we reached port. I felt like having been reborn. I wrote home as I continued to write from almost every port.

Christmas Eve we were sailing south in the English Channel. Well after midnight a sailor—who was on watch—bursts into our quarters and shouts: "All men on deck. We have collided with another ship." We dress rapidly and run up on deck. The sea is relatively calm and the stars are shining. We had collided with a French sailing ship with eighty hands on board coming loaded from Africa, which sank in five minutes with all eighty men except four, who in the moment of collision jumped over onto our deck. We lowered two lifeboats, but they could not find any survivors. The front of our iron ship was slightly damaged, where we had hit the middle of the wooden boat. We limped into Freetown, England, for a week of repairs and official inquiry. I never found out the result of the inquiry. It had been a clear night, but, being Christmas, they might have drunk too much. The Frenchmen were at the end of a six month journey, one day short of home.

We were now in the Atlantic on the way to Tenerife. First thing in the morning, we had to wash the decks. The sailors had rubber boots, but I, poor deckhand, washed barefoot. As we moved south the water got warmer, and the task pleasanter.

One calm, sunny day we noticed smoke coming out of one of the hatches. On investigation, it was found that the ship was on fire. The coal bunker was burning. The sailors were swearing about the ship and this voyage. We then pumped seawater into the bunker for about three hours, until the ship was safe to continue its voyage.

Africa

We visited Sierra Leone. Accra on the Gold Coast (now Ghana) was a small town. Its only imposing building was the British governor's residence. I made friends with a young African and told him I would like to see an African jungle. He took me for a long walk through a forest, and when we came back at about six, it suddenly turned dark as it does in the tropics. A British official, dressed in white, approached us with a flashlight in hand, and scolded my companion and then hit him in the face. He told me that it was a rule that after dark he had to carry a light. Witnessing that treatment and the poverty around I lost sympathy for colonial empires. For an old, torn undergarment, or a few slices of white bread, we could get a large bunch of bananas or a couple of pineapples.

We sailed for about two weeks up the Niger, collecting peanuts. At one of our stops about six of our crew were invited to visit a tribal chief. We were taken in two dugout canoes through dense jungle for about two hours in narrow streams to his camp. He was taller than I, about 80, with grey hair, had ten wives and was called King George. Since I was the tallest in our group he gave me special attention. The heat made us perspire constantly. I told myself this is a good place to catch malaria.

Our last stop was Port Harcourt. Three sailors got malaria. I had to bring them food and water. ... I did not get sick, therefore I had to return to Hamburg. For three months work I had earned forty-five dollars. It made me feel rich. Besides I had a discharge paper, making me feel like a seasoned sailor.

But my passport had expired. No other ship would sign me on without a valid passport. I went to the Romanian Consulate and asked for an extension for six months. Since I was due to apply for military service, the consul was supposed to extend it only sufficiently for me to return to Romania. Through an oversight he signed it for six months and I felt ... in seventh heaven.[6]

2

MONTREAL

EMERIC, in Hamburg, Germany, was willing to take any ship, anywhere. He finally was able to sign onto the SS Cairngowan, bound for Canada.

Meanwhile, the Gillies family lived on tree-lined Jeanne-Mance Street in Montreal. Malcolm, a captain with the Anchor Donaldson Steamship Line and his wife Catherine had immigrated to Canada from Glasgow, Scotland in 1906 with their children, Helen, Margaret and Mary. Now, years later, in the spring of 1926, young Mary was teaching kindergarten. She could not know of the youth crossing the Atlantic on the SS Cairngowan. It would not be long before they would meet.

Emeric's account continues:

We would land either in Halifax or Montreal, depending on ice conditions in the St. Lawrence River early in May.

I was to wash the dishes and clean the officers' mess, which seemed to me like a palace compared to the primitive quarters on the SS BURUTU. I slept in a cabin with bedsheets. ... I ate together with the steward and chief steward who, as he knew me better, suspected that I will skip ship and told me so, but I pretended not to understand his English. At five every morning I had to take a cup of tea with two pieces of toast up to the officer on the bridge. When the sea was rough it was a difficult balancing act to hold it all, and myself, on the rails.

We moved through icefields, saw seals and icebergs, as we approached the American continent. The Captain entered the Gulf of St. Lawrence and proceeded to Montreal. More than a year had passed since I left Sibiu on my way to Australia. I had seen and traveled a lot but was now farther away from my goal than when I left home. Australia was ... far away not only in distance but also in my mind. I had two paramount objectives: survival and escape from Europe. If Canada was the way, so be it.

We arrived in the evening of May 6th, 1927, in the harbor of Montreal. The first thing I saw was the lighted cross on Mount Royal. The next day, after washing the lunch dishes, I had a shore leave of about four hours. After seeing Berlin, Hamburg, Antwerp and Rotterdam, Montreal appeared to me like a provincial barrack city. Its only modern office building was the Sun Life Building. ... There were no traffic lights. What I liked best was Mount Royal and I wanted to climb it at the first opportunity.

I bought the Montreal Daily Star for two cents and looked for rooms to rent. On Saturday I got an advance of five dollars as spending money and decided to desert the ship on May 13th, which I considered a lucky number. I left behind my small suitcase with my belongings. I also left a letter for the purser, cook and assistant cook, apologizing for any inconveniences, and assuring them that I had to take this step due to circumstances beyond my control.

I was wearing my winter coat and had $20 and the three English pounds in gold, which was worth $15, in my pocket. On the wharf were several large signs of warning that deserters of ships will be prosecuted, jailed and deported. I had no other alternative. I could not realize that because of this illegal act of mine I would save not only my own life but also the lives of my brothers, sister and parents. We all would have perished in the holocaust of Hitler, which was also illegal.[1]

First Months in Montreal

Emeric abandoned the Cairngowan, leaving behind his passport and few belongings. He knew not a single soul in the new city and he barely spoke English or French. He was legitimately afraid of being discovered as an illegal alien. Across the ocean were family, friends and all that was familiar. What he had was his strength of character, his self-discipline, the courage and hope of a 21-year old. His chronicle continues:

I took a room ... as far away from the harbour as possible, on St. Antoine Street, near the CPR tracks, for $2.50 per week. A black man was my neighbour with whom I shared the bath. Later I found out that the immigration office with its jail for detainees was on the same street. Until my ship left harbour I kept myself low, fearing encounters with crew members who might report me. Even after the ship sailed I kept away from policemen, having left my passport with picture and description with the purser; I feared it may have been circulated among them.

For reasons of economy I went back to my vegetarian diet, eating in my room mostly milk, cheese, dark bread, oranges, apples and bananas, and I felt well and happy. Since my funds were running out I had to find work. I stopped at every construction job and offered my services with no result.

Then I bought myself a pair of overalls and work shoes, and was employed on Bishop Street to carry bricks up a ladder to the second floor for 30 cents an hour, 10 hours a day. The third day, the owner and his son came to inspect the job, in riding boots and costume. By this time my movements were very slow, and looking at me they did not like what they saw. At one o'clock I was paid out and told not to come back Monday. I was fired. The next morning, Sunday, I could not get out of my bed. My back and shoulders were aching. I was glad I was fired, as otherwise I might have collapsed on the job.

After three days rest I felt strong enough to try for another job. ... I found work digging ditches with pick and shovel for the foundation of a building. As we dug deeper I thought I could hide from the eyes of the Swiss foreman. I could not keep up with the others. On the fourth day he moved me to an easier job, unloading and sorting lumber. Two more days and I was told there was no more work for me.

Since landing I bought the Montreal Star every day, partly to practice my English, but mainly to peruse the "Situations Wanted" column. I was looking for openings for an office boy, or hopefully, for a German stenographer or correspondent, which never appeared. I wrote dozens of letters listing my European experiences, to no avail.

Finally, a letter arrived from the Czechoslovak Manufacturer's Company, on St. Paul Street, that I should present myself for a job as office boy. It was an agency business run by an elegantly dressed bachelor from Prague. I would be the only employee at seven dollars per week. He dictated letters in German, I had to dust his samples—mostly glass and ceramics, clean the office and wash his car. My income was less than half that of a laborer but I didn't mind, since I was at the bottom of the ladder I wanted to climb. About 10 days later, while Mr. Mason was out, a customer phoned whom I did not understand. He hung up. The next day I was fired, because this important customer told my employer: "What kind of a stupid bloke do you employ who does not understand English."[2]

Eventually, Emeric was hired as a stenographer by another importing company.

Mr. Kuna dictated long letters in German to Prague, and short collection letters in English. He did not mind correcting my English letters which I had to rewrite. Since his English vocabulary was limited, within a few weeks I could transcribe his letters without the need of correction. There were three more employees in that office and warehouse which made life quite pleasant.³

As many newcomers to Canada did in those days, Emeric decided to change his surname. Szalavetz became Sala. He continued to read the newspaper every day. He was now searching for free lectures to improve his English language skills and one day he found a notice that would change his life.

As soon as my ship lifted anchor, I went to all advertised free lectures to hear and learn English. I even went to church services to hear the sermons. That is how one Sunday afternoon at four I went to hear a Bahá'í lecture in the Guy Block building on St. Catherine Street. There were about 15 well-dressed, middle aged or older Anglo-Saxons among whom I felt out of place. The speaker was George Spendlove. All I understood was that he was against nationalism and militarism, with which I agreed. On the way out I took a free pamphlet with me which contained the basic Bahá'í principles [see Appendix A]. Reading them in my room ... with the help of a dictionary I realized they were my own.⁴

A Speaker and A Book

Emeric kept going back to these lectures. One day, the speaker was May Maxwell. She was introduced by her daughter, Mary.

...a very distinguished and elegantly dressed lady was sitting in the speaker's chair. I was charmed by her radiance, and could not take my eyes from her face. Then, to my surprise, a beautiful young girl ... stood up to introduce the speaker. She spoke with great ease and confidence with opening remarks on the subject "Interracial Marriage". I was also amazed by the close and loving rapport which I felt between these two people, and thought that perhaps they were related to each other. Then the lady stood up. There was silence. She spoke and the atmosphere in that room gradually changed. Most of her words I could not understand, but I sat there spellbound, not wanting to miss a second of that unique and new experience. There was a tremendous love radiating from her, and I wanted a part of it for myself. She embodied to me the ideal Mother, and I was telling myself how fortunate the person who has a mother like her.

I left after the talk without speaking to anyone. I was and felt like a foreigner in that room. Not only because of the language, but I also felt the barrier of culture and class. ... It was only months later that I discovered that the beautiful lady was Mrs. May Maxwell, and her chairman was her daughter Mary, then seventeen years old.[5]

The next Sunday [while I was] looking at books, Mrs. Cowles, the librarian offered me Dr. Esslemont's *Bahá'u'lláh and the New Era*. I was very impressed that she trusted me, a total stranger, with a book. I read with great interest all I could with the help of my dictionary, and when I tried to return it the next Sunday, there was a notice on the door stating that the lecture series would reopen in October. Thus, I had three months at my disposal to study this Bahá'í book.

I was happy in my tiny basement room. It was no larger than a ship's cabin. It had a cot, a kitchen chair and a small table. It had no closet, but then I had no clothes either. A bare bulb hung from the ceiling. There was a small window facing the entrance stairs, giving some light but not enough for reading. Next door was the laundry room where I could shave and wash.

Reading in this room for the first time about the suffering, exile and imprisonment of Bahá'u'lláh, I felt guilty about my comfort. Compared to the torture, humiliation and execution of so many of the early Bahá'ís my life was easy. The deeper I got into this book the more I liked it. I felt that here was something worthwhile to hold on to. I felt spiritually at home, although at that time I would not have used the word "spiritual."[6]

Bahá'u'lláh was the prophet-founder of this new faith. Reading about 'Abdu'l-Bahá, Bahá'u'lláh's eldest son, Emeric realized that he had heard of Him some years before.

When I was sixteen years old, my best friend told me that he had read in a German newspaper that a wise man died in Palestine who believed in the same things as I did: a world peace, a world government, a world religion. But he could not tell me his name. I told him that I would like the clipping, but he could not find it anymore. [Now from Esslemont's book] I found out it was in 1921 that Abdu'l-Bahá had passed away and that newspapers reported it all over the world.[7]

By now Emeric had finished reading *Bahá'u'lláh and the New Era* and as he said in an interview a few months before his death:

> I felt in my own heart that that is where I belonged, there is my home. I was not fully reconciled with God. I came as an agnostic and therefore it was difficult for me to accept Bahá'u'lláh as a messenger of God. But May Maxwell and Mary Maxwell both helped me to get over that hurdle. From September - October I felt myself a follower.[8]

Emeric was attracted as well to the Bahá'ís themselves. He found among them a space of welcome for newcomers from other cultures as he stated in this excerpt from a video interview by his nephew Rick Sala:

> In the Bahá'í community I felt there was no anti-Semitism. As any other member of a minority, I was sensitive to discrimination. Any people senses if another group considers itself superior. Canadian Anglophone society at that time was democratic, liberal, educated. They never said insulting words expressing anti-Semitism, but it was there. One could see it in the eyes, sense it in body language. Among the Bahá'ís, however, I did not feel this. To me, this was one of the proofs that the Bahá'í Faith was genuine. It brought together people who were very different, and made of them genuine brothers. I had formulated these ideas of brotherhood intellectually; here I saw them in practice.[9]

Emeric by now must have considered himself a Bahá'í. The process of enrollment in those early days in Canada had not yet been formalized. One day, when Emeric decided that he wished to contribute to the Bahá'í Fund, he came across a stumbling block. Only Bahá'ís are permitted to contribute to the Bahá'í fund.

> In December, I gave a check of $2.00 to Ernest Harrison [treasurer] as a contri-

bution to the Faith. He said, "I am not supposed to take it because you are not on our list." A week or so later he let me know he did bring up my name, I assume in the Local Spiritual Assembly, and they accepted me, and accepted the check, and he wrote a beautiful letter of acceptance. It was different then in 1927. People came to the meetings, some thought they were Bahá'ís, some didn't.[10]

Ernest Harrison wrote this beautiful letter to Emeric. In it, aspects of contributing to the Bahá'í Fund are clarified:

> Dear Brother,
> Until I had first brought your request before the Local Spiritual Assembly, desirous of being considered a BELIEVER, no Bahá'ís would ever accept or permit me as Treasurer to accept one cent from you, or from anyone but a believer, for the Cause. I hope this is now understood. I was very happy to place before them your verbal declaration and really there was no need for me to say very much - they all realized that you were at heart a believer and wished to be heart and soul in the Cause, so that just as soon as I voiced it they agreed.
> Your letter was not placed before the Spiritual Assembly nor was the amount of your cheque - that is a matter of confidence between the Treasurer and each contributor – only the total on hand at the bank is reported to the believers. Each individual contribution is a matter between him and God and is not made public by the Treasurer.
> Your Baha'i brother
> E. V. Harrison[11]

With no clergy, no equivalent of rabbi, priest, or mulla, the Bahá'í community is administered at a local level by freely elected councils called Local Spiritual Assemblies. The same system operates at the national and international levels. The Local Spiritual Assembly of Montreal, the first in Canada, was founded in 1922.

In those early days, there was not yet an elected leadership internationally. A young man only thirty years old headed the Bahá'í Faith. 'Abdu'l-Bahá had appointed Shoghi Effendi, His eldest grandson, to lead the Faith following His passing. Shoghi Effendi, known as the Guardian, guided the Bahá'ís, in part, through his many letters.

Shortly after enrolling, Emeric wrote Shoghi Effendi a letter. Here is a section of the reply:

March 7, 1928
My dear co-worker:
I wish you from all my heart the fullest success in your efforts to teach and spread our beloved Cause, and trust that you may some day undertake the pilgrimage to the Holy Land and visit the Bahá'í sacred Shrines and there obtain a clearer vision of the mission and significance of the Faith.
Your true brother, Shoghi[12]

It Began With A Dream

I will now pick up the threads of Rosemary's story. I wish she had written about her early years in the Gillies household. She was an unusual young woman for those times. Although suitors were available, she did not marry early. Rosemary longed to become an architect. In the 1920s, only Columbia University in New York City would accept women as students in that field. Her parents would not allow her to move so far from home. She decided instead to become a teacher, graduating from Macdonald College, outside of Montreal. Soon she was teaching kindergarten in an inner city school. Having a profession gave her independence, with a mind open to new ideas. Photographs show her with her hair in the fashionable 'bob' of the times seated at the wheel of a car.

Rosemary tells of her first encounter as a child with the Bahá'í Faith describing a childhood dream.

> I had a dream about 'Abdu'l-Bahá. I dreamed I was in a foreign country ... I was in the shadows, very timid and afraid to have found myself in such a strange place. I was terrified and so cold. Then, I saw a bright light come along the road, and this Figure walking. He looked at me, and with His eyes, He drew me out of that dark, cold cavern, into the sunlight. I realized years later that it was 'Abdu'l-Bahá. I was a child at the time.[13]

In 1912, 'Abdu'l-Bahá travelled for several months through North America, with Montreal the sole Canadian city on His itinerary. Although we have no way of knowing if Rosemary's dream occurred at that time, there nevertheless was a Gillies family connection to His visit. Rosemary's mother had an opportunity to hear 'Abdu'l-Bahá speak. Rosemary continues:

One day in September, 1912, our doctor who was also a family friend, and was very interested in esoteric movements, came to visit. He told my mother that this wonderful person who came from Persia was visiting the Maxwells and he had been invited to their home to hear him, and wouldn't Mother like to go? She rather hesitated, her Scotch Presbyterianism and her love for Christ coming before her - and she said no.
Then he said, "Well, won't you come in my carriage and we'll drive past the house and perhaps see him walking outside." Again, she refused. She told me this years afterwards when I had become a Bahá'í, that she had had this opportunity, and perhaps she had made a mistake in not agreeing to his request.[14]

Rosemary's first visit to the Maxwell home was not promising. One of her friends suggested they go to a youth group that was meeting that evening. They were curious about the group, and the daughter, Mary Maxwell, who was considered an "unusual teenager".

But Edith and myself (Edith became a missionary later to China) we decided that they were just a little bit too fluttery for us. That was my first entrance into the Maxwell house... But I remember Mr. Maxwell and Mrs. Maxwell being very kind and very hospitable.[15]

Bahá'í Youth Group

Sometime later, Rosemary and a friend, heading to the movies, became sidetracked:

One evening en route to the movies with a friend from Newfoundland, we got off the streetcar and walked down Union Avenue when I saw Bahá'í Hall. I suggested we go there rather than the movies, and we did. It was in the fall ... I remember I was wearing a coat and hat that I felt a little warm in. We sat down, and I saw Rowland Estall, George Spendlove who was the leader, and Emeric Sala, who could hardly speak English.

When I looked at Emeric a voice said to me, "This is the man you're going to marry." I was rather indignant at this; I had sentimental feelings towards someone else at the time, and here was someone who couldn't speak English! But I was so captivated by the manners of these three young men who of course were delighted to see a new fish swim into their pool. I went back again and again and again.[16]

That eventful evening, Rosemary had stumbled upon a meeting of the new Montreal Youth Group. Earlier that year, Emeric had met Rowland Estall, also a recent Bahá'í, who had just returned to Montreal from his summer job as wireless operator on ships in the St. Lawrence River. Together they teamed up with George Spendlove, who had become a Bahá'í in the Maxwell home following his years serving in the First World War.[17]

Here is Emeric's version of how the Youth Group began.

Rowland Estall and I felt very strongly that our Faith was not growing in Canada as fast as it should. We felt that our only hope was with young people. We both had youth and enthusiasm with no experience and little knowledge. We asked George Spendlove, who was nine years older, to join us and with the assistance and encouragement of Mrs. Elizabeth Greenleaf [a Bahá'í who had come from the United States to assist the growing Bahá'í community in Montreal] we obtained permission from the Montreal Local Spiritual Assembly to hold a weekly study class - for youth only - at the Bahá'í Hall ... We have never read of any similar Bahá'í youth activity anywhere else in the Bahá'í world prior to 1927.[18]

From a biography of the Maxwell family of Montreal published in 2012, we learn that May Maxwell was a force behind the scenes. "She loved them; she encouraged them; she even indulged them. At times she also admonished them."[19]

One of Shoghi Effendi's letters had a profound impact on the young Bahá'ís of Montreal. Rowland Estall had written to the Guardian about the youth group and in the Guardian's reply was this sentence:

"I urge them to study profoundly the revealed utterances of Bahá'u'lláh and the discourses of 'Abdu'l-Bahá and not to rely unduly on the representation and interpretation of the Teachings given by the Bahá'í speakers and teachers"[20]

Emeric reflects on the Guardian's letter:

This surprising statement of Shoghi Effendi confirmed our feeling that we were at the threshhold of a change. We felt that a new wind was blowing, and did not want to mix it with the old. In my own life the above statement left an abiding impression, and I have ever since listened to every fellow Bahá'í's written or oral statement with the above reservation.[21]

Since we invited many non-Bahá'í young speakers often to share the platform with a Bahá'í youth, this feature attracted many new young people and our attendance grew until by 1931 we had an overflowing audience of up to sixty-five. As we were in the Depression the predominant questions were along economic and social lines. ... Rather than lose control of such large audiences, our Youth Committee decided in the Fall of 1931 to have henceforth only Bahá'í speakers on our platform with the purpose of direct teaching of the Faith. Those [guests] who were more responsive we took to meet Mrs. Maxwell, and many we invited to the Friday night deepening classes which were for old and young alike. Freddie Schopflocher invited many of us to his Sunday morning brunches. We had many Sunday picnics at the Back River... We held many anniversaries and parties in the Maxwell and Schopflocher homes. About this time the number of young Bahá'ís increased from three to nineteen.[22]

Emeric sent a report on the Youth Group's activities to the Guardian. Here was Shoghi Effendi's response, written on his behalf:

Haifa, Palestine,
1-4-32
Shoghi Effendi was very glad to read and obtain first hand information

as to the way the young people in Montreal have succeeded to attract many souls and inspire them with the spirit of service to our beloved Faith. Once the youth learns that this Cause is their Cause, and that through it they can ensure their future social tranquility and spiritual progress, then they will arise and consecrate their life to the promotion of this Faith. And as you clearly state in your report, no one can awaken the youth of the world to a consciousness of this road to salvation except from their own numbers – youths already inspired with the Bahá'í spirit.[23]

Today I see the twenty-first century youth of Montreal, working energetically with groups of neighbourhood children and young teens, providing leadership as Local Spiritual Assembly members, as coordinators of island-wide activities, even serving on provincial organizing bodies. There is a link back to that first audacious youth group of Montreal. They have learned well "that this Cause is also their Cause."

Within a year of encountering the Montreal Youth Group, Rosemary joined the Faith. There had been some hesitation in inviting her, as Emeric's friend, Rowland Estall describes:

Neither Emeric or I had had any experience of enrolling anyone in the Faith, but one day, in discussing it together, we decided it was high time that Rosemary should be given the opportunity to declare herself. We were not entirely sure of her reaction and so, neither of us wishing to bell the cat, so to speak, we tossed for it. I won, and invited Rosemary to become a Bahá'í. She simply wondered why we had waited so long to ask her.[24]

Rosemary describes her first visit to Green Acre, the Bahá'í School in Eliot, Maine.

George Spendlove took me to Green Acre, and that was a tremendous experience. There was a gift shop at that time, and he was in charge of it, so he asked me if I would go down with him and help him look after it. My parents were in Europe and I asked Helen, my sister, if she had any objections to my going. She said no, she was so busy studying for her McGill exams that it didn't interest her. That was how I got plunged into Green Acre, and that of course was a real plowing up. One day I'd be floating on cloud nine, and the next day I'd be grubbing in the earth – the soul going through this process.[25]

Siegfried (Fred) Schopflocher was an industrialist who had been born into a Jewish family in Germany. He came to Montreal as a young man, eventually developing a manufacturing process for bronze powder. He played an important role in the life of the Bahá'í community, and in the lives of Rosemary and Emeric. Rosemary recalls:

> He was so sweet to me as a young Bahá'í. I was brought up in a very church-oriented home. You know on Sundays one went to church three times a day. Then I became a Bahá'í and it was rather difficult. He was so sweet and he used to invite me to his home for brunch. ... Emeric was sometimes there and other young people. ... Freddie would talk about the Guardian. He had beautiful music and all the Bahá'í books. It was a perfect haven for me.
>
> After our brunch we'd go down to the Bahá'í Center for the meeting at three o'clock in the afternoon. If it was raining, we took a taxi, but if it was not raining, we all came down by streetcar. This again was wonderful; he gave us a lesson in economy. He was a very wealthy man; he didn't give indiscriminately to charity. Once he became a Bahá'í, the Bahá'í Faith was his charity. He would give individually to people we don't know about who were in straits and difficulties but his whole devotion went to the Faith.[26]

Rowland Estall was a master storyteller and would hold audiences spellbound with his tales of these early days. In his irrepressible manner, Rowland would recall the beautiful Mary Maxwell, and how all the young men in the Montreal community were captivated by her. Emeric would have been one of these, perhaps wavering in his feelings between her and Rosemary. No one could know of Mary Maxwell's special destiny.

Another example of caution and reticence on the part of Emeric and Rowland concerned a young man from England, David Hofman.

> It was Mrs. Bolles [sister-in-law of May Maxwell] who meeting David Hofman then a contact only ...walking with Rowland and Emeric, invited him to a meeting commemorating the martyrdom of the Bab. The two Bahá'ís were sure that this would

be the worst possible approach to one of David's intellectual brilliance and hoped he would not come - He came late just as Mary [Maxwell] had begun to speak. Then he left immediately after the talk; Rowland and Emeric were in agony, sure that their contact was lost forever! About a week later, David phoned Rowland to say that he was so deeply moved that he had had to leave![27]

David Hofman soon joined the Bahá'í Faith. Some thirty years later, in 1963, he was elected to the Universal House of Justice, the chief governing body of the Bahá'ís of the world.

Emeric and Rosemary's friendship developed in the early 1930s, though we know few details. May Maxwell, ever-perceptive, wrote to Emeric of a dream she had had. Did she have a premonition? Was she aware that in the Jewish faith, the wedding ceremony takes place under a special canopy called a chuppah, symbolizing the home the couple will build together?

May 10, 1933

Emeric – I cannot go to sleep without writing you this line. Last night I dreamed of you – or should I say I saw you in the world of reality – so strong so young – with that strange power around you which has had so deep an effect upon my life. You were with Rosemary under a kind of canopy beneath a clear blue sky – and she took your hand and said, 'Come' and as you arose to go with her you turned and looked at me.

You have both become so rare and beautiful – and oh! – so dear to me!

Ever in His path

May M.[28]

Emeric writes:

Rosemary Gillies came from a strict Scots-Presbyterian home. Her father ran away from home at fifteen and hired himself on a sailing ship. Later as captain he was transferred from Scotland with wife and three daughters to Montreal as ship's superintendent. ... As a member of our Youth Group, Rosemary became a Bahá'í ... She was a sweet and lovely girl, and among her many admirers she had four serious contenders. Her parents and relatives would have preferred any of the other three, not only because of their more desirable background, but also because I had no funds. Rosemary, however, remained steadfast and loyal to me to the end.[29]

But before thinking of marriage, there were some practical matters for Emeric to consider. Though he was now working for a wealthy manufacturer, his employment struggles continued.

Mr. Reinblatt had just returned from Europe with many agencies which he wanted to develop. Most Czechoslovak and Austrian manufacturers corresponded only in German which he could not speak. He hired me at $17.50 per week, and I saw a greater opportunity. We sold tie silk from Austria, woolens and linen from Czechoslovakia, felt from Poland, lace from Belgium and velvet from France. We were just starting when the crash of 1929 depressed all business.

The crash was followed by the great depression of the 1930's. Reinblatt was heavily hit. Business was sinking, unemployment was skyrocketing. ... To earn my salary I volunteered to go out selling. I sold rayon tie silk material, ladies woolen coating, and buttons to manufacturers.

I kept my job.

One day, Nick Szalavitz, my second cousin, a bon vivant whom I had not met before, came to visit me from New York. Looking at my family pictures, he saw a photo of my sister, Blanca, and said that this was the girl he was going to marry. I took it for a joke. Some time later I was informed in a letter from home that they were engaged to be married. I mailed them my savings for a wedding present, thus contributed to their fare to America. ... In 1931, their only child Norma was born.[30]

One of Emeric's pressing goals was to convert his illegal alien status to Canadian citizen. Emeric writes:

Mrs. Elizabeth Greenleaf, the renowned Bahá'í teacher, through whose intervention we obtained permission from the Montreal Assembly to hold our Youth meetings in the Bahá'í Hall on Union Avenue ... was very close to me. She was the first Bahá'í and also the first person in Canada, to whom I told very confidentially that I was illegally in the country. ... She arranged an appointment [with a lawyer friend of hers] and assured me that I could fully trust him. He was an imposing figure with white hair and beard. After hearing my story, he said to come back in 10 days; in the meantime he would inquire at the Immigration Department in Ottawa, without giving my name as to what would be best to do. When I returned he told me to do nothing, keep quiet and wait. About a year later, I asked another lawyer ... and got the same answer. This meant there was no way to get an exception in my case.

Reinblatt was now taking advantage of me. I earned my salary of twenty dollars, I felt, in the office. Besides I went out selling, for which he refused to pay me a commission. One day, I gave him an ultimatum: twenty five dollars or I would quit. He let me go. I did not look for anymore desk jobs. I saw my future in selling. My next job was with the Fuller Brush Company, selling from house to house. I did not earn much, but it provided an excellent training in selling, and in breaking my shyness of meeting strangers.[31]

Rosemary provides some context:

While cooking breakfast this morning, I thought of Emeric's struggles when he first came to Canada and thought I should write of them. Part of his nervous reactions and outbursts sprang from that time; though like his brothers Paul and Ernest, he was always a Hungarian in temperament and a Sala!

In Europe he was the eldest son with the certain authority of respect accorded to that station. He arrived in Canada, poorly dressed to the standard of the time, with no English, desperately shy, feeling alienated as a foreigner. He poured out his loneliness in letters to his mother and was assuaged by her loving replies. He carried bricks up a ladder for a building company and was sworn at for clumsiness; he washed dishes in the kitchen of the Queen's Hotel, lower Windsor Street. When we were engaged, he took me to dinner there, (it was a good hotel at that time, convenient to the station for travelers). The doorman, major domo, was his onetime companion in the kitchen!

Then he became a Fuller-brush man. ... To his shock, one day, Mrs. Cowles, a Bahá'í, answered the door - by this time he had found the Bahá'ís. His embarrassment was acute but she was kind and invited him in for tea but had no money to buy brushes.

His dream had been to go to college or become an air-pilot, but the urgency of the European situation and his longing to rescue his family drove him into business. Like your father, business was not his forte, he did it because it had become his skill, though even as late as our stay in Port Elizabeth, he had to conquer this shyness in his salesmanship.³²

In the early 1930s, Emeric had finally saved enough money and acquired the confidence to take a first step into business for himself.

I decided to start my own business as foreign manufacturers' representative. I had a savings of about one hundred dollars. First, I had to have a name. I submitted to Rosemary a list of five names, and she chose the one I liked also best, Transatlantic Agencies Company. I registered it in the City Hall, giving my boarding house address and telephone number. My next expense was the printing of letterheads, envelopes and the purchase of a secondhand typewriter ... Mornings and some afternoons I continued selling on commission to cover my daily expenses. The rest of the time, except when I had Bahá'í commitments, I wrote hundreds of letters, asking for samples, price lists and agency contracts.

After eight months of hard work Transatlantic received its first commission cheque of twenty eight dollars. This did not discourage me, as I was on my own. The second year I had enough lines to keep me busy ... Before the end of the year, I had my own office in Fred Schopflocher's office building ... and my own telephone. Soon after I hired a stenographer for mornings only.³³

Citizenship

It was 1933. Emeric's illegal status loomed while at the same time he was engaged to be married and the owner of a new business.

Rosemary's brother-in-law, Dr. Rolland Kennedy, had a good friend Mr. Gabouri, a French-Canadian lawyer, and he arranged an appointment for me. Mr. Gabouri checked again with the Immigration Department and then asked me to write the story of my life, the reason why I had come to Canada, and to collect as many character references as I could. I got one from Mr. W.S. Maxwell, President of the Canadian Architects Association, designer and president of the Montreal Arts Museum; one from Mr. Fred Schopflocher,

Vice-President of the Canadian Bronze Powder Works; one from Captain Malcolm Gillies, one from Dr. R. Kennedy, another from Dr. Charles Johnson, another brother-in-law to-be, and one or two more. When I brought these to Gabouri with a rough draft of my life's story, I thought he would edit my draft and correct my English, but instead he took it as is – considering it more genuine – and mailed it all to the Immigration Department in Montreal, which, according to law, issued a deportation order and mailed it all to the minister in Ottawa for a final decision.

A few weeks later, I found a letter in my box from the Immigration Department. I opened it with trembling hands. It was very short. All it said was that referring to such and such a letter the application had been rejected by the Minister.

My heart stopped beating, and I must have turned white. My world had come to an end. All my struggle was for nothing. I phoned Mr. Gabouri. He was very surprised, and said he would ask for an explanation, and would phone me back. After about ten minutes of desperation he phoned to tell me that not my application but the application for my deportation has been rejected by the Minister. Therefore I was free, and could apply for naturalization and a passport. Never before or since have I travelled in such a short period from the darkest pit in hell to the seventh heaven.[34]

Shadows of War

Emeric's goals of Canadian citizenship and financial stability were realized, but new challenges remained. He foresaw another war. His father and mother and two brothers remained in Europe and he was anxious to bring them all to Canada. At the end of 1933, he travelled to Europe on business and to see his family.

My mother was very conscious of family. Although they all lived in the Old Hungary [the extended family lived in Hungarian sections of Romania, and Czechoslovakia as well as in Hungary itself], distances, measured in train-time, was for them very far. They did not see each other, often for periods of ten years or more. Instead contact was maintained by regular correspondence. My mother shared with us news she received from her sisters and brothers, and although we did not see all our various cousins and other relatives, they were engraved very deeply in our consciousness.

I told a cousin of mine to pack up and leave Europe before it is too late. He laughed at me. He and his wife were later exterminated in the Holocaust. I told it to others but they would not believe me. If I had told them that my authority was 'Abdu'l-Bahá, it would have meant nothing to them.[35]

'Abdu'l-Bahá, in 1920, had written these prophetic words: "The ills from which the world now suffers will multiply; the gloom which envelops it will deepen. The Balkans will remain discontented. Its restlessness will increase. The vanquished Powers will continue to agitate. They will resort to every measure that may rekindle the flame of war."[36]

From a letter on behalf of Shoghi Effendi, we learn that Emeric had written him about meeting Bahá'ís in Vienna.

November 13, 1933
…He thoroughly appreciates the opportunity you have been given to visit some of the important Bahá'í centers in Europe and particularly Vienna where the friends are growing both in number and influence.

… He has always advised and even urged the friends to emphasize in their Bahá'í activities the necessity of strengthening, through correspondence and particularly by means of frequent and warm visits, the bonds of cooperation and amity between various Bahá'í centers and groups. This, he feels, is an essential step towards the further extension and consolidation of the New World Order.[37]

And in Shoghi Effendi's own words:

I wish to add a few words in person in order to confirm my deep sense of appreciation of what you have done and are still doing in the service of our beloved Faith in Europe. If you could arrange to visit some of the groups in the Balkans, such as Sofia, Tirana, Budapest and Belgrade, there is no doubt that the friends in these centres will feel greatly stimulated and grateful. Miss Root, Miss Jack and Mrs. Gregory are very active in these regions.[38]

Emeric was able to respond to the Guardian's request in a small way.

On reading the biography of one of the first Bahá'ís of Hungary, Emeric recalled that he had met her in Budapest on another trip in 1937, with his young cousin, Pista:

> I just finished reading "Rebirth" by Renee Szanto-Felbermann. ... In 1937, on my way to Haifa, I phoned her and arranged to meet in a Budapest coffeehouse. My 10 year old cousin (who died in the Holocaust) asked me how will I recognize her since it is a very large coffeehouse. I said 'Don't worry. Bahá'ís have a special light in their eyes.' He took me very seriously. When we arrived there were about 60 people sitting around. On entering I saw a young lady sitting alone, looking at me since she was obviously waiting for somebody. I looked at her. She kept on looking at me. I proceeded toward her and she still looked at me. It was Renee Felbermann. For my cousin it was a miracle."[37]

Also in 1937, Emeric visited Sofia, Bulgaria. We do not know if he ever went to Tirana or Belgrade. One of his last wishes, before his death, was to visit the emerging Bahá'í communities in Romania and Hungary.

Emeric's description of the 1933 trip to Europe continues:

> I visited Aunt Natalie in Budapest, the youngest sister of my mother. She lived above their store with her husband Jeno Bolgar and their son, Pista, who had been born deaf. He was highly intelligent; he could read our lips when we spoke in Hungarian. ...He knew Budapest well and took me around on my business errands.
>
> From among our mother's seven brothers and sisters, we felt closest to Natalie. While my father was in the First World War, I was ten, I saw my mother taken away in an ambulance, ill with typhus. We four children were left like orphans under the care of the young maid until Aunt Natalie arrived. She was like our guardian angel ever since. ... When she entered a room she brought sunshine with her.
>
> I discussed with her, as I did with every other relative when the opportunity arose, the possibility of their leaving Europe, which in my eyes was a powder keg. She answered with anxiety in her eyes that Pista could not learn with his handicap another language. Therefore his and their place would have to remain Hungary.
>
> Returning home after seven years absence was a great experience. ... I obtained my parents approval to marry Rosemary which I required according to Bahá'í law. My

next obsession was to bring my brothers out, and then my parents. There were only two obstacles, money and visas, both very hard to get.⁴⁰

Marriage

On June 27, 1934, Rosemary and Emeric were married twice. First by a Presbyterian minister in the Gillies home, and then on the same day in the Schopflocher home, the simple Bahá'í ceremony. In those days the province of Quebec did not recognize Bahá'í marriages as legal, thus the reason for two ceremonies.

What did Adolf and Charlotte, being observant Jews, think of their son's conversion to another faith, and furthermore of his engagement to a "gentile"? When, in later years, I questioned family members, none felt this had been a major issue. Malcolm and Catherine Gillies might also have had reservations, yet they too accepted their daughter's conversion and marriage. This parental consent on both sides would have a positive impact on the extended family, paving the way for intercultural and interreligious marriages to follow. I wonder though, if the two sets of parents, Szalavetz and Gillies, ever meet?

May Maxwell was delighted with the marriage, and wrote to Emeric, regretting that she could not attend:

> June 9, 1934
> You are too close to me not to understand my deep disappointment in not being with you and Rosemary on the day of your marriage. I shall see you two glorious young people in the ranks of Shoghi Effendi standing with your faces uplifted to the light of the future, the hope, the promise, and the strength of our sacred Faith.⁴¹

In a separate letter to Rosemary May Maxwell again expressed her pain at not attending the wedding, "for very deep reasons in the Cause related to my work over which I have no control…" She continued with these insightful words about the youth, words that could be used today:

June 9, 1934.
Oh Rosemary, sometimes I think that vision is given only to the youth, that, as Helen Bishop wrote from Haifa, the Guardian's great hope lies in your generation, unveiled by ancient prejudices in the Cause, untrammeled by our early habits and tendencies, free from personalities, dogma and strife....
...my whole heart's love to you, our precious beautiful Bride.⁴²

Rosemary and Emeric moved to a house on Riverside Drive in St. Lambert, across the river from Montreal. According to Will van den Hoonaard, Rosemary and Emeric were "perhaps the first homefront pioneers in Canada"⁴³, moving to another locality to help expand the Faith. Here they held community firesides in their home.⁴⁴ In 1938, the fourth Local Spiritual Assembly of Canada was formed in St. Lambert.⁴⁵

In the late 1930s, as the world drifted relentlessly towards another war, Emeric continued his efforts to bring his family from Eastern Europe to Canada. This was difficult. Canada was not the multicultural nation it is today; anti-Semitism and racism were widespread. In the ten years from 1935 to 1945, fewer than 5000 Jews were accepted into this country although hundreds of thousands applied, desperate to leave Europe.⁴⁶

In his unpublished autobiography, Emeric describes his struggle to bring his family members to Canada during that time.

Heavy Doors Open

Using friends and lawyers I knocked for over two years on the heavy doors of the Immigration Department in Ottawa to obtain a visa for Ernest but the answer was always no. Finally, I obtained the visa under the condition that Ernest bring with him two thousand dollars in cash. Since I did not have such liquid money, Freddie [Schopflocher] loaned it to us and Ernest arrived in Montreal in 1936.

In the meantime I had been working on a visa for Paul. The only [Jewish] immigrants Canada accepted at that time were bona fide farmers. Since Paul had been working for the last 10 years on our uncle, [Armin] Valko's estate, and was interested only in agriculture, I thought it should be easy to obtain a visa. We were turned down. We were made to understand that there were no Jewish farmers in Canada, or anywhere else. That the few Jews who did come to Canada as farmers, as a pretext to get in, soon disappeared in the cities. After guaranteeing that I would buy a farm and Paul would stay on it, we finally got his visa. Paul arrived in 1937, we bought his farm in Rivière Beaudette, where an immigration inspector kept checking on him for a number of years. It turned out that Paul remained on the farm over 40 years.

By this time, the [three] Sala brothers were well known to the Immigration Department, and when we applied for a visa for our parents it was granted without difficulty. They arrived in May 1939, four months prior to the outbreak of the Second World War, and settled on the farm.[47]

The farm, situated near Rivière Beaudette, close to the Quebec/Ontario border, became a rallying point for the Sala family. Emeric and Ernest built summer cottages. Blanca and family visited every summer. Ida Kaplan and her family were among the small number of Jews accepted into Canada during those pre-war years. The Kaplans arrived in Williamstown, not far from Rivière Beaudette, just weeks before World War II began. Paul Sala and Ida Kaplan met and eventually married. They were my parents. Three generations lived on that beautiful farm; my parents, my sister Renée and I, and our grandparents.

I have fond memories of my paternal grandparents, Adolf and Charlotte. German was the one language in which the adults could all communicate, and thus it was my first language. I remember watching Charlotte (whom I called Oma) light sabbath candles on Friday evenings. Sometimes, Adolf (Opa) would take me with him to a Sabbath service in the small Montreal synagogue he attended. I recall going for walks with him at the farm, holding his hand. The temper for which he was noted was of little concern to me. He was an intelligent man who liked to keep up with world events, and in Canada, regularly read the Kanader Adler, a Yiddish newspaper. Two stories of Oma stand out for me. In Europe, at a time when there was little food, probably during World War I, she provided the family with a meal of pork, which observant Jews avoid. She had a streak of pragmatism. She also had courage. Another time, also during the First World War, she took the children to her parents' village home in Slovakia where conditions were safer. Then she bravely returned to Sibiu, a day's train ride away, to collect much-needed winter clothing.

One of my earliest memories takes place after World War II ended. I was watching my grandmother read a letter, her tears falling on the thin blue airmail paper. She might have been reading about her brothers, sisters and their families who had perished in the Holocaust. What suffering there must have been in the family as they heard of nieces, nephews, brothers and sisters, aunts and uncles who perished. Of the six million Jews exterminated by Hitler during World War II, 43 were members of Emeric's family.

3

THE MAXWELL FAMILY

On the slope of the mountain close to the center of Montreal is the only Bahá'í Shrine in the western hemisphere. Here 'Abdu'l-Bahá resided at the beginning of His week-long stay in the city in 1912. He said, as He entered the house for the first time, "This is My home." The building was also home to May and Sutherland Maxwell and their daughter, Mary. This family had a profound impact on the early Canadian Bahá'ís. And their impact continues.

May Bolles Maxwell

May Bolles learned of the Bahá'í Faith in the last year of the 19th century in Paris, France. It was there she met her future husband, a Canadian architect from Montreal, William Sutherland Maxwell. Rosemary describes how May had early intimations of the Faith in a "remarkable dream":

> We belonged to a discussion group of close friends and naturally we spoke of the Faith to them. It seems that I told these friends of Mrs. Maxwell's dream when a child ... The members of the group were somewhat skeptical, so the whole group was invited to Pine Avenue to meet May Maxwell. One of the members said: "Rosemary told us of a remarkable dream of yours when you were twelve years of age or so, and we would like to know if it is true." May turned to me and said, "Rosemary, tell me the dream as you remember it." This is the way I told it:
> Just after [May's] birthday ... she dreamed that an angel took her up into the sky. There she saw the earth revolving in space. On top of the earth was a birthday cake. The angel had a sword; with his sword he cut the cake into many pieces. From the center of the cake rose a blue-violet mist which encircled the world writing the name "BAHA". Then the angel declared, "The knowledge of the glory of God shall cover the earth as the waters cover the sea!" From all corners of the globe came people dressed in the different

national costumes to take a piece of this cake. The child was so overcome by this dream she woke up startled and cried out. Her mother heard the sound and the child told her dream so the mother could record it.

After I had ended the story, Mrs. Maxwell said, "That is exactly right!"[1]

May Maxwell was part of the first group of Westerners to visit 'Abdu'l-Bahá in the Holy Land. On her return to Paris, she set to work letting people know about her new-found Faith. Rosemary highlights May's impact as a teacher and as a person:

> ... it was 'Abdu'l-Bahá Who sent Abu'l-Fadl [the great Muslim and Bahá'í scholar] to Paris to teach the devoted group there but with special emphasis on May Bolles. May so often used to say that it was this great and wise teacher who taught her to first try to weed or eradicate the prejudices in the seeking soul that might prevent it from accepting the Faith. May would do this, so wisely, questioning one so gently and subtly until finally the seeker would give an answer amazing to himself or herself. May would exclaim joyously, "That is what 'Abdu'l-Bahá said!" and quote His words.
>
> One felt so elated to find that one had had the joy of realizing an aspect, a facet of truth for oneself, through one's own perception! It could by no means be called manipulation, than that one could say the sun "manipulated" the seeds to grow from the earth. Truly, she had such a love for the seeking soul, and this love, like the warmth of the sun, caused the soul-seed to sprout.
>
> Juliet [Thompson] told me how the Master placed His hand on May when Juliet also was present, with closed eyes as though praying. When, after a second or two He removed His hand He said, "I have planted in you the seed of love. This you will impart to everyone you meet!"[2]

The bond between each member of the family, their love for one another was also part of the "magic" of their home, though May was the radiating center. Her daughter, now Rúhíyyih Khánum, wrote these words: "Many people inspire more or less love in others but I don't think I ever knew anyone who inspired the love mother did - so it was like an event when one was going to see her. This I felt all my life, day in, day out, and it never became commonplace!"[3]

We in the Montreal community would get a little disturbed or perhaps jealous at times of the love and attention May would shower on someone who seemed to us a dried up bulb. Suddenly this dried bulb would give forth green shoots and blossoms! The amazing quality, the universal scope of this love: She wouldn't restrict it only to Bahá'ís, it was showered on everyone...It was like a garment around one, warmth without restricting weight.[4]

May spent a great deal of time away from Montreal, partly due to her work for the Faith, and partly because the winters affected her fragile health. Emeric remembers her:

[Without Mrs. Maxwell] the Montreal community appeared to me like a club, consisting mostly of well-brought up elderly ladies, enjoying their firesides, consisting of prayers and reading the Writings of the Master (one seldom heard the name 'Abdu'l-Bahá) and tea with polite social chit-chat, entirely innocent of the fact that they were members of the most world-shaking and revolutionary movement of the century.

The central figure around which the community revolved was May Maxwell. She was an excellent teacher and raconteur. But her overriding quality was love. If we accepted her love, as I did, we had the feeling that she loved us more than anyone else. We knew that this was not true, but she was drawing from an inexhaustible Source, as no one else I know could, such unending, all-encompassing love and concern and sympathy, that we were helplessly overwhelmed, and were anxious to do anything to please her. What saddened us all was that she spent only a small part of each year in Montreal. Most of the time she appeared to have been away to teach and also on account of her delicate health. With many others I felt very close to her. We had many private sessions, since she was my spiritual mother. When she left Montreal, which was often, there was a general letdown. We somehow felt like orphans.

In a letter, May wrote to Emeric about human and divine love:

August 26, 1931
... Earthly love at best is but a poor imitation of that sacred essence which once it penetrates the human heart transforms the whole life. Human love separates but divine love unites; human love is possessive, but divine love

gives all – even life, in the path of the Beloved; human love brings often bitterness and pain, but divine love brings the ecstasy of joy and self release and its pain is sweeter than honey! 'Abdu'l-Bahá said to me that the human intellect is a fine and valuable instrument of human progress, but that only the rare soul attains the supreme gift of divine love." [6]

Anne Savage was a member of a less prosperous branch of a well-known Montreal family. Rosemary and Anne would meet together for tea and talk about their beloved May Maxwell. Rosemary recorded some of Anne Savage's memories.

"The first time I saw May Maxwell was at the University Settlement. She came to tell stories to the children in the library and how entranced and spellbound they all sat and listened! She took me home in a cab and in those days a cab drive was a great treat to me.

"In those early days, before 'Abdu'l-Bahá's visit, I saw a great deal of her. She taught me everything I know of the Faith. As she talked I felt such a wonderful exhilaration and when I walked home it was as if on air. ...

"One time when I was driving on the mountain with her, she pressed a twenty dollar bill into my hand, which in those days was a fortune to me. She could not keep money if others were in need!

"Once May said, "If only I could ride in the streetcars!" I asked, "Why?", thinking of the many unpleasantnesses of riding in the streetcars. With a sort of ecstasy she answered, "Oh the people, to be near them!"

"Her sympathy and understanding of the poor was remarkable. Once I asked, "Could you go about smelling unclean?" I spoke from experience. She answered, "If I was a mother of a family living in one room and the only water would be in a small basin at the far end of an entrance hall, the basin about six to eight inches, I'd smell to heaven!" [7]

May Maxwell was involved in philanthropic work in Montreal. In those days the mortality rate of children was very high. Milk dispensaries were created (in French, *Gouttes de lait*) where mothers could get pasteurized milk and medical care for their babies. Colborne Street Milk Station was a dispensary that May helped maintain.[8]

May was active in the Negro Club of Montreal, and was honorary president for a period of time.[9] Once, a visitor arriving at the Maxwell home was told that Mrs. Maxwell could not be disturbed. A woman was upstairs about to give birth. Because she was black, all the hospitals had refused her and Mrs. Maxwell was bringing in her own doctor. The baby would be born in her home.[10]

May's thinking could be called 'cutting edge'. Enthusiastic about a new system of education started by Italian doctor, Maria Montessori, May brought a teacher from New York, converted the top floor of the house into a kindergarten, and thus started one of the first Montessori classes in Canada.[11] In areas of health, she made use of homeopathic treatments. In a letter is this sentence: "...to me there is no medicine outside homeopathy."[12]

There is much we can learn from May's ability to deal with gossip and backbiting; from the way she would dig to the source of a misunderstanding through her directness and candor. Rosemary shows one way that she handled backbiting:

> May Maxwell's disregard of some really dreadful criticism and gossip is a glowing memory with me, alas not always followed. I heard her listen politely to someone telling her of so-and-so saying such-and-such about her. Immediately the story was ended, May unruffled, would talk with joy of some aspect of the teachings. What interested me was that she did not make the narrator feel guilty as a gossiper, she just relegated the subject as one of unimportance to greater things.[13]

Violette Nakhjavání, in her book, *The Maxwells of Montreal*, provides some of Rúhíyyih Khánum's comments about her mother's frankness:

She was unspeakably frank—a trait often misunderstood by those who are not by nature themselves frank. If she heard that one of the Bahá'ís, or any friend for that matter, was upset over something...which she had actually or supposedly said or done, she would go to the telephone, ring them up and say, "What's this I hear that you, etc." She always said it to one's face, whether flattering or otherwise...One of our young Montreal Bahá'ís—who as it happened was her spiritual child—told me that: "Mother almost killed me the other day. I telephoned her from a booth downtown and she was mad at me for something I had done and she gave me a terrific lecture and the combination of the heat of the lecture and the telephone booth, almost suffocated me!" Needless to say he did not object to her "lecture" at all![14]

One More Step

Despite frail health, May set out in 1940 on a teaching trip to South America. Rosemary recalls a visit:

Shortly before [May] left on her journey to South America, and we to Venezuela, we sat on the blue velvet couch in the Maxwell living room ... She told me how she knew the Guardian wished her to take one more step and she prayed she would be worthy to take it! She told me that she knew that God in His mercy would permit her to die before the real forces of war were released; that she could not bear the cruelties and suffering of humanity; that she hoped she would die in February, her favourite month. As we know, she died on March 1st.[15]

Emeric wrote about the last time he saw his dear friend:

Early in 1940 I happened to be in New York, and was the last Canadian to see Mrs. Maxwell prior to her embarking for her fateful journey to South America. I shall never forget her deep blue eyes and her encompassing love for all of us, including those who are as yet unborn, but will arise to serve His Cause.[16]

Not long after arriving in Argentina Mrs. Maxwell passed away suddenly. She was buried in a suburb of Buenos Aires, in obedience to Bahá'u'lláh's decree that Bahá'ís be buried close to the site of death.

I cannot end this section about May Maxwell, without adding a personal story. My father, Paul, Emeric's younger brother, immigrated to Canada in 1937. Two years later, he became very ill and needed an operation. One day, as he was recovering in the Royal Victoria Hospital, May Maxwell came for a visit. She sat quietly with him, reciting some prayers, not staying long. Until that time, he had regarded the Bahá'í Faith as a logical set of principles with which he was in intellectual agreement. But a shift happened during May's visit and his heart was touched. He became a member of the Baha'i community not long after, and remained a staunch Bahá'í to his last breath.

William Sutherland Maxwell

Sutherland Maxwell was a distinguished Canadian architect. His work includes Canadian landmarks such as the Chateau Frontenac in Quebec City and the Parliament Buildings in Regina, Saskatchewan. However, it is a golden-domed building on the slopes of Mount Carmel in Haifa that remains his preeminent work. Mr. Maxwell designed this superstructure over the resting place of the Báb, Manifestation of God and forerunner to Bahá'u'lláh.

Here are some of Rosemary's impressions of Sutherland Maxwell:

[Mr. Maxwell] was President of the Art Association of Montreal; as an architect, his work was known and services sought all over Canada. ... May always rejoiced to dwell on 'Abdu'l-Bahá's promise that her beloved husband would confer great distinction on Canada. Distinction to her was to teach the Faith and she would look for those signs and be happy in his services to the Faith as a member of the Local Spiritual Assembly, as Treasurer, as Chairman, etc. but would seem to wait expectantly for further flowering as a teacher. The full-flowering of his talent and service to the Cause was only to become known when the outer edifice of the Báb's sepulcher was built. The association of Mr. Maxwell with the tomb of the Blessed Báb reaches all over the world ... Most assuredly Sutherland Maxwell brought distinction to Canada! ... Sutherland Maxwell ... loved beauty, art. His exquisite sense of form and color reflected in every aspect of his home, built and furnished as a setting in which 'Abdu'l-Bahá would be more than a guest! ... How wonderful that the Master's words on entering the Maxwell home, "This is My Home'"should find completion in the Guardian's words naming it a Shrine![17]

Emeric adds to the picture:

What was he like? He was a gentleman, the ideal of a gentleman. Reserved, reticent, never showed his emotions. He did not attend firesides, didn't participate in discussions or study of the teachings. Mrs. Maxwell would say he is a wonderful Bahá'í but does not know it. He buried himself in his study and his art which he loved. When we had public speakers, sometimes he would be chair, introduce. Later he became more active, member and chair of the LSA of Montreal. Very proper, gentlemanly, created an atmosphere of dignity and respect.[18]

A Bahá'í House of Worship was being constructed in Chicago, the first in the Americas. All costs were borne by Bahá'ís around the world: a challenge during the Depression of the 1930s. Rosemary recalls:

We used to have what we called economy dinners. Each Bahá'í family would invite other Bahá'ís to come and share a meal. We each vied with one another to find out who could provide the cheapest, most satisfactory, most gourmet meal for the least amount of money. And everyone would come and pay [something for the Temple Fund]. ... We did this apart from Feasts you know, just as a little way of meeting one another. And I remember the Maxwells coming too and sharing in that, and Sutherland who was quite a gourmet in his days, would approve and flatter one ...One felt immensely flattered if Sutherland said he enjoyed a meal particularly for 32 cents. Which it would sometimes cost in those days of the Depression. ... It was a sacrificial penny, it was that sacrificial mite that ... gave the spirit to the body of the Temple.[19]

One of Mr. Maxwell's duties was treasurer of the Local Spiritual Assembly of Montreal:

One of the members of the Montreal community was a labourer's wife. She had six children to bring up on a very meager salary. As her husband was a non-Bahá'í she wished to give her own services to the Faith. She herself cleaned offices to make extra money. I remember Mr. Maxwell, as Treasurer of the LSA, asking it if the members would accept Mrs. —'s offer to clean the Center and the LSA fund would contribute the $3.00 pay into the Fund in her name. This was Mrs. —'s sacrifice. I was so touched to see Sutherland Maxwell place the receipt in the donor's hand with a special word of appreciation.[20]

Not long after May Maxwell's sudden death in 1940, Shoghi Effendi invited Mr. Maxwell to come and assist with the work in Haifa. His letter to Mrs. Dorothy Ward, first custodian of the Maxwell home, illustrates his practical, business-like side and attention to detail.

> May 9, 1940
> Dear Dorothy,
> Regarding your living in Pine Avenue during my absence abroad, these are arrangements between us.
> You are in charge and are to see that the house is kept clean, free from moths, locked up at night.
> Regarding heating—I shall pay for winter coal only (use ½ coke and ½ Welsh)
> Regarding Bahá'í use of house—The Spiritual Assembly may use the house for its meetings, for Feast meetings, and special meetings. It may keep books and pamphlets there. Fireside meetings may be held.

Regarding keys. Only the following may have them. ...
Report anything out of order to Mrs. Brooks [Mr. Maxwell's secretary][21]

Mr. Maxwell arrived in Haifa during the early days of World War II. Once the war ended, he hoped to return to Montreal for a visit as indicated in his reply to one of Rosemary's letters:

Greetings and Baha'i love to all the friends. ... I have spent many an hour prowling around the old haunts and having imaginary conversations - and re-creations - of the good old times and friends in Montreal...

If I shall have the pleasure and satisfaction of returning to Montreal for a visit, it will be a great happiness to me - and a joy to see all the old friends again. I have been very busy here, doing all sorts of things - including architectural work.[22]

Mr. Maxwell remained in Haifa for 12 years. During that time he assisted the Guardian in a variety of important matters culminating with the design and construction of the superstructure to the Shrine of the Bab. In the early 1950s, he returned to Montreal from Haifa, because of failing health. Rosemary recalls:

In the Canadian Archives are some lovely designs made with bright blue ink that he doodled one afternoon when a group was gathered in his library. ... I saw him drop them in the wastepaper basket, later gathered them and kept them for years until I sent them to the Canadian Archives. Even when he returned to Canada ... and I would have the privilege of sitting with him when the nurse was having an afternoon's respite, he would arrange pieces of paper he had collected for their texture and color and play with them, commenting on the balance or contrast of color![23]

Occasionally he startles one by his perception. After a Regional Conference which had not been too successful, he said, "The Cause will never grow unless the friends show spirituality, enthusiasm towards each other and their guests." He greets people, smiles his sweet angelic smile but cannot converse beyond a few moments [because of his ill-health]. But his sweetness wraps itself around one's heart!²⁴

The Hands of the Cause of God performed a unique role in the Faith. These were exceptional men and women appointed by Bahá'u'lláh, 'Abdu'l-Bahá and later by the Guardian, charged with the duties of protection and propagation of the Faith. Rosemary describes a poignant moment:

On Christmas Day, 1951, Emeric and I called at the Maxwell House to say goodbye to Mr. Maxwell and his nurse as we were leaving the next day to attend the Winter School at Beaulac.²⁵ We sat down on the high-backed Italian couch in the study, one on each side of Mr. Maxwell. He had come downstairs, but sat there so folded in, so pale and lifeless, our hearts ached. The nurse said that he hadn't slept. Then the telephone rang so the nurse asked me if I would please go and answer the telephone. (She was Swiss and spoke almost no English). So I picked up the telephone and heard the message:
"*Pleased to announce your elevation to the rank of a Hand of the Cause of God.*"
... I wrote it down; ... I showed it to Emeric and the nurse, and the nurse pulled out of her pocket the same message which had arrived the day before, but she had been afraid to give it to Sutherland for fear it would upset him, so we had the joy of doing this. Emeric wrote in beautiful big letters on a piece of paper, "THE GUARDIAN HAS APPOINTED YOU HAND OF THE CAUSE". It was wonderful to watch Sutherland. He sat up, his chest filled out and his face lit up. Then he said these beautiful words: "I didn't do it all alone, there were so many others to help me."
When Emeric told the nurse the distinction the Guardian had bestowed on her beloved patient, her eyes filled with tears as she expressed her joy. My own eyes were filled with tears as I sat clasping Mr. Maxwell's hand in both of mine. I could not resist kissing his hand! It was a deeply moving moment. He was strong enough to walk to the door with us, shook our hands, waved goodbye smiling. He was so full of life, spiritual life. What a privilege for us to be there by happy accident. One of God's bounties.²⁶

The Alabaster Box

Mr. Maxwell passed away in the spring of 1952. Rosemary describes the Guardian's request made during her pilgrimage later that same year:

> When I was a pilgrim in Haifa, the Guardian gave me an alabaster box containing a piece of the wall of the Prison of Máh-Kú, wrapped in a silk handkerchief ... [He] asked me to take it back to give to the National Spiritual Assembly of Canada, and to have it interred in the grave of Sutherland Maxwell. So here on Mount Royal we have some of the soil of Máh-Kú. And when you go to visit that grave, to think of that connection with the Báb, the sense of the Báb's nearness is present. Sutherland Maxwell most certainly brought distinction to Canada and to the world.[27]

An article in the September 1956 issue of the *Canadian Bahá'í News* reported that:

> On Saturday, June 16th, friends from the Montreal area gathered at the grave of our beloved Hand of the Cause, Sutherland Maxwell. This gathering was held for the purpose of fulfilling the instructions of the Guardian for the placing, under the headstone of Mr. Maxwell's grave, of a piece of plaster from the walls of the prison in Máh-Kú where the Báb was incarcerated in 1847.
> The Guardian had sent this piece of plaster enclosed in an alabaster box to the National Spiritual Assembly. The Guardian pointed out that another piece of plaster from the same source had been placed under the first golden tile of the dome of the Shrine of the Báb on Mount Carmel. The superstructure of the Shrine of the Báb, as we know, was designed by Sutherland Maxwell. ...
> The box containing the plaster was placed in a special excavation in the foundation stone under the headstone and attar of roses, sent by the Guardian for the purpose, was poured over the alabaster box which was then permanently sealed with tile and cement in the foundation stone in the presence of the friends.

Mary Maxwell – Amatu'l-Bahá Rúhíyyih Khánum

Mary was destined to become the wife of Shoghi Effendi, 'Abdu'l-Bahá's grandson and successor. She would become known as Amatu'l-Bahá Rúḥíyyih Khánum. *Amatu'l-Bahá* means "handmaiden of Bahá'u'lláh", *Rúḥíyyih* means "spirit", and *Khánum* means "lady."

"A Very Wonderful Son"

Rosemary tells the story of an event when Mary was two years old. It was May Maxwell's last meeting with 'Abdu'l-Bahá in the fall of 1912, shortly before He left North America.

May carried Mary in her arms as she entered the Master's presence. He had held the two-year old child in His arms, kissed and embraced her, calling her His daughter, His own dear daughter. May said her farewells and had reached the door, which had been opened, to leave the Master's presence. Suddenly He called out, "Mrs. Maxwell, someday you will have a very wonderful son." Again, in a stronger voice, "Mrs. Maxwell, someday you will have a very wonderful son!" Then again, in a voice so resonant and full, He exclaimed, "Mrs. Maxwell, Some day You Will Have a Very Wonderful Son!"

As she left the room, overcome by these words which she understood to mean she would have another child, she saw Montfort Mills and Horace Holley [two American Bahá'ís] standing looking a little embarrassed as the Master's voice had reached them also. As time passed May realized that the words could only mean her son-in-law to be! Though she said that the thought of a connection with the Family of Bahá'u'lláh was beyond her reach.[28]

A Dream

One evening, seated together on the blue velvet couch in the Maxwell Home, waiting for a Feast to begin, Mary told Rosemary about a remarkable dream she had had. It was in 1932, not long before the passing of Bahíyyih Khánum, the beloved daughter of Bahá'u'lláh, known as the Greatest Holy Leaf.

Mary (as she was then) appeared to be in Haifa. She entered the room of the Greatest Holy Leaf who was lying ill in bed. At the foot of the bed was a table laden with all shapes and sizes of bottles of different coloured medicines. Mary, longing to help, asked if she could give Bahíyyih Khánum some medicine, indicating the table.

The Greatest Holy Leaf smiled gently, shook her head and replied, "That will not help me. That is the world's medicine!" Then she asked Mary to go to a table in another corner of the room, remove an exquisitely carved silver or ivory screen and behind it she would find her medicine. Mary did so and saw a goblet of such pure crystal filled with a liquid so clear and pure that one could not know where the goblet began and the liquid ended!

This precious goblet Mary carried with both hands and gave to Bahíyyih Khánum. The Greatest Holy Leaf took a sip, handed it to Mary saying, "Drink it, drink it all up!" Mary then said she could never describe the taste of that divine elixir.

The significance of this dream was dimly realized some years later. When one compares the Guardian's tribute to the Greatest Holy Leaf and his tributes to Amatu'l-Bahá Rúhíyyih Khánum, the station of one incomparably higher but both serving the Guardian with equal devotion in her own sphere.[29]

The Guardian's Marriage

Following an extended teaching trip in Europe in 1937, May and Mary were invited by Shoghi Effendi to visit Haifa. Rosemary describes the evening in 1937 when Mr. Maxwell left to join them.

The Montreal community met in the Maxwell home for a Feast, the same night Mr. Maxwell left for Haifa, to attend, unknown to us, the Guardian's marriage. He stood at the door, hat in hand, overcoat on his arm, about to get into the waiting taxi. Goodbyes were said, then I called out impulsively, "Are you going to bring May and Mary home with you?" For one brief moment, one glimpsed a dark look of pain. It vanished, and with a smile and a wave of his hand, he left.

We realized afterwards what that brief glimpse of pain meant when we learned of the Guardian's marriage, and that Mary, Rúhíyyih Khánum, would not be home again, one of a unit of three.[30]

May and Sutherland both felt the separation from their beloved daughter, though it did not sadden them. They accepted it as the price of great bounty. [31]

Emeric once had a dream before the marriage of the Guardian, that the whole Montreal Spiritual Assembly was seated in a circle outside the Master's house, but Rúhíyyih Khánum wasn't among us. She was standing behind the Guardian. Emeric wondered why. He thought she had been doing something, stepping out of line. This was his immature interpretation at that time.

Then, of course, the cable came. I happened to be secretary of the Montreal Spiritual Assembly. I grabbed up the mail that day and was dashing out of the house to do something or other with some Bahá'ís. ... I suddenly noticed that one envelope was from Haifa. So I stopped in the middle of crossing the street, opened up the envelope and it said:

"Announce assemblies celebration marriage beloved Guardian. Inestimable honor conferred upon handmaid of Bahá'u'lláh, Rúhíyyih Khánum, Miss Mary Maxwell. Union of East and West proclaimed by Bahá'í Faith cemented.'

(Signed) Ziaiyyih, Mother of the Guardian."

What great excitement! It's a good thing it wasn't a main highway. I dashed back home again to telephone all the friends.[32]

Rosemary recalls conversations with May Maxwell on her return to

Montreal, following the marriage:

> May Maxwell, when she came back from Haifa, told me [that] after she and Mary had been traveling in Europe ... teaching ... the Guardian wrote saying that he hoped that after they had completed their teaching plan, that they would visit Haifa. And May, in speaking to a dear old Bahá'í friend, said, "When I read this, I felt something in my heart!" ... Then she told me that when they went to Haifa, the Guardian greeted them both very lovingly and warmly. One day the mother of the Guardian, Zia Khánum, invited May to tea. She alone, not Mary. After the tea was over, Zia Khánum put down her cup very formally and said, "And now Mrs. Maxwell, would you consent to the marriage of your daughter with Shoghi Effendi?" Well, you can imagine May's feelings. She sat there silent for a moment and then she said, "I will have to consult with Sutherland and it is for Mary to decide." She went across to the Pilgrim House and Mary was standing by the window, looking up at Carmel. She told Mary. And Mary said, "If the Guardian so wishes."[33]

Here are glimpses into the shared life of Shoghi Effendi and Rúhíyyih Khánum.

The Swiss nurse who accompanied Mr. Maxwell to Canada on his return in 1951 shared this with Rosemary:

> One day when in her presence the Guardian chided Rúhíyyih Khánum for something she had done, he turned to the nurse with a beautiful smile saying, "Mais je l'adore!"[34]

Rosemary recalled an incident from her Pilgrimage in 1952:

> The Guardian spoke of the Báb for whom he had such love and reverence. In the conversation he lightly touched a turquoise and silver bracelet which Rúhíyyih Khánum was wearing, saying that it had been a present the Báb had given to His wife. The tender touch he gave to the bracelet and the sweetness of the smile he bestowed on Rúhíyyih

Khánum was again a glimpse into the privacy of their shared life. Rúhíyyih Khánum sat with bowed head, in such touching humility.³⁵

May Maxwell told Rosemary that:

The Guardian wrote her [May] that the time would come when a little scrap of paper on which Rúhíyyih Khánum had written would be precious.³⁶

Rosemary would use stories such as this one to illustrate the nearness of the afterlife:

The interrelationship between the worlds is a thin veil, like an onion skin separating the layers, as May used to tell us the Master said. I give this illustration: Rúhíyyih Khánum told me that one day (in Haifa) after her mother's passing, [while] tidying her cupboards she came upon some of the little gifts her mother had sent her from time to time. She began to weep, realizing that now she would no longer receive such gifts. Then she seemed to hear her mother's voice telling her that of course she would send her gifts, but through others. A few days later, a Persian pilgrim came to her with some little gift, excusing herself saying that when in downtown Haifa shopping she had felt impelled to buy it for her. Rúhíyyih Khánum then felt it was as a confirmation of her mother's words to her.³⁷

After World War II ended, Rosemary and Emeric were able to go on a teaching trip to South America. Thus they had the opportunity to visit the grave of May Maxwell, in Quilmes, a suburb of Buenos Aires.

Argentina, Dec. 31, 1945: We had breakfast in our room ... then dressed to go out to Quilmes to Mrs. Maxwell's grave. It was a pleasant trip by train through lovely suburbs like the lakeshore with palms and firs alternating almost. We bought four dozen small roses which I placed on the grave, naming each one for a Canadian person or family, for Rúhíyyih Khánum and Mr. Maxwell ... I got the feeling that used to flood the Maxwell home some years ago - that golden flood. The wings express pure joy...³⁸

Emeric had ended a report to the Guardian by describing May's gravestone as "the wings of Quilmes". Rúhíyyih Khánum referred to this phrase in a letter. (See the next chapter for an excerpt of Emeric's report on the South American teaching trip.)

Haifa, March 22, 1946

I just read what you said of the "wings of Quilmes" in your letter to our beloved Guardian

Did you know I modeled the wings? For many, many years I felt whenever Mother died I wanted to make for her the figure of an Angel with wings as her tombstone. When she did die I realized it was a purely Christian motif. So Daddy and I together worked that out.

I thought "how close he is to Mother" when I read your words. Indeed a hand everlasting binds you to her, dear Emeric.

To me she is what Swinburne wrote once, "the angel that presided at my birth..." She was the angel of my whole life!

You are doing so much to serve the Cause and I am so proud of your book! And how lucky you are to have Rosemary by your side – she has such a deep devotion to the Faith and so constantly strives to wing her way ever higher spiritually. I admire that so much as sometimes one sees the believers complacent, anxious to reform the world and neglectful of the ever-constant necessity of self reform!

I owe you both a proper letter – but am so terribly, terribly busy![39]

The Shrine

As mentioned before, when Mr. Maxwell moved to Haifa in 1940, he placed the Maxwell House in the care of Mrs. Dorothy Ward. A letter from Rosemary to Dorothy contained words of premonition:

I'm so excitedly happy to hear ... that you are in the Maxwell home! ... Pictures of you moving about, up and down stairs, working in the familiar kitchen, acting as hostess fill my mind as well also as the indescribable atmosphere of the home the last time we visited it, the very evening of the day we left. Then, even the tables and chairs, every object in the room was bathed in heavenly peace. Emeric said its atmosphere reminded him of the Holy Shrines.[40]

In 1953, Shoghi Effendi wrote to the Canadian National Spiritual Assembly saying that the Maxwell home in Montreal:

> ... should be viewed in the nature of a national Shrine, because of its association with the beloved Master, during His visit to Montreal.[41]

Adolf and Charlotte Sala, Emeric's parents.

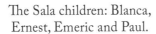

The Sala children: Blanca, Ernest, Emeric and Paul.

Catherine and Malcolm Gillies, Rosemary's parents

The Gillies family.
Back: Dorothy, Rosemary, Helen
Front: Catherine, Malcolm and Jean.

May Bolles Maxwell

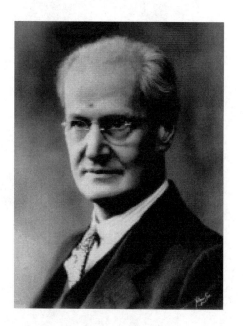

William Sutherland Maxwell

Left: Montreal Youth Group, photo taken by Mr. Maxwell, March 20, 1932.

Back row: Eddie Elliot, Walter Lohse, Emeric Sala, Norman McGregor, Tom Lee, Edward Lindstrom.
Middle row: Ruth Cunningham Lee, Rosemary Sala, Alberta Sims Dubin, Ilse Lohse, Bahiyyih Lindstrom, Dorothy Wade.
Front row: Henry Bergholtz, Mary Maxwell, Glen Wade and Lorris Dear.

Rosemary and Emeric at the Wilmette Temple site, 1935.

Left to right: E. Noyes, Rosemary, Emeric, Marion Holley and Kenneth Christian at Louhelen Bahai School, 1937.

Above: the St. Lambert Local Spiritual Assembly. Photo taken by Mr. Maxwell in the drawing room of the Maxwell home, 1938.

Left: The Salas in Venezuela with refugee friends from Germany, 1940.

Below: Gayle Woolson, Emeric and Rosemary in Costa Rica, 1945.

Top: Emeric giving a talk in Havana, Cuba, 1946.

Middle: Beaulac Bahá'í school, Rawdon, Quebec, 1947.

Bottom: First Canadian National Convention on the lawn in front of the Maxwell home, 1948.

The Sala Family, 1947

Wedding at the Sala's in St. Lambert, August 1952.

Left to right: Emeric, Norma, Klaus (Harry) and Rosemary.

☙ 4 ❧

ST. LAMBERT—1930'S, 1940'S & 1950'S

FOLLOWING their marriage, the Salas moved to St. Lambert where a few Bahá'ís already lived. I have only a few childhood memories of the cozy house on Riverside Drive. Across the road was the St. Lawrence River, the city and Mount Royal in the distance. I remember a special spot near the kitchen which Rosemary called the "sunroom", filled with plants, where breakfast was served. A side door led to a large garden surrounded by trees.

By 1937, St. Lambert had nine adult believers, the exact number needed to form a Local Spiritual Assembly. However, there were growing pains. The friends were reluctant to loosen their warm ties with the Montreal community. Former St. Lambert Bahá'ís, the Lanning sisters, recalled a letter sent by the Montreal Assembly, suggesting that St. Lambert hold a Feast in their community "rather than always going in to Montreal".[1] Meanwhile, Rowland Estall, in Vancouver at this time, remembered a "tearful letter" from someone, perhaps Rosemary, lamenting that "we are separated from Montreal."[2]

May Maxwell was concerned about those growing pains and raised the issue in a letter to the Guardian. When she learned that Emeric would be traveling to Europe on business, she urged him to make a pilgrimage to the Holy Land to visit the shrines, and meet Shoghi Effendi. This he agreed to. In her letter to the Guardian May wrote:

14 December, 1937
... Not one of the Bahá'ís living in St. Lambert wishes to form an Assembly, for obvious reasons; they love the Montreal Community where they are all active workers; the Montreal Community has an outstanding prestige and is the Mother Group of Canada and they dread to disassociate themselves from the communal life and activities of Montreal. Some of the St. Lambert members frankly admit this, others make various excuses. ... May I beg you to discuss this matter with Emeric Sala when he is in your presence in Haifa, that is if it is in accordance with your wisdom.[3]

I have found no mention of this issue in Emeric's notes made during his pilgrimage.

Emeric's Pilgrimage and a Question

Before Emeric set out on his voyage to Europe and Palestine, this letter arrived from Mary Maxwell, now married to Shoghi Effendi, and known as Rúhíyyih Khánum. She wrote:

> Haifa, 22/11/37
> Dear Emeric & Rosemary,
> Thank you for the program of the meetings and the snaps of the youth group. I love to hear news of Montreal, as you can well imagine! Now that Mother and Dad are home I am sure it is a perpetual feast of love and discussion of the Cause!
> It will be lovely to have Emeric here and he will take back, I am sure, a rich harvest for you both.
> I know how active you both are and am always eager for news of Canada's progress – there are so few there to do the work compared to America!
> My love to all the friends and a great deal to you both,
> Lovingly,
> Rúhíyyih[4]

The following descriptions of Emeric's journey and pilgrimage are based partly on reports and the autobiography, but mainly from a talk that he gave at a special conference on the subject of the Guardian.

The Maxwells' and the Schopflochers' were the only [Canadian Bahá'ís] who knew Shoghi Effendi up to that time. There were not many in the USA either. Not only because of the cost and time (there were no planes then), but we just did not think or dream of the possibility of a pilgrimage.[5]

In December 1937 I had to cross a rough Atlantic on a business trip to Europe. Mrs. Maxwell suggested since I will be visiting my parents in Romania, why not continue to Haifa and see Shoghi Effendi, which I did.[6]

While en route to Haifa, Emeric had the opportunity to visit Marion Jack, the Canadian pioneer who lived in Sophia, Bulgaria. On December 25 and 26, 1937, Emeric spoke at two meetings in Sofia; one of which was attended by over fifty people. In his biography of Marion Jack, Jan Jasion records this letter from her to Shoghi Effendi.

> Everyone was most pleased with dear Mr. Sala, he gave a remarkably fine talk on Justice which I hope he will some day write up ... the talk was forceful and big & fine ... It was quite satisfactory that we had over fifty in this busy season with very few invitations ... It was a real treat to have a visit from such an earnest & enthusiastic believer.[7]

Emeric continued on to the Holy Land:

> I travelled on the Orient-Express to Istanbul, and from there by train through dozens of tunnels to Tripoli in Syria, and from there by bus over a tortuous coastal road with a reckless Arab driver, to Haifa. In Beirut I bought a dozen oranges for one piaster. When we came to the border of Palestine a British customs official took my oranges and threw them into the Mediterranean Sea. No citrus fruit could enter this British Protectorate.[8]

Nearly 50 years later, at an Association for Bahá'í Studies conference in Ottawa, in 1984, Emeric gave a talk entitled "Shoghi Effendi's Question". Here are excerpts:

> The Guardian told me that the main purpose of my pilgrimage was to visit and pray at the Shrines and Holy Places. In my own mind my main purpose was to visit Shoghi Effendi. Actually I never met Shoghi Effendi. However, having been the only Western pilgrim, I had the undivided attention of the Guardian for about three hours of each of the five nights. [Pilgrims from the west and east would meet with the Guardian at separate times, probably because of language differences.] Gradually I gained the feeling

that Shoghi Effendi, the man, had sacrificed himself long ago for the Faith and the Guardianship. I have never before or since met a human being who had given so much of himself for the Faith, obliterating all personal desires or aspirations. ...

I asked the Guardian many questions, most of them prompted by my immaturity, having been a Bahá'í only ten years. One night, Shoghi Effendi asked me a question, which I could not answer, nor did I understand its significance at that time. Shoghi Effendi asked me: "Since after the martyrdom of the Báb the authority of the Faith was passed on to Bahá'u'lláh, and after His passing to 'Abdu'l-Bahá, to whom was it transferred after the ascension of 'Abdu'l-Bahá?" I answered, of course, Shoghi Effendi. He said no. I then said, the Guardian. He again shook his head. I then ventured the Universal House of Justice. He again said no, and I could see from his expression that he was disappointed with my inability to answer his question. Then he asked, are the friends not reading my letters? The answer he said, is clearly stated in *The Dispensation of Bahá'u'lláh*. It is divided into four parts: Bahá'u'lláh, the Báb, 'Abdu'l-Bahá, and the fourth part is entitled 'The World Order of Bahá'u'lláh', which is the answer to his question.

The Guardian spoke a beautiful Oxford English. I spoke English with a terrible Hungarian-Canadian accent, which the Guardian found difficult to follow. Rúhíyyih Khánum, who had known me for nine years, had to interpret on several occasions.

After returning to Montreal, I wrote seven pages of the usual pilgrim's notes, but I did not mention the above question as I did not see any importance in it. As time passed, I could not forget his question, nor the sad expression on his face for my inability to answer. I was also puzzled as to why he had asked me that question.

As the years advanced, especially after his passing in 1957, I realized increasingly that the greatest lesson I learned was not during the many hours of exclusive conversations, most of which were based on my questions, but it was the question the Guardian asked me and which I could not answer. For the last forty years or so, I have asked the friends the same question on four continents, at untold firesides, summer and winter schools, and I received, with one single exception, the same wrong answers that I gave the Guardian as far back as January, 1938.

It is obvious that 'Abdu'l-Bahá in His *Will and Testament* stated very clearly that all Bahá'ís should turn to Shoghi Effendi, that *"whoso obeyeth him not ... hath not obeyed God"* and again, *"He that opposeth him hath opposed the True One."* It is also indisputable that Shoghi Effendi was the head of the Faith during his ministry of thirty-five years. Yet, he wanted to impress upon me at that time, that the authority of the Faith did not rest upon him but on the World Order of Bahá'u'lláh, which was based on two pillars: the Guardianship and the Universal House of Justice. His vision of the future went far beyond the Guardianship, and our failure in all these years to visualize the significance of his question should indeed make him feel sad.

Our Faith was centered in the Guardian as a father figure, oblivious of the other pillar and its implications, which was a distortion if not a mutilation of our vision of the World Order of Bahá'u'lláh. Shoghi Effendi described this condition as follows:

To dissociate the administrative principles of the Cause from the purely spiritual and humanitarian teachings would be tantamount to a mutilation of the body of the Cause, a separation that can only result in the disintegration of its component parts, and the extinction of the Faith itself.[9]

These are strong words. ...

'Abdu'l-Bahá, who was also called the Mystery of God, was, as I understand it, the last father-figure in the Adamic cycle, which carried humanity through its stage of immaturity. In all dispensations for thousands of years, religious communities centered around a pope, a caliph, an archbishop, a rabbi, a priest or a minister. In many congregations even today the leader is not only looked upon as wiser and more learned than anyone else but is also called "the Father", whose authority is unquestionably followed.

Shoghi Effendi wanted neither to be treated nor followed as a father figure. He signed many thousand letters as "your true brother Shoghi". ... One possible reason for his refusing to meet Bahá'í communities on any of his journeys, was probably to de-emphasize the importance of his personality in relation to the World Order of Bahá'u'lláh. He told us on various occasions that the main difference between the papacy and the

Guardianship is that the Pope has exclusive authority to legislate and to interpret, while the Guardian's authority is limited to the interpretation of the sacred writings only.

Guided by the vision of Shoghi Effendi and the events of history, the Bahá'í world community, having been personality-centered, the characteristic of an immature society, has become assembly-centered, which is a precondition for entering the age of maturity.[10]

After his return home, Emeric received the following letter written on behalf of the Guardian:

> March 17th, 1938
> Dear Mr. Sala,
> The Guardian was indeed pleased to receive your letter of the 25th February, and to know of your safe return to Montreal, and to realize that the impressions you had carried back from your visit to the Holy Land are still very vivid in your mind. He hopes as years go by your realization of the great privilege you have had of visiting these Holy Spots will deepen, and that you will be increasingly stimulated as a result to work with added devotion and with a clear vision of the task that lies ahead of you.
> It is now that you are back home that you can look at your visit in its true perspective, and appreciate its full significances. Gradually you will also be able to find the answer to certain questions which may still puzzle you. These inner struggles of the soul are indeed a necessary part of the spiritual development of a believer, and if faced and overcome with resolute will and deep faith they can be of an immense asset to his growth in the Cause.[11]

This section on Emeric's pilgrimage began with a segment of May Maxwell's letter to the Guardian regarding the formation of the St. Lambert Assembly. When Shoghi Effendi asked Emeric the question he could not answer, what seeds were planted in Emeric's mind? It should be noted that the Local Spiritual Assembly of St. Lambert was formed in 1938, a few months after his return from pilgrimage.

And, finally, being curious, I once asked Emeric who that single individual had been, who had given the correct answer to the question Shoghi Effendi had asked. Emeric replied, Douglas Martin. Mr. Martin would go on to serve the Cause in innumerable ways, including being for many years a member of the Universal House of Justice.

A National Convention in 1938

Just as a Local Spiritual Assembly administers the affairs of the local Bahá'í community, so too, a National Spiritual Assembly governs at a national level. Every year, delegates attend a National Convention to elect the nine members of a new National Spiritual Assembly and to consult on the affairs of the Faith in the whole country. Rosemary and Emeric attended an historic National Convention in the spring of 1938. At that time Canada and the United States were still under one body – the National Spiritual Assembly of the United States and Canada. Here is Rosemary's account:

Emeric and I were attending the National Convention in Chicago in 1938. We were invited by a group of very devoted and loving Bahá'í teachers to attend a special meeting, not open to all the friends, to take action on a very important issue to present at the Convention. As we loved the friends who invited us, older, well-known teachers in the Faith, we agreed to join them. When we arrived, I went about kissing and being embraced by these precious Bahá'í teachers. After a few minutes, Emeric came to me, took my arm and said, in most decided tones, 'Come, we are leaving!' Bewildered I went. Then outside the room I asked what had happened to upset him. He told me that those dear Bahá'ís were planning an open attack on Horace Holley for his pre-occupation with administrative functions instead of the teaching work.

This was one of those early stormy conventions. After the formal opening, and the agenda voted upon, one of those dear souls stood up and very emotionally chided—attacked—the secretary (Horace Holley) for not emphasizing or concentrating on teaching methods in the agenda. The majority of the delegates and visitors were horrified, while Horace stood there motionless.

Then came a cable announcing the death of Munirih Khánum, the wife of 'Abdu'l-

Bahá. This message brought sanity into the Convention as all were united in their sadness at the physical loss of this tie to the days of the Master.

One more dramatic event added the final uniting force: Grace Robarts Ober, who had just returned from an extensive teaching tour, was called to the platform. She stood before the assembled delegates and friends, sweeping all up with her into the wonder of the Cause of God and the bounty of being one of His vessels. She lifted up her arm (in a characteristic gesture) crying out: Yá Bahá'u'l Abhá! Then collapsed into her husband's arm as he was sitting on the platform. While the assemblage, deeply moved, repeated the Healing Prayer, she rode out of this world on the waves of those holy words to the Abhá Kingdom. Stirred to their depths, cleansed, purified, the friends arose as the Prayer for the Departed was recited. There was never any more openly expressed feeling against Horace Holley.

The Guardian valued Horace's services and would have liked to have him in Haifa to assist but realized the tremendous value of his services in America and Canada. Shoghi Effendi addressed him "My most precious brother" and mentioned his and his wife's services as being "heroic". [Some years before] in 1925, Horace became a paid full-time secretary of the National Spiritual Assembly at a time when its members and fellow believers could feel free to and did criticize! Shoghi Effendi was fully aware of this and paid tribute to the work he did in assisting to build up the Administration to fulfill its sacred function in the establishment of the world order of Bahá'u'lláh![12]

Year in Venezuela

Emeric's parents arrived in May of 1939 to settle in Canada on the farm. World War II was looming. A few months later, as they drove back to Montreal from Green Acre, Rosemary and Emeric made a decision that would align their lives more closely to a new Plan of the Guardian's. Emeric writes:

While driving home, we heard on the car radio Chamberlain declaring war on Germany. ... War, hatred, killing, destruction were the antithesis of what we were trying to do. It made us so despondent that I suggested to Rosemary, let us go pioneering in Latin America, as far away as possible from all this madness. Rosemary agreed with enthusiasm, though with some trepidation, leaving behind a jewel house, a hundred and fifty year old French Canadian cottage which Mr. Maxwell had renovated for us.[13]

 Emeric mentioned "pioneering", a word we will come across often in this book. Pioneers are adventurous souls who arise and move to new locations, whether in nearby communities or across the world. They set up a home, find employment and integrate into their new surroundings. They meet new people and make new friends some of whom may be attracted to the Faith. Thus gradually, new Bahá'í communities come into being. Marion Jack, the pioneer whom Emeric had visited at Christmastime in Bulgaria, was upheld by Shoghi Effendi as a "shining example to present and future generations."

 Shoghi Effendi, in 1937, launched a teaching campaign for the Bahá'ís of North America, entitled the Seven Year Plan. Bahá'ís were asked to share the teachings of the Faith, at a time when most people had no idea of its existence. In this Plan, the Guardian called for one Local Spiritual Assembly to be created in each province in Canada, in each state in the United States, as well as in every Latin American country and in the Caribbean, by the end of the Plan in 1944. Rosemary reflects on the Guardian's Seven Year Plan, which motivated many Bahá'ís to pioneer across the Americas:

> It was the first Seven Year Plan which woke up the Bahá'ís of North America from the rather parochial vision of the Cause only being confined to America. Now the pioneers were asked to go to (Latin) America, to establish a centre in every country ... and we were part of that. ... It was a very exciting and thrilling motion, because for the first time the American and Canadian Bahá'ís were brought out of their own little world ... So many Bahá'ís went out, mostly women, which was amazing. Women, not young, ... not speaking the language, who had the daring to go out in a continent that was consumed by machismo, for the men ruled; and yet, they conquered the continent. Many men went out too, of course."[14]

 Rosemary and Emeric gradually reoriented their lives in service to this Seven Year Plan, and from here on, to other future Plans. Rúhíyyih Khánum wrote to Rosemary and Emeric when she heard that they were planning to pioneer to South America.

10/11/39
Since returning home I have been longing to write ... and tell you how thrilled I am at the news of your intended flight to the South!

You don't know how I love and admire you both for your wonderful courage and devotion. I know it involves sacrifice, that is what makes it so precious! So many of us suffer an arrested development – some never get beyond just becoming Bahá'ís, others do some one service and rest on their oars – others reach a high level and bask in their glory! But how many of us go on and up till the last day of our lives like Martha Root?

...We have demonstrated, so far, to the Guardian that we not only do what he tells us but even more! And I assure you that has rejoiced his heart and greatly encouraged him. I am so happy over this. How wonderful if he could come to feel he could rely on us. That implies a great deal. There is a big difference between relying on someone to do something and being sure whatever you ask them they will do without fail!"[15]

After months of preparation, Rosemary and Emeric left Canada for Caracas, Venezuela. Montreal Bahá'í Elizabeth Cowles wrote them a letter of farewell. It was a poignant time, as word had come of the death just days before of May Maxwell in Argentina:

March 3, 1940
Emeric dear,
You must not go away without one more little word of au revoir from me.

...Some day you will go to Buenos Aires and visit the tomb of our beloved May. Sutherland has just told me that she is to be buried there and he will design the monument. How lovely and wonderful!

Much as we shall miss her we can but rejoice that she has entered a new and much fuller life in the 'Kingdom of lights'.

We must all be more vigilant, more devoted to the great Cause of Bahá'u'lláh. We shall think of you and pray for you very often in your new field of work as I am sure your thoughts and prayers will often turn to the friends in Montreal, St. Lambert and all of Canada and elsewhere.

With fond love and every good wish to you and Rosemary

Your true sister
Elizabeth Cowles[16]

They also received this note from Anne Savage, written shortly after the passing of May Maxwell:

March, 1940
My darling Rosemary and my beloved Emeric,
You are really going this evening! You understood Rosemary dear, I know, on Saturday, just why I felt I could not go with you. I just could not (illegible) any more!

On reading over letters from May I have come across some very beautiful things and I think I shall ask the friends if they would not like to come together & hear them. Possibly I can send them to you by mail. There was such a very close bond between us that I feel as if part of myself has gone with her!

This is just to tell you that we shall pray for you as I know you will pray for us & may Bahá'u'lláh abundantly bless you dears.
Yours always, Anne[17]

Emeric wrote from their new home in Caracas, Venezuela.

25th of March, 1940
What I like best in this country are the people. They are wretchedly poor, but kind, their voices melodious and pleasing, their movements graceful and their eyes gentle... Once I asked a poor candy vendor — an aged man with white hair — [for directions] and he in the most courteous Spanish, with an exquisite bow and the gestures of a nobleman of the 16th century, showed us the way..."[18]

April 27th, 1940
Dear Friends :
You did not receive my letter No 2. It described our visit on Easter Sunday to the Anglican Church of Caracas. My description of our reception, as strangers, which reminded me of many things but the Spirit of Christianity, was according to the mature judgement of my beloved wife not for Canadian consumption. I, therefore, destroyed Let-

ter No. 2, and posterity will never know its contents. ...

For the last four Fridays, we have been going to the meetings of the Theosophical Society. It consists of three young Venezuelans. One of them does most of the talking, teaching us the workings of the divine law. They are broad-minded and tolerant. Therefore they listen to us. My Spanish is still very poor, but sufficient to convey to them some of the Bahá'í principles, and thus, although they don't know it, we are constituting the first Bahá'í Study Class on Venezuelan soil."[19]

June 29th, 1940
News from Venezuela will appear uninteresting in contrast with events which are taking place in Europe. Rosemary describes our maid, Antonia, who does not know what "Hitler" means. She never heard that name. And there are many like her in this blessed country. And yet we call them backward, uncivilized. For after all Hitler is a product of our glorious civilization. We made him great. He represents the forces we generated. Kill him and the evil remains. ...This is [why we are] "shortsighted". And this is why disillusionment will spread.[20]

Rosemary writes to her family:

May 27, 1940
What wealth – to receive two letters from home in four days. Mail was held up of course on account of the war. ... We are busily keeping up with European events. Emeric's room, one wall at least, is lined with maps and he moves pins about. The papers here print dispatches from Germany, England and France and we try to pick up the truth from all sorts of conflicting statements. I do not think I could bear to think about it, if I was not trying to live in Bahá'u'lláh's concept of a New World Order and which has been the eternal plan for mankind. ... I do not like to think of Charlie [her sister Margaret's husband] going off to the battlefield. Let me know the news.[21]

During their eleven months in Venezuela, Rosemary and Emeric made many contacts. They compiled a list with the names and backgrounds. Here are a few:

> A former lawyer from Barcelona, Spain; an author-professor of Philosophy at the University, also from Spain; the economic advisor to the Minister of Finance and professor at the university; a teacher poet; a Venezuelan physician; a post office employee; a professor and cancer specialist; a tailor; a chiropractor; a Venezuelan owner of mines; the director of the National Library; businessmen; secretary of the Theosophist Society. Several were from Spain, others were refugees from Nazi Germany, some from Austria, some were Venezuelan-born.[22]

Emeric tells of crossing the Andes to visit a Bahá'í pioneer in Colombia:

> ... traveling from Caracas to Bogota in Colombia ... eight days by car on a gravel road—one-track; we traveled from sunrise to sunset. People told us we would be killed by banditos, as there was no police protection. It was a mountain road, very steep, with precipices to the right; a car, human bodies, possessions could easily disappear. They told us if we decided to go, we should take weapons with us, at least a machete. But all we had were prayers. Rosemary said everywhere the Greatest Name [see Glossary]. We were the first Bahá'ís traveling in that part of the Andes. Martha Root had gone further down, in Chile.[23]

Rosemary takes up the story:

> I remember on one mountain top I said the Greatest Name nine times... with all my heart. Suddenly, such a silence came. The birds seemed to stop singing, and the leaves stopped rustling. The silence was like a tremendous void. Then everything began again. You felt yourself there in a tremendous moment of destiny, to hear this Word go shouting out over the mountains.[24]

Emeric's vision was far-reaching. Here he reflects on the year in Venezuela and on into the future:

Most of us limit ourselves to the short-range view which is necessary for everyday life; we think also in terms of a week, a month, or a year. But the long-range view, if we perceive it, visualize it, includes our whole life cycle, and goes beyond it. Reading the Bahá'í Writings, seeing and following the vision of 'Abdu'l-Bahá, the prophecies of Bahá'u'lláh, we can correlate world events with the teachings. This extends, lifts our vision to a greater distance and when crises or calamities face us, individually or collectively, they can be faced so much more easily. Because you see all these troubles as part of life, as necessary for our own and for the development of the human race. It also helps us not to fear. With faith, and belief in God, and His Plan, and His Prophet's vision, fear is no longer needed, is no longer necessary. ...

We went to Venezuela ... an unknown country, tropical, malaria-infested, great poverty. We ... had to learn a new language, adjust to the climate, culture, conditions. It looked foolish, ridiculous, no one else would do it, normally. And yet, that one year was one of the highlights of our lives. We look back to it with ... joy. It was a great adventure, we took great risks. We could have been afraid and worried but we were not. We had confidence; we felt we did something from the point of the long-range view for future generations.[25]

First Summer School in Canada

After a year, Rosemary and Emeric returned to Montreal and Rosemary expressed her feelings:

When we returned from Venezuela, I was heartbroken, and I thought, surely we'd return again. When I heard Spanish on the radio, I used to weep, tears would stream down my cheeks. Of course we made two or three trips, one trip all around South America, visiting each country, and we could speak Spanish at the time; so we were in touch.[26]

Their friend Rowland Estall wrote to them, referring to another element in Shoghi Effendi's Seven Year Plan—the settlement of Bahá'ís in each province of Canada:

February 26, 1941

Now what are you and Rosemary going to do when you get back to Canada? That's the question! Well, first of all perhaps you'd like to have the enclosed reports of my recent travels and begin to get a new perspective of the tremendous tasks waiting .... in this country of promise. I've taken the liberty of suggesting to both Regional Secretaries in the Eastern and Western Regions that they should at once consult you regarding the prospects of your both making a coast-to-coast tour of the country. .... Then there is the prospect of Summer Schools, only in the idea stage as yet, for Canada. I feel very strongly that we should begin to draw much closer together throughout Canada as a possible prerequisite to an N.S.A. at the end of the Seven-Year Plan period, provided our objectives of an Assembly in every Province have been reached. ...

I'm sure I don't see clearly these personal futures of ours though in the Faith I know our bonds are eternal ones. For the rest, I think we cannot see or plan too far ahead in these changing times. ...

Be sure of this! Nothing you have both done, or tried to do is lost to the Faith. And for yourselves, you must know and feel the rewards of your own historic sacrifice. We shall feel it here when you return. So -

Welcome home![27]

Rowland in later years, recalled this period. He told how during the War the Canadian government had restricted foreign exchange, and thus travel to the United States. One could only take $25 across the border, and thus it was nearly impossible for Canadian Bahá'ís to attend the well-developed American summer schools at Green Acre, Louhelen and Geyserville, as had been the pattern. An east-west movement was beginning for Canadian Bahá'ís, rather than north-south.[28]

Emeric reflects on Rowland's suggestions:

When we returned after our year's stay in Venezuela, in the spring of 1941, we found conditions of the Faith in our mother community in the doldrums. Montreal could not recover, not only from the loss of Mrs. Maxwell, but the whole Maxwell family. For Mr. Maxwell was living also in Haifa.

Rowland Estall had also just arrived from Winnipeg, for a longer visit. We were both very concerned about the state of affairs, and together with the Regional Teaching Committee, of which I remember only Amine DeMille of Rouyn, Quebec as a member, we organized the first Canadian Bahá'í Summer Conference which was held over a weekend ... We had a very encouraging response. About three friends came from Moncton [New Brunswick] about six from Ontario, including a new believer, John Robarts, Rowland representing the West, and the rest from Quebec, making a total of close to thirty. ...

This conference not only gave us all a new lease on life, but next summer we arranged a successful week-long conference at Paul Sala's farm in Rivière Beaudette, Quebec, with Dr. Glen Shook as guest speaker. ... Ontario, not to be left out, started their yearly summer sessions at Rice Lake.[29]

World War II – Impact on Family

In one of my earliest memories, I am seated across from my grandmother Charlotte. In her hands she holds a thin blue airmail letter. Tears are rolling down her cheeks. In those days after the War, news of what had happened to family members must have come gradually. Emeric describes that time:

Eugene Umstadter arrived just before the outbreak of the Second World War ... His wife Lily, [Emeric's cousin] the only survivor of her family, arrived after the war. ...
Ernest and Lillian visited Budapest in 1946 and they brought out Yvonne Solt, a seventeen-year-old cousin, who was again the only survivor of her family. Later Ernest was instrumental to bring Mike Klein to the U.S.A. ... Mike, his sister Babi and another two cousins in Budapest [and their mother] were the only survivors left from my father's family.[30]

In later years, visits were made to surviving family members in Europe, stories accumulated and Emeric gathered them.

In the Astoria in Budapest I met Erzsi [a cousin] first, who told me that her mother, Mariska neni, died a week before my letter arrived. Erzsi and her younger sister

Sari escaped while on a march to an extermination camp, returned to Budapest and were hidden by Gyula Varkonyi, a Hungarian communist, who later married Erzsi. For three months they were hiding in a cellar living on raw potatoes. Sari has never fully recovered and is still sickly. Their mother Mariska was also arrested and held for deportation. Gyula Varkonyi saved her life also. ...

We had lunch with Judith Huba, ... formerly a nun. She now works as an English [translator]. Evenings and weekends she keeps her devotions as a nun just as though she was in a convent. There is not a bitter strain in her. She is positive, cheerful, practical and a person of faith. We both liked her very much.[31]

In 1963 I saw Natalie in Budapest for the last time. Her son and husband were dead. They were picked up during the War and disappeared without a trace. Natalie suffered now from diabetes and angina, but her soul was as radiant as ever. She met Rosemary for the first time. They could not communicate by tongue, but they took to each other like fish to water.

My mother had four sisters and three brothers. Between them they had twenty-five children. Every one of these families was totally or partially exterminated in the Holocaust except my mother's. My father had three brothers and three sisters, who had among them sixteen children. Every one of these families was totally or partially exterminated except my father's. None of these families lived in the same city, but they were clustered together close to their roots. The world is now not unlike it was then. The lesson that the new generation can learn now is not to cluster, but to disperse, the farther the better.

Among the Bahá'ís I met in Budapest there was a woman whose infant child was thrown into the Danube [during the war]. Sometime later, the Hungarian Gestapo visited her, and when they saw some Bahá'í books they asked her what are these, she answered: "These books teach me that you are my brothers." The police then left.[32]

I do not recall Emeric talking about the War or about the Holocaust. He was not one to show emotion. Many years after, in one of our last visits before he died, Emeric and I sat together at the dining table while he talked about his father Adolf, his difficult life, his fierce temper.

In Emeric's voice there was only compassion as he now talked about his father, (my grandfather) Adolf. How during the depression he could not adequately support his family. Then, before World War II, he had to leave his six brothers and sisters and their families behind to join his children in Canada. After the war came news of the loss of most of his loved ones. Today, we are aware of the psychological trauma that comes with times of crisis and tragedy. My grandfather could well have suffered from post-traumatic stress disorder. But such conditions were unknown then, so he was characterized as bad-tempered. He eventually moved to a small apartment in Montreal, ostensibly to be close to his synagogue. My grandmother divided her time between her children's homes.

This Earth One Country

The three Sala brothers took action during the war and post-war years. Ernest brought to Canada those family members who wished to leave Europe. Paul regularly sent parcels to Hungary to help out the relatives who remained. And Emeric wrote a book.

The book was called *This Earth One Country*. These words from the preface show its far-reaching vision:

Events culminating in two devastating world wars are forcing a change in our outlook. ...

A world government, a supranational government, is the ultimate goal from the point of view of the needs of the people. But to work towards this, a new world-ethic is required. Such an ethic must be idealistic in its emphasis upon humanity, and practical in its ability to lessen the great divisions which keep men apart.

This book does not contain a new utopia, nor does it propose another postwar plan. Its aim is to draw the reader's attention to the existence of a supranational community with a plan already agreed upon, which is being put into execution on a world scale.[33]

Emeric explains why he decided to write a book while World War II raged.

During the middle of the war, a young Oxford graduate who was stationed in Ottawa, came to Rivière Beaudette one weekend. He was an intellectual type, not religious, but was interested in the Faith. He asked me for a Bahá'í "primer" but the type of book he wanted we did not have. We agreed that such a book was needed. Thus I began writing This Earth One Country. My income had been frozen due to wartime measures, with anything extra subject to 100% income tax. This allowed me free time to write.

The book explained how the religions in the past developed in mankind a personal conscience, by touching the heart and modifying our behaviour as individuals. Now, for the first time in religious history, the Bahá'í Faith provided the means whereby this individual conscience could be translated into a collective one. Many of my talks and lectures would be based on the book.[34]

Getting the book published was not a simple matter. Publishers, being short of paper due to the War, readily turned down this manuscript by an unknown author about a strange religion.[35] Finally Bruce Humphries, Inc. decided to accept the book—and to sell it for $2.50 a copy, hardcover! This letter was sent to Emeric's agent:

I have looked over Mr. Emeric Sala's manuscript, This Earth One Country, and I am reading it in more detail slowly and carefully. It is really a very good piece of work. It is well written and, while the market is perhaps somewhat specialized, I happen to know that a book of this sort, which will strongly appeal to Bahaists, ought to have some sales possibilities. ...

Meanwhile, please tell Mr. Sala that I am really impressed with the value of the book, and it is quite possible that much more might be done with it in the long run than the ordinary commercial publisher might imagine.[36]

Emeric continues:

For reasons I cannot explain, Mr. Brown, the owner of Bruce Humphries, Boston, read and liked the MS and agreed to print 5000 copies (a fact for which any sensible business man would have said his head should have been examined). They might have broken even, but certainly made no money. ...

This book should have been reprinted by the Bahá'ís in the 1950's, when the first edition was sold out. The Indian NSA was planning to issue such an edition. The German and the South American NSAs were considering a German and a Spanish edition. Then came the Guardian's Ten Year Crusade and a ruling that all efforts and resources should be concentrated exclusively on the Plan. Even the World Order magazine had to be discontinued.[37]

When the book was published, many people wrote Emeric and I have excerpted some of their comments.

Recently I loaned a copy of your book "This Earth One Country" to Mr. Henry C. Beecher of Fort Lauderdale, Dorothy Baker's father, and his comments were so interesting and unusual I wish to share them with you. He wrote:

"What a book! Especially for the stranger or beginner! Beginning on a most interesting but innocent looking note of politics and economics, he drifts naturally into world problems and leads gradually up the mountain, knocking aside the obstacles of prejudice and ignorance on the way, until he lands one, breathless and panting, at the top. There he `pops the question' and performs the `common law' marriage. If the reader fails to say `yes' it is just his mistake and misfortune."[38]

Have just had a chance rapidly to glance through your manuscript ... and wanted to write you to say that I think it is excellent. ... so often you bring to their logical conclusion arguments which have more or less been wandering around in my head searching unified expression. ... Particularly did I like your chapter on "The Christian Individual in an Immoral Society" - which seemed to me to be the crux of the whole matter of the place and need of a social religion such as Bahá'u'lláh teaches. The phrases I liked too – "social legislation is no substitute for moral education."

Last November I was told about the Cause... Then I was given your book,

This Earth One Country. ...
    I had been a law enforcement officer or a soldier all of my adult life and at the time I was given your book I was Coordinator of Law Enforcement Agencies for California. I tell you this because of what is to follow. When I had finished reading page 73, "America tried but failed to live without liquor. It had apparently forgotten...;" I was convinced of the divinity of the Prophets.[39]

The excerpt mentioned above comes from the chapter in the book devoted to Islam. Here Emeric referred to the failed attempt by the US to prohibit alcohol use in 1919 through the National Prohibition Act. In contrast, Muhammad's forbidding the use of intoxicating beverages still had an effect of his millions of followers some 1400 years later. Emeric wrote: "That a modern democratic state, disposing of unlimited funds, having use of the pulpit, radio, press and the police, could not compete on a moral issue with a poor, untutored camel driver of Mecca, is one of many proofs that we have not yet found the key for the reading of history."[40]

    From Island Workshop Press:

    We are preparing to publish a pamphlet by Leroy J. Montgomery on "The Negro Problem: Its Significance, Strength and Solution". The author is a Negro minister, and we believe that he is making a real contribution to the study of this problem.
    He wishes to quote from your book, "This Earth, One Country"...[41]

I have discovered this pamphlet by Leroy J. Montgomery online! At the end of the pamphlet Montgomery states: "My personal belief is that the Bahá'í faith, in so far as its racial and social idealism is expressed by Emeric Sala, is destined not only to teach, but also to demonstrate to America and the world how to solve the race problem."[42]

A student who used the book in a scholarly article on the Faith wrote:

I was recently asked to write an article on the Faith for the magazine

Common Cause published by a group of faculty members at the Univ. of Chicago who are interested in world government. ... I relied to a very great extent on your book in preparing my article. Your presentation, aimed at the intelligent, thinking person, was exactly what was required in this case.[43]

Dr. Ross Woodman, longstanding member of the Canadian Bahá'í community, wrote me a few years ago about *This Earth One Country* and about Emeric:

> I read Emeric's book as soon as it appeared and when I met him we talked at length about it. He was so fundamentally shy and I was so moved about his stories of how he had learned to speak English by going to any meeting where English was being spoken. He worked hard on his pronunciation, not knowing that he was at the same time working on digging his own intellectual foundations deeper and deeper. English was the language that taught him the Bahá'í Faith and the Bahá'í Faith was the "archetypal" language he had known from birth.[44]

Marion Hofman in England sent Emeric a copy of a book review she had written, with a little note jotted in the corner:

> I sent this to "World Order" [magazine] today, in case they haven't a review already. The book is a grand job, and I'm loaning it right and left.

> Emeric Sala's book, "*This Earth One Country*", reaches England on the eve of the convening of the General Assembly of the United Nations (January 10, 1946). Although written apparently before the San Francisco Conference, the book could not be more timely. All the world now knows that the institutions embodied in the United Nations Charter are far from adequate to meet the threat of atomic war. But what does the future require? ...
> "*This Earth One Country*" is a book for our day. It speaks in practical and understandable terms to all those who are concerned with society and the direction of world events...[45]

Mr. Maxwell wrote from Haifa :

Before I forget it, tell Emeric that among the books I have read from cover to cover in Haifa – and I have not read a great many – was his book – and I enjoyed every page of it.[46]

Rúhíyyih Khánum sent Emeric this letter, referring to his book as well as to his pilgrimage 10 years earlier:

Recently I had a chance to read your book quietly and I was so proud of you! I think you wrote it very well and it is a very useful book to give to a type we never had anything to begin with before! ...

How blessed your life has been since you sat on that blue velvet sofa in our drawing room so many years ago and were thirsty for the Cause! (I don't mean the sofa blessed you!) To me it is a true object lesson of the words of the Bible "seek ye first the Kingdom of Heaven and all else will be added unto you." It is a never failing rule – how true it has been in my life too: for however much I loved other things, I loved the Cause most and see what it has given me! ...

You know when you were in Haifa I was quite worried over you. You asked the Guardian such very pertinent questions and I felt the answers you practically forced him to give you were – for you – a rather hard pill to swallow! But if they were not what you had figured out they would be, they never-the-less did you good and carried you forward into a deeper realization of the Faith. I have had, in these ten years, more than one "straightening out" of my concepts by Shoghi Effendi and at times it was a wrench, to say the least! For only he can see the Cause as a whole and balance all its component parts; we are sure to have biases on our own pet angle of it that fits most comfortably into our individual psychology.

To go on always developing, deepening ... what a challenge that is! Mother used to put it in such a cute way: she said the Faith was a university she had been studying in for over 35 years! ...

Well Emeric dear, God bless you! And go on growing as you are – I think you are another laurel in Mother's crown of spiritual children – but don't get conceited![47]

Finally, this excerpt of a letter written on behalf of the Guardian to Emeric refers to *This Earth One Country*:

March 24, 1946
The many valuable services you are rendering the Faith—through your book, your teaching trips, and your local Bahá'í work—are very deeply appreciated by him, and he rejoices to see you and your dear wife toiling so faithfully in the service of our beloved Cause. In this connection he wishes to thank you for the copies of your book which you sent him and which he placed in various Bahá'í libraries here.[48]

As a child I was proud of having an uncle who had written a book, though I had no idea what it was about. Some years ago, while going through my own process of examining the Bahá'í Faith, I found a copy of *This Earth One Country* in a library in Miami, Florida, where I was living at the time; reading it helped me in my personal investigation. In those days, the book could be found in libraries far and wide. Bahá'í's arriving as pioneers in South Africa found a copy in the Johannesburg library, filed under Muhammadanism.[49]

1944 Centenary

Emeric almost did not attend the 100th anniversary celebrations of the Declaration of the Báb. On hearing he might not go, a friend, Bahíyyih Ford, urged him, in no uncertain terms, to go.

Once in a hundred years the activities and spirit of the Cause reach a climax—It is the Plan of God that it should be thus—In this country a gathering together of the believers in a Convention. ...

There are crowds, there is much small talk, but these are not things to matter—we are there to learn, to serve, to drink deeply, to be ignited with the Spirit as we have never been before. To be inspired! To pray. To be ready to take up the greater tasks that lie ahead. This is our opportunity!

How can we stay away? It is like deliberately deciding to have spiritual anemia.[50]

Rosemary of course was delighted, and wrote to Audrey Robarts:

Bahiyyih Ford's letter convinced Emeric to make the trip. He even thought of a gift for the Centenary—to visit all the countries of the Americas.[51]

Rosemary's description of the 1944 Centenary was glowing:

... we walked outside to go up the steps into the Temple. ... and my heart was crying out ... for guidance to greater service; my body was conscious too of being crowded by 2000 Bahá'ís, as we more or less gently inched our way inside. I always thought I would have to wait to be in the other world to see so many Bahá'ís! The Temple was so beautiful - ferns, palms in the centre ...[52]

Travel to Latin America

A soft brown, beige and white rug made of llama wool was a gift from South America. I kept it for years until it wore out. Rosemary and Emeric made several trips to Central and South America, now equipped with the Spanish they had learned during their year in Venezuela. Wherever possible, they would visit Bahá'ís and their friends. In those days before television and computers, public speakers were in demand and Emeric gave many talks. Here he describes that gift offered during the Centennial celebrations:

In [October 1945] Rosemary and I left on a four month tour visiting Bahá'ís in every country of Central and South America, except Paraguay [due to illness]. It was all on DC3's, which cruised at about 150 miles an hour. ... It took two days to fly from New York to Mexico City. We stayed overnight in Corpus Christi, Texas ... since there was no night flying.

We joined Dorothy Baker[53] in Mexico City for nine days. After reading my prepared talks in Spanish I had to answer questions in my bad Spanish. Dorothy advised me not to read my talks in the future, since I could hold my audience with my bad Spanish, while I lost them when I read. ... My delivery improved from place to place, and by the time we reached Lima, Peru, I was proficient.

In La Paz, Bolivia, we got into trouble. It is the highest capital in the world at

14,000 feet. ... The mountains around rise to twenty thousand feet and more. When we reached the airport at 6 a.m. the only pass through which the plane could fly out was fog bound. We went back to our hotel for another day, but my lecture at the University of Santiago in Chile had to be cancelled. There was a large audience, we were told, waiting.

Flying from Chile to Argentina we had to cruise for several hours through a canyon at ten thousand feet as the mountains on both sides rose to around 20,000. We had again and again the sensation that the wings will scrape the sheer rock on both sides. It was the most spectacular and exciting part of our journey. Today's passengers flying over thirty thousand feet miss it all.[54]

Emeric was an unusual speaker. He would talk thoughtfully, leaving pauses which allowed the listener to integrate his often complex ideas. His talks were lightened by his self-deprecating sense of humor. The early training received in the Montreal Youth Group would be put to use. A report in Bahá'í World, 1944-1946 shows what Emeric accomplished on this particular trip:

In the nineteen Latin-American Republics included in their comprehensive itinerary, Mr. Sala gave seventy-nine Bahá'í talks, ten over the radio, to audiences ranging from fifteen to two hundred and twenty. All possible channels of publicity were utilized to their fullest, resulting in at least forty-seven free newspaper articles, covering from one to five columns, seventeen of which were accompanied by pictures of the speaker.[55]

While Emeric gave lectures, Rosemary provided backup support and encouragement. Her travel notes were filled with detail. Here are Rosemary's impressions of flying in the mid-1940s, of praying in Mexico City, of the tremendous inequalities in Central America, and of Bahá'ís that they met:

St.Lambert, October 20th, 1945: Otto drove us to the Colonial Airways. The first part of our plane trip was not auspicious! The plane flew low because of the clouds and we pumped along rather miserably. In fact, when we stopped at Burlington for customs inspection, I was sick for the first time in my life! Emeric looked rather white too! ...

Got to La Guardia Airport ... were squashed up in a poky waiting room and finally got away by eleven thirty. Thoroughly enjoyed our trip—the plane stopped about every two hours. Meals were delicious. ...

Mexico City, October 26: Octavio arrived. After breakfast, he, Dorothy Baker and I walked to the Plaza Reforma to find a bench on which to sit and pray for Mexico. I said the Tablet of Ahmad, Dorothy read the powerful Long Healing Prayer of Bahá'u'lláh, newly translated.... Then Octavio said the Remover of Difficulties 95 times. The effect on us all was so tremendous - we were wrapped together in confident peace, as though set in a pillar of light from the world of God. The voices of vendors, or children playing, came to us as though from a great distance...

[Octavio] told us of his first Feast. He had expected that he would enter the doors of heaven and become a new being. But there was a fight over a very insignificant question of a picture of the Master. He was heart-broken and awoke at dawn sobbing. ... Then he suddenly felt himself to be in a vacuum of silence and a voice said, "It is nothing. You will become an igniter." Dorothy told us of her first experience on the NSA. How X told a few off-color stories and there was a fight over Temple contracts. Dorothy suggested prayer, X said, "Trust a woman to go mystic on us". She drew herself up and insisted. After they prayed, the solution came to cable the Guardian as some kind of precedent was to be established.

San Salvador is the most pathetic distressing country to visit. Stark, ragged, dirty poverty is everywhere. The contrast after Guatemala City is appalling beyond words. No wonder there is no distinctive art to be found - a people so cracked by poverty can't do anything else but exist. The stores are filled with cheap American products, the streets filthy. ... Truly, it is a miracle that the Cause is established here - a triumph for Clarence which God alone can reward. He has been here six years and only been home once - that is true service.

... Miss Montalvo came hurriedly to the hotel to tell me that she had a note of invitation to the reception for President Rios of Chile at the University. ... I dashed about changing my dress. When we reached the University, the Hall was filled so we were too late. But we stood in the balcony. ...One saw the general public of El Salvador! Mixed in with students, mostly well-dressed, were ragged workers from the streets and ragged is a literal term. Hundreds of curious dirty ragged children pushing their way ... The President spoke. We were too far away to hear clearly, but it seems to me that everytime he mentioned the word "democracia" there was loud applause from the audience - except the army men and their cohorts. ... The young students had the brightest most alert looking faces, courageous too! For moving among them, listening to comments, watching the ones who applauded were several secret police. As President Rios left there was applause, and cries from the students for "Romero". It seems he is an exiled San Salvadoran. ... I somehow do not feel the University will be permitted to have "open doors"again.

Tegucigalpa, Honduras: T. seems to be full of energy to give in the service of the Cause. He has a dominating nature but I was told a little incident about him which pleased us. Young Natalie [Natalia] de Chavez, the only woman Bahá'í on the L.S.A. told me that T. had felt very hurt over some remark ... about there being no leaders, no directors in the Cause. He complained to Natalie. Being a wise young woman, she told him this was an opportunity for further spiritual growth for which he should be grateful. Whereupon he made a compact with her that she was to signal to him whenever she felt he was being domineering!

Managua, Nicaragua, Nov. 15: Elizabeth came at 5:30 to visit before dinner and our meeting. She told us stories of the bloody revolution staged last Saturday to coincide with Pres. Rios' visit. It seems the government placed placards on the walls, as coming from the people denouncing his arrival but when the people tried to tear them down the soldiers attacked them. People lay dying in the streets. She told us how two Bahá'ís' lives were saved because she and Gayle (Woolson) warned them not to mix in politics! Because of this warning they avoided all contact with the revolutionists. They both said, "Now we believe in miracles!"

Costa Rica, Nov. 20th: I had a very nice breakfast in bed and enjoyed the comfort of it.

X visited this afternoon. ... In speaking of Y she said something about him not being spiritually developed because he was not interested in her talk on the Seven Valleys. I imagine she has the conception of many that a "spiritual"subject relates to prayer, soul, immortality, etc. Wait until she hears how Emeric can make the subject of government spiritual! ... This same evening a meeting took place at the Theosophist center. Two speakers preceded Emeric. .. About 43 were present, including seven Bahá'ís. ... Poor Emeric sat through them with his eyes closed—exhausted. Raul looked across at him anxiously while I said the Tablet of Ahmad. I whispered to Emeric to speak only 15 minutes as everyone looked so sleepy. However, his first words so attracted the audience that an electric charge took place. Sleepiness vanished and how they sat up and listened! ... Emeric continued to speak for 40 minutes. There was a wonderful atmosphere and everyone was full of enthusiasm and interest. Raul's face became again the face of the Centenario - all lit up. We went to sleep in that wonderful glow that always follows a successful meeting.

Costa Rica, Nov. 21st: R. came at eleven and brought (two other Bahá'ís) with him. They expressed themselves very freely over the situation and their hurt feelings... Emeric spoke with them very frankly telling them there was place in the Cause for everyone and that their troubles with the rest of the community lie in themselves as well as the others. He went on to say that the others needed more training of their minds and the three strong-minded ones needed more heart! They looked at us open-eyed for a moment and slowly nodded their heads.

...Then we went to the meeting—there were 52 present. The priest hurried in again and listened absorbedly as did most of the audience. Emeric spoke beautifully, very powerfully on "A World Faith and a World Plan". He introduced the subject with the three phases of civilization as spoken of by Ortega y Gasset, then went on to ask three questions—why a Christian would not kill as an individual, but would as a citizen of the state; also, not robbing as an individual, will as a group or as a national unit; give gifts at Xmas as an individual but never as a nation. He spoke the most cleverly and tactfully on the difference between Christ's gift of love to the individual and Bahá'u'lláh's [gift of] justice to society.[56]

In one of Rosemary's letters, Emeric added this loving note: "My sweet wife forgot to finish this letter. She also left out the date. If she would not forget things sometimes she would be perfect. And that would be too much to bear. I love her as she is."

This little flaw showed up from time to time, and we do not know the time and place of a significant visit with two refugees who were related to my mother's side of the family. My mother's older sister Bertha had married Willy Bergman, a refugee from Germany and survivor of Dachau Concentration Camp. One of Willy's brothers had fled to South America. Rosemary provided the following description with no date, no location. According to my cousin, Willy would receive letters from his brother in Saõ Paolo, Brazil, so that most likely was the site of the meeting.

About seven, we went downstairs to pay our bill. To our surprise the office man told us that Mr. and Mrs. Bergman had called yesterday twice and stayed some time waiting for us! He never thought of telling us, and they never thought of leaving a card or note with their address or telephone number. We hopped into a taxi and dropped in on them. They live in two small rooms of an upstairs apartment, their supper of bread and coffee was on the table. Willy had not written so they did not know our connection with Willy and Bertha. They did not even know the baby's name! She reminded us of Bertha a little - not as pretty or as young. He suffers from rheumatism as a result of his stay at Buchenwald. She works also. Thoughts of their struggles possessed me all during dinner. What a struggle those refugees have in these countries![57]

Emeric wrote to Shoghi Effendi, reporting on the trip.

Dear Shoghi Effendi:
As requested in your letter of Dec. 13th which reached us in Caracas, I would like to add the following to Rosemary's detailed report.

Having visited 19 Latin American Republics, we can report that the Faith for which Mrs. Maxwell gave her life in Buenos Aires has caught root in every Latin American republic. (Although we did not visit Paraguay, we met a Paraguayan believer in Argentina, another in Uruguay, as well as two pioneers who had lived in Asuncion. We therefore, feel that we can speak for Paraguay as well.)

We have found in only six countries, communities with functioning Assemblies, which held Spiritual Assembly meetings regularly and were able to exert collective effort...

We have found nine countries with nominal Spiritual Assemblies which did not meet for lack of perseverance or of a quorum or, if they did meet occasionally, they were unable to generate a collective will, much less to transform it into community action....

Our most cheerful news is that we have found in at least 12 countries resident believers, mostly natives, with great spiritual capacity, firmly rooted in the Faith and moved by an irresistible desire to serve the Cause of Bahá'u'lláh. They are already taking over much of the task which was initiated by North Americans. Several of these friends, because of their linguistic and cultural background, will be invaluable for future pioneer work.

Another notable fact which came to our attention was the overwhelming number of men among the active believers, while in North America the women outnumber the men. The same applies also to the communities.

We have also found that the Latin American believers, being mostly men, are particularly interested in the social teachings of Bahá'u'lláh, while the North American pioneers, being mostly women, stress the individual teachings at the expense of the former.

The striking difference between the two continents of the New World might eventually prove that neither can find its spiritual poise without the other. The common destiny of these two continents is tied together by more than a strip of land. There is a spiritual and cultural correspondence of the two Americas which Christianity was unable to exploit. Apparently this is left for the standard bearers of the New Faith.

We have met practically every pioneer in the field. They are a group of devoted and sincere souls. Their accomplishment in the face of almost insurmountable difficulties were momentous. They had to overcome also great handicaps. For instance:

Insufficient knowledge of Spanish. I know pioneers who have lived for several years in Latin America without being able to follow, much less participate in a Spanish conversation. Such teachers cause many misunderstandings. Natives also resent foreigners who live among them without taking the trouble to learn their language. Pioneers who cannot learn to speak a new language could be used to better advantage in countries where they are understood. Example and the language of the heart may be sufficient for the individual teachings of Bahá'u'lláh but the Administrative Order needs to be explained.

Although the Latins do not like to be taught by North Americans, especially women, it was almost miraculous to see to what extent our pioneers endeared themselves among the friends. ...

I cannot close this report without mentioning again Mrs. May Maxwell whose influence we felt throughout the journey. One of our most satisfying days throughout these memorable four months was our visit to Quilmes, one hour out of Buenos Aires. The photographs we have seen of the tomb do not do it justice. Those wings arrest and hold one's eyes... There is nothing sad nor somber nor heavy about this monument. Those outstretched wings cheer the onlooker to new heights and bolder ventures. ...

In all, it was a great journey, the greatest and perhaps the most fruitful we have undertaken. To have been there and seen only the "Wings of Quilmes" was in itself full compensation.

Gratefully yours,
Emeric Sala.[58]

This response written on behalf of the Guardian anticipates the great future contributions to be made by Latin Americans. Three current examples are the Ruhi Institute, an educational institution whose approach and curriculum are being used worldwide, begun in Colombia in the 1980s; FUNDAEC (Spanish acronym for Foundation for the Application and Teaching of the Sciences) with its focus on training and development, also founded in Colombia; and, Nur University, with its many educational innovations, originating in Bolivia.

March 24, 1946
Dear Bahá'í Brother:

Your most welcome letter of March 5th was received by our beloved Guardian, and he has instructed me to answer it on his behalf.

The graphic and to-the-point description you have given him of the conditions you found in Latin American Bahá'í Centers helped him very much to see the picture of the work there as a whole, and he feels your recommendations to the Inter-America Com. are excellent.

He has felt from the very beginning that these gifted, sensitive Latins, who are capable of being both spiritual and intellectual, have a great contribution to make to the future progress of the Cause everywhere, and he is very anxious that they should become strong enough to manage their own affairs.

...

He will pray that your labours for the Faith may be ever-increasingly blessed and fruitful.

With Bahá'í love,
R. Rabbani

And these words in the Guardian's own hand:

Dear & valued co-worker:
The services which you & your dear wife have rendered in Latin America are highly meritorious, & evoke my heartfelt admiration. I pray you may have similar opportunities in the near future, and that the Beloved may, wherever you labour, bless abundantly your notable activities and accomplishments. Persevere in your work, rest assured & be happy.
Your true & grateful brother,
Shoghi[59]

Another letter written around this time, on behalf of the Guardian refers again to the qualities of the Latin American people:

The Latin American friends have many fine traits of heart and mind, and he believes they will, in the future, when they become firmly grounded in the World Order and their numbers multiply, contribute much to the general progress of the Faith the world over.[60]

My own experience with Bahá'ís from Latin America occurred in the early 1990s when I spent some months in Romania as a pioneer. Youth from Central and South America were serving in towns and cities throughout Romania. They picked up the language almost immediately, and their warm personalities were embraced by the local people. They made a tremendous contribution. One dear friend remained, married a Romanian, and has served for years on the National Spiritual Assembly of Romania.

Visits to Eastern Canada

There were teaching trips in Canada as well. Rosemary would visit her sister Margaret and family in Prince Edward Island and combine these expeditions with teaching.

Rosemary describes a trip to Moncton, New Brunswick with Mabel Ives. Mabel's husband, Howard Colby Ives, had been a Unitarian Minister who gave up a successful ministry after meeting 'Abdu'l-Bahá in 1912.

> I was privileged to assist [Mabel Ives] in opening up Moncton to the Faith—oh, she was so beautiful, so highly brilliant in presenting the Faith, I only operated as an errand girl and felt honoured to do so. In those days, the NSA of the US and Canada felt that it could not pay teachers, except for traveling expenses. In Moncton, people flocked around Mabel Ives, not always for interest in the Faith, but for her beauty and charm. We were flooded with invitations. One day at breakfast she said to me, almost in tears, "Oh Rosemary, I am expected to sell these beauty products I carry with me to pay my expenses! When do I ever have the time? I will not sell them to those who come to me to learn about the Faith and you see how I have no free time." I was truly horrified at her situation - she refused help, except from the small sum her daughter could send her.[61]

One delight for Rosemary would be to see her friends, Willard and Doris McKay:

> Willard and Doris came to Prince Edward Island to pioneer - bought a not-too-productive farm but it was a joy to me to visit them, especially during the Fast. The old iron stove was hot and we all sat around it, each reading three verses at a time of the long dawn prayer. It was heaven and I am sure we'll recapture the essence of those days again. Doris told me how Willard (a lover of music and poetry, the soul of an artist) took some very menial job. They could only afford a room in New York at the same level of the elevated railway that passed by their window. Sleep was impossible; they were distracted until Willard discovered the rhythm of the Greatest Name hidden in the heart of the wheels clattering by their window! During these days in the farmhouse on P.E.I., Willard played the Caesar Franck Symphony and pointed out how the repetition of a climactic phrase was a chorus of the Greatest Name.[62]

In Halifax Rosemary met Annie Romer:

> Annie Romer spent some time travel teaching in the Maritimes, helping also to consolidate the nascent groups. I usually went on a few weeks teaching to assist, but it

was in Halifax I had most contact with Annie. Even now I picture her slight slim figure walking up and down the hilly, ice-clad streets of Halifax, seeking halls suitable for meetings, haunting newspaper offices with articles on the Cause, notices of public meetings.

She would explain to me the training her husband gave her. [Harry Romer] was an editor for the Associated Press and trained her in the importance of printing date, page and newspaper headings for every clipping! ...

Harry and Annie spent the years from 1926-1935 in England, a critical period for the Cause. ... Harry had introduced to the friends there the value of the right type of publicity on the Faith, giving it prestige as well as attracting the public. ... They did wonderful service for the Faith, indeed Annie told me that the Guardian had said they had re-created England! ...

The Guardian wrote Annie after Harry's death, "Harry will help you with increasing power from the other world." This she felt. This she felt. At moments of difficulty, she would hear, with inner ear, Harry singing his own special song to her.

Martha Root, shortly before her death, wrote Annie that she had a dream. She and Harry were standing together in a beautiful place trying to get a message through to Annie who was speaking to a large audience.⁶³

Visits to Western Canada

In Canada Emeric found ways, during the war and afterwards, to integrate his business responsibilities with the needs of the Faith. The following selections from Emeric's papers show how few Bahá'ís there were in the major cities of Canada, and how the numbers, little by little, grew:

When the Bahá'ís decided to open up Toronto, I established a branch office there, which paid for my traveling expenses. Later, when it was decided to open every province to the Faith, I would make regular trips across Canada, selling during the day and visiting or (giving talks) at night. One Sunday, I had to give three talks in the Vancouver area. Next morning, Monday, I had business appointments in Edmonton, and had to give a public talk the same evening. We were young, it was a pleasure.⁶⁴

While flying across Canada during the war on DC3 passenger planes, civilians were often bumped in favour of the military. When the check-in girls asked me if I was flying for the war effort I answered, "No, the peace effort, to prevent World War III". Since I had speaking engagements all along I was never bumped.[65]

Emeric gave a talk in Regina, Saskatchewan, in 1939:

When I arrived in Regina, Saskatchewan, an arrangement had been made for me to lecture before the Institute of International Affairs. I remember standing on the platform, facing about fifty strangers, with no other Bahá'í in that room or, for that matter, in Saskatchewan, to proclaim for the first time the Call of Bahá'u'lláh.[66]

I had always had the moral support of Bahá'ís in the audience. Now I had no one to lean to for support, for encouragement. I turned to Bahá'u'lláh, nobody else. For me it was a spiritual experience to turn to Bahá'u'lláh for help. I think I gave a satisfactory talk. It was perhaps the first public talk where the Bahá'í Faith was mentioned in Regina. After that I often went to Regina and I have a special affinity for that city.[67]

Excerpts from a report of a trip to Western Canada in 1946:

I was not happy in Vancouver on this trip. Some Bahá'ís compromised with the teachings during the war. The others tolerated it. The result is spiritually depressing. Since all the Bahá'ís in Vancouver are of British stock, I suggested that they concentrate each year on one of the minority groups, like the Chinese, Japanese, Jews. If they will succeed to attract and absorb at least one of each group, their spiritual health could be restored. ...

There are only five Bahá'ís in Victoria. Bruce Hogg is confident to form an assembly soon. ... Both meetings, we felt, were successful. There were many genuine inquirers. Almost all our free pamphlets were taken. Even a book was sold. ...

There are now six Bahá'ís in Calgary. ... Doris Skinner, pioneer in Calgary since eight and a half years never looked as happy and confident as now. One of the new believers is Noel, our first Canadian Indian. Rev. Dr. M. of Hungary and his wife were our new contacts. Both showed unusual interest in the Faith and promised to study it.

I was staying at the Palliser where Mrs. Maxwell stopped several years ago.

When the hotel manager asked whether her husband is Mr. W.S. Maxwell, the famous Canadian architect who designed the Palliser Hotel, she answered that he is her husband all right but Mrs. Maxwell never knew that the hotel she was staying in was built by her husband. ...

My heaviest engagements were in Regina and my stay of one and a half days was to end in physical exhaustion. Providentially, however, my plane was delayed four hours, which gave me the necessary sleep to restore my strength.[68]

On this trip to Regina, Emeric accomplished the following in one day: held a press interview resulting in an article in the Leader-Post; met a former Bahá'í; gave a dinner-talk at the Institute of International Relations, a club for men only, on "Latin America and World Affairs"; and finished off the day with a fireside on Bahá'í Administration at nine in the evening. The next day began with a 10 a.m. visit to the first Japanese Canadian Bahá'í, Mr. H. Takashiba, and his wife Sunshine, "who looks close to her name"; followed by a luncheon with "a brilliant young man which might have more far-reaching results than my subsequent talk ..." In mid-afternoon Emeric spoke to 260 grade 11 and 12 students at Central Collegiate on "World Government" and in the evening, gave a public lecture on "World Peace on Trial".[69]

In 1949, Emeric made another trip to western Canada. Here is a draft of a report with comparisons to his teaching trips in the previous ten years.

Regina: No Bahá'í was living in Regina in 1939 when the Institute of International Affairs first heard of Bahá'u'lláh. [Ten years later] after many trials and hardships the Regina Assembly stands firm though small in numbers. ... Leslie and Mabel Silversides of Regina have just made a momentous decision. They are going to sell their house and move to an Indian Reservation as school teachers...

Saskatoon: Mary Fry, our new pioneer with two Bahá'í university students arranged a meeting which was attended by nineteen. Several left their name wishing to attend a regular fireside.

Calgary: The history of this city will always be linked with the name of Doris Skinner ... In 1939 Doris was a newcomer in Calgary. She had no one to invite to meet a speaker, much less arrange a public meeting. And now 65 attended a Bahá'í public meeting, while 150 businessmen were at the Kiwanis luncheon to hear Emeric Sala speak on "Civilization on Trial". ...

Vernon, B.C. has the unique distinction of being Canada's smallest isolated assembly-city. Situated in the country's largest apple valley which harvested last year seventeen hundred carloads. Loudspeakers, spot announcements, radio interviews, placards on the street and on a Bahá'í's truck, telephone calls and newspapers were used by Vernon's valiant community of nine (of whom three were bed-ridden) to assemble 55 people to a public meeting on a foggy night.

Vancouver has the second oldest Assembly in Canada and has developed qualities of solidarity and confidence. It featured a Bahá'í luncheon for men only. Some Seattle friends operated a tape recording machine during a discussion with the purpose of sending the tapes to the friends in Japan with special greetings from Canada. It was probably the first time that the voice of Bahá'í Canada was carried across the Pacific to Tokyo. ...

Victoria, B.C. our most western city, has a community of barely nine. Yet there were about eighteen at the meeting for Bahá'ís, since so many live in the outskirts. Sixty came to the public meeting.

Comparing the trip of 1939 with the one just completed, we find that against the five cities visited in 1939 there were ten in 1949. Instead of eight talks, now 24 were delivered and the total audience of 250 in 1939 increased in ten years to over a thousand.

These figures may not be impressive, but the Faith is established. Its roots are set. Western Canada has a solid foundation on which thousands of years of Bahá'í history can be built.[70]

The anniversary year, 1944, commemorating the declaration of the Báb 100 years before, was fast approaching, and with it the end of the Seven Year Plan. By January of that year, many of Canada's goals had been met, but the Maritimes still were an issue. The Robarts family made an offer, Rosemary, as member of the Regional Teaching Committee of Eastern Canada, was elated. In this letter, John Robarts advises Rosemary of the family's plan, with his well-known humour in full evidence:

> January 6, 1944
> After receiving your inspiring letters yesterday two people in Toronto

put their heads together for the nth time on this pioneering subject, and the following wire was sent off to Charlotte Linfoot: "If Moncton situation desperate we will move as last resort. Please advise".

Perhaps I should tell you who signed the wire!! They were 'John and Audrey Robarts. As you know, we volunteered before, but our offer was not accepted. ... It would be a big move, taking our family of six down there and giving up a marvellous job. But if it is the will of Bahá'u'lláh, that's all we want, and I have no doubt a house will be found in Moncton, and that I will be able to make a living some way."[71]

Soon Rosemary replied:

January 12, 1944
Dear John and Audrey,
I cannot tell you, or Emeric either how deeply moved we were to hear of your re-decision. The final move is out of your hands but I truly feel that your wonderful, loving sacrifice has set in motion a tidal wave which will sweep over and obliterate all our problems. ... I am silenced in awe before you, stunned at the magnitude of what you have offered to Bahá'u'lláh.[72]

Then the National Spiritual Assembly of United States and Canada decided against the offer. The Robarts remained in Toronto and other pioneers moved to Moncton. Experiences like this were fairly common in those early years of establishing the first Local Spiritual Assemblies across Canada.

A further cause for celebration in May, 1944 was the completion of the Seven Year Plan with its goals for all of the Americas. Two months earlier, Rosemary had written to Rúhíyyih Khánum about the Canadian goals:

March 26, 1944
Praise be to God - the Seven Year Plan in Canada has reached its objective! It was a thrilling moment for us when Emeric and I welcomed the last settler - Mrs. Netta Powers of St. Lambert with her three small children (seven, four and eight months old) - to make the ninth believer in Moncton. The ninth believer for Charlottetown arrived a few days before. We were all so exhilarated and intoxicated. It was indeed a happy

Naw-Rúz. Mrs. Powers left St. Lambert on Naw-Rúz. St. Lambert is feeling very happy at sending two settlers and four children out into the field. Of course we realize steady work of consolidation remains to be done. Charlottetown as yet has no native-born believers. Moncton has only five, and Halifax only two. ...

The intensity of my longing to be a settler abated somewhat when I realized Bahá'u'lláh had permitted me to be with Mrs. Ives when she opened the Plan in the Maritimes in 1937 in Moncton and at the end when the last settler arrived in Moncton to complete the Plan. Emeric assisted in opening the Plan in the west and was the one to add the final touch of confirmation to the ninth believer in Regina. So weren't we blessed? I am happily acquiescent not to be a settler for it is as though Bahá'u'lláh recognized my longing and accepted the spirit of my intention.[73]

Beaulac

Emeric tells the story of Beaulac, Canada's first Bahá'í School, and of Bill Suter:

We visited Bill Suter, a Bahá'í living 200 miles north of Toronto on "Rosemary's Farm". He called it that way because we helped finance its purchase. Bill was a colourful person, a Swiss immigrant, who got tired of the city ... and wanted to make his living in the country. It was also his dream that when he died his farm should become a retreat for Bahá'ís. He worked from sunrise to sunset and got nowhere. We then suggested to him that he sell his farm, and we will buy him one in the Laurentian mountains, about sixty miles from Montreal. ... [We] and other Bahá'ís will visit him in the ski season and when we both die we turn it over to the Bahá'í for a summer and winter school. He agreed and within six months his farm was sold.

When Freddie Schopflocher heard about the scheme he liked it and suggested that he join me half and half. He also wanted us to buy it in the name of the soon to be formed National Spiritual Assembly of the Bahá'ís of Canada, and to start with the winter schools at once. We were delighted with the idea and proceeded accordingly. [Together with Freddie, in 1946] we bought the Beaulac farm near Rawdon and had the first winter week including Christmas and New Year, for about 18 in very close quarters. Our schedule was study, skiing and fun. The Rakovskys, Salas and Bill chaperoned the young. A non-Bahá'í young man, Noel Ryan, ... could not understand how New Year could be enjoyed and celebrated without liquor. Afterwards he admitted that he never had nor could have conceived of a more hilarious New Year than this one without alcohol. [Noel later became a Bahá'í]. After running out of water, we shoveled snow into the well, and survived.

The farmhouse was improved and enlarged, two additional cottages were built, another two wells were dug, part of the barn was rebuilt into a lecture hall, regular winter and summer sessions were held for more than twenty five years. It was also offered and used by the Canadian Youth Hostel Association.

Bill kept cows and goats, which were his special love, and sold Swiss herbs. His inseparable companion was Quinty, a lovely dog. Young people loved Uncle Bill, and he enjoyed their company. He died of a heart-attack ... while repairing his roof. His French-Canadian neighbours brought his body down, and the Bahá'ís buried it. He was over seventy, having lived the way he wanted to and being useful to his fellowmen.[74]

The January 1951 edition of *Canadian Bahá'í News* includes an article on a winter session at Beaulac from which the following is excerpted:

A very interesting topic which resulted in much discussion was, "A new form of leadership - Group work". Here we discussed the sponge type of personality who sits back passively, absorbing and receiving benefits, without contributing, as compared to the radiator personality who has discovered that the way to enjoy oneself to the full is by contributing to the general welfare of the group.

The Recreation Committee planned its activities with the view in mind of encouraging the development of radiators rather than sponges. It was generally observed that more enjoyment was derived from activities requiring participation rather than passive enjoyment...Informal sing-songs broke out on the least provocation. Everyone enjoyed the Beaulac yell that Bert Rakovsky devised. All were encouraged to try some skiing...[75]

Ask anyone who attended Beaulac as a child in those early days and you can be sure they will mention Bill Suter and his goats; playing in the fields and hills while the adult sessions took place; the delight of sleeping in bunk beds; trips to Rawdon Falls; some might even remember passing the prison on the old highway from Montreal to Rawdon.

The National Spiritual Assembly of the Bahá'ís of Canada

The Bahá'ís of Canada and the United States used to be administered by a single national body. Now the time had come to separate and for each country to elect its own National Spiritual Assembly. In the spring of 1948, the first Canadian National Convention took place at the Maxwell home. Nineteen delegates from all provinces came to vote. The nine members elected to Canada's first National Spiritual Assembly were Laura Davis, Rowland Estall, Lloyd Gardner, Doris Richardson, John Robarts, Emeric and Rosemary Sala, Siegfried Schopflocher, and Ross Woodman. Rosemary and Emeric would continue to serve in this capacity for the next five years. Rosemary reflects on the relationship of this first election of the National Spiritual Assembly of Canada to the first election of the Universal House of Justice that would take place 15 years later in Haifa, in the home of 'Abdu'l-Bahá:

And only once in writing a report I saw the connection between the Universal House of Justice, which was elected in 'Abdu'l-Bahá's home in Haifa and the National Spiritual Assembly of Canada which was elected in the place that 'Abdu'l-Bahá called his home in Canada. I think it's very lovely to dwell on this relationship and to think of the significance of it. That the [National Spiritual] Assembly was formed in the home of 'Abdu'l-Bahá. ...

Rosemary recalls early National Spiritual Assembly meetings:

We went [to Toronto] about every month I figure, in the beginning and it was very heavy going. I think we were all exhausted, we usually began Friday evening and carried through for the weekend. ... And also we were not used to such concentrated activities.[76]

Ross Woodman, one of the members of the first National Spiritual Assembly of Canada remembers Rosemary:

> When I was in Beaulac one summer teaching a course with Rosemary, I told her (of a dream about the Báb). We were sitting on a large rock near a very small waterfall and she interpreted the dream as a birth dream. I had, she said, been born again. I shall never forget the way she talked to me that day, moving her arms in large arc-like motions that seemed to be conducting the sound of the water. It was a moment of profound bonding which I carried in me throughout our days together on the National Spiritual Assembly, Rosemary and I being what the other members thought to be the most 'mystical' of the nine. We were always trying to find the spiritual meaning of any problem which rather interfered with more practical matters demanding very immediate decisions. Freddie (Schopflocher) was quite bewildered by the two of us and sometimes impatient. John (Robarts) was never impatient as he circled the table by inviting each of us to speak. Then Rosemary would suggest some lovely restaurant for lunch, but quite often it was decided that we did not have time. I, of course, was eager to go to any restaurant that Rosemary would suggest.[77]

The following letter from Rúhíyyih Khánum was written a year after the formation of the Canada's National Spiritual Assembly.

> Dear Emeric:
> It did my heart good to hear you and Rosemary had helped ---. The reality of Bahá'í love is so much more important than anything else in the world! I guess it would make your and my spiritual mother happy too!
> My book[78] is coming out – and I have cold feet. Did you feel this way about yours? Or are you sure of yourself and don't get frightful inferiority sensations at such moments?
> I could stand hearing from you more often. Rosemary is such a comfort and gives me so much welcome news. Tell her I have a letter to her under way.
> I am so busy. No day seems long enough to do all that must be done and the correspondence is a burden - but a pleasant one, for I know how much the Guardian's letters mean ...
> I admire the Canadian N.S.A. It is near the Community and loving and

natural, may it always remain on this high pillar. There is a tendency to manufacture too much tape, red or otherwise, in the administration process.
Much love,
Rúhíyyih[79]

"Here is your home"

Rosemary made notes during her pilgrimage from December 1 to 9, 1952. Here are extracts:

At last one enters the Shrine of the Báb. Rich soft carpets cover the floor, the soft glow of the lamps illumine the crystals of the chandelier, the vases of flowers, the petals strewn over the white cloth on the threshold, the brilliant scarlet of the rug which covers the very core of the Tomb. ...

The pilgrims' first dinner in Haifa is a tremendous occasion. It is then one usually first meets the Guardian. The members of the household gather in the sitting room waiting for dinner to be announced. This is a signal that the Guardian has come. ... As one turns the corner, one looks into the dining room still a few feet away ...The Guardian is seated at the upper right hand of the table, rises, and with a smile of welcome and a warm handclasp greets each friend and motions one to a place at the table. Rúhíyyih Khánum is seated on his right, the pilgrims usually sit at his left or opposite him.... When he begins to speak on some aspect of the Faith, sentence sets on sentence, phrase on phrase with such clarity and power one's vision of the Cause seems to stretch as space does, into aeons and light years. ...

...Arriving at Bahjí, that heavenly Spot, Saleh, the keeper, greets the pilgrims. At all of the Holy Places, one is touched and humbled by those who serve. They awaken an even deeper appreciation of the treasures they guard and care for. As one walks about Bahjí, rejoicing over the beauty everywhere, Saleh outlines amidst the digging and planting, the new beauty the Guardian is designing. With a voice warm with love he would say, "My Guardian said this..." "My Guardian wishes that..." Then with a laugh, "My Guardian asks us to do the impossible, but because he asks it we do it!"

A simple supper is served in the caretaker's home, with the birds flying in and out of the open windows as they did in the days of the Master. This is a touching link with Him, bringing the past and present together in this world as they are in God's.

The moment comes to enter the Most Holy Tomb. As soon as one steps into the entrance one has an impression of light and space and life. The living green of the trees from an indoor garden reaches up to the sky-light. ... The Tablet of Visitation stills the restless waves of one's heart...

...One leaves Bahjí after a night sleeping in the Mansion. One leaves Haifa and the Holy Land after nine days' pilgrimage. The price of pilgrimage is to have an eternal hunger in one's heart. ... Memory becomes one of the most precious gifts of God, for through it Shrines and Gardens blossom forever in one's heart. Nine days are over, pilgrimage ends, yet as with all endings, means only a new beginning.[80]

Before going on my first pilgrimage in 1984, Bahá'í friends gave me advice and told stories of their own experience. Rosemary wrote this to a friend about to depart:

> Perhaps you may feel the real impact of your experience only months after you arrive home, but know that the impact will be there in every pore of your body. Don't let your imagination try to create this power; just relax into the will of God as a leaf, a flower, a bird does! It will flow into you and through you I hope to touch everyone you meet. And remember dear that the time will come when Bahá'ís will not be permitted to enter the Qiblih itself, except for certain occasions, or certain individuals. As spiritual consciousness is deepened in us, we would or will not be able to bear the spiritual power there condensed in the Holiest Spot on this earth. You have heard how some Bahá'ís could not remain long in 'Abdu'l-Bahá's presence at times...[81]

Green Acre

One day I heard that my aunt and uncle were taking Tip (the seven-year-old son of good friends of theirs) with them to Green Acre. I wanted to go too and must have expressed this in no uncertain nine-year-old terms! As a result, I was included in the expedition. As we drove through Vermont and New Hampshire, with heavy rain pelting the roof of the Buick, Tip and I worked hard at memorizing prayers. Rosemary had created a competition to see who could learn a prayer first—was it the obligatory prayer? Or the healing prayer? At Green Acre we attended children's classes. One afternoon, we were taken to Ogunquit Beach where we reveled in the Atlantic Ocean. I have a vague memory of visiting a very kind, very interesting elderly man who paid special attention to Tip and me. This must have been Hand of the Cause, Roy Wilhelm, who lived close to Green Acre. I also have a vague memory one day, of Rosemary telling us that she and Emeric would be going to a funeral, and that we would remain behind at children's classes. Here are Rosemary's recollections:

> It was so wonderful to be at Green Acre again. We brought Tip, a seven year old boy, and Ilona, a nine year old girl with us. They were so excited to be in a place where 'Abdu'l-Bahá had been that when we entered the room He occupied, they walked over every corner of the floor so that they could say they had walked in His footsteps. Green Acre was the place where I was more deeply confirmed, so that the children's joy was a fountain to me with which I refilled the well of my soul. We visited Louis Gregory the day before he died. Do you know his story? He is the Negro lawyer who became a Bahá'í before the Master's visit to America. The Master married him to his white wife, also a Bahá'í. He was on the NSA for years. When we saw him, his wife was so troubled for he had refused food for several days saying that 'Abdu'l-Bahá was healing him and had told him not to eat. The next day he was with the Master after eighty faithful years, over fifty of them in service to the Faith."[82]

Emeric adds details:

> When we visited Green Acre with you and Tip we visited Louis Gregory who was sick in bed and a few days later we attended his funeral. He spoke to us from bed and said that 'Abdu'l-Bahá is waiting for him and he was anxious to meet Him again.
> We also visited Roy Wilhelm in his large summer estate not far from Green Acre. He took us around his property and tried to surprise you with all kinds of

jokes and tricks and surprises. We all enjoyed him very much.[83]

Norma

A much-loved niece, Norma Sala, was the first of the younger generation in the Sala family to become a Bahá'í. She did so at the age of fifteen. Norma was the daughter of Blanca (Emeric's sister) and Nick who lived in New York. For various reasons, Norma was educated in Canada, attending St. Helen's School, an Anglican boarding school in the Eastern Townships near Montreal. Rosemary wrote about an experience at school following her declaration as a Bahá'í that showed her strength of character:

When Norma went back to school, she decided by herself that she would no longer take communion in church. This is a Christian ceremony, a very beautiful one, in which the church members eat a tiny piece of bread, and drink a sip of juice, saying that they do this to remind them of the sacrifice which Christ made ... And the Christians say, during this ceremony, the words of Christ, that they will do this until Christ returns to earth as He promised He would. What do you suppose Norma did? She told the principal that she would not take communion. The [principal] was shocked and surprised, and asked "Why not?" Norma replied, "I am now a Bahá'í and believe that Christ has come again in Bahá'u'lláh, so that I do not need to do it any longer.'" The principal then said, "But why don't you do it with the rest of the girls? After all it is only a form, and doesn't really matter." Norma must have sounded a little rude, but she was very sincere in her response: "Why do you do it then if it doesn't matter?" I was proud of Norma.[84]

Rosemary conveyed happy news to her friend Amine:

Our big news is that Norma offered to leave her "super" job in the States and pioneer in Verdun. She made the offer last summer, planning to arrive this summer. At Beaulac she met our wonderful young German pioneer, Klaus Liedtke. He has been pioneering in Verdun since his arrival in October. She and Klaus are announcing their engagement at Ridván. They are both such eager and devoted Bahá'ís it is a joy to see and hear them plan."[85]

It was the early 1950s - stunning that a marriage could occur so soon after World War II between two youths, one of Jewish background, and the other who had grown up in the Nazi era in Germany. The Bahá'í teachings emphasizing the oneness of humanity made this possible.

Norma and Klaus married in 1952, and moved into an apartment in Verdun. At the end of March, 1953, the news came that Norma had given birth prematurely. There were complications and soon after, she died. I have a few memories of that time, being with my sister and younger cousins in a darkened living room, curtains drawn against a very sunny cold spring day. But I have no memory of hearing the news. Long afterwards, I asked my father, "Who told me that Norma had died?" He thought for a minute, then answered, "Maybe no one." The adults were in shock; at the same time, children were 'protected' from anything to do with death. It can be understood that we were overlooked. Rosemary again wrote her friend Amine:

> I still can't believe that Norma is not here! She would phone me twice a day, or I would phone her, echoes of her everywhere. We learn to rejoice somewhat in these memories and the closeness of her spirit. For over a week I would wake up in the morning with tears on my cheeks and the pillow damp. Then one night I had such a comforting dream: Norma walked into my bedroom in an old grey dressing-gown and got into bed with me to share my breakfast as she did so often during her engagement period, this time last year. We were talking and laughing happily together. Suddenly I stopped, looked at her and said, "But you are dead!" She continued to smile, giving a little shrug saying, "What difference does that make?" Then into the room walked Rúhíyyih Khánum and behind her May, carrying a baby's chair. I was cross and wondered who would be permitting May to carry the chair. Then again I said, "But May is dead!" Death, our concept of it as separation, became suddenly so ridiculous that I woke up laughing![86]

Emeric often would talk about the importance of "being strong", of developing character. In the month of March, 1953, his mother and his niece both died. I do not remember him showing emotion. However, near the end of his life, Emeric writes about this period in the early 1950s:

> In 1952, my father died at the age of 77. The next year, which was the opening of

the Bahá'í Ten Year World Crusade, mother died ...

[Three weeks later] Norma died giving birth to Keith. The shock was tremendous and paralyzed all those who were close to her. ...

But why did it happen? Why was this devastating suffering necessary? Looking back ... one can say that this tragedy touched the deepest core of our beings, and we emerged more sensitive and human. Suffering is necessary for growth, and the deeper the pain, that much closer do we become conscious of our own inner reality.[87]

A few months after the death of Emeric's father, Rosemary's father followed. Here she writes Rúhíyyih Khánum in Haifa:

Emeric and I had just returned from my father's funeral. He had been ill for so long, and so unhappy for even longer at the state of the world and the dissolution of his beloved British Empire! It was his whole world, and the only one he wanted. He had been completely bed-ridden for four months; my mother has retired into a foggy world where past and present are one in an effort to face the inescapable fact of Dad's illness. We all feel that she will recover now and regain some of her old spirit and capacity to enjoy life once more. Death is truly "glad-tidings" when one has lived out one's span and though I felt that with all my heart there is a peculiar sense of losing something of one's physical self. It is a psychic experience. Dad became so lamblike and appreciative for anything done for him, that I feel he was prepared for the great journey.

I was speaking to Dorothy this morning; she was so eager to learn how you were, especially your father. ... D. wanted me to tell you that the chestnut tree is a glory of bloom just now, and even yet, hyacinths and tulips bloom from the ones you planted so many years ago.[88]

Emeric describes some different encounters with death:

In the beginning of the fifties through some strange turn of events, my wife and I were privileged to say farewell shortly before their death to three outstanding Bahá'ís: Montfort Mills, Louis Gregory and Sutherland Maxwell. Two of them were Hands of the Cause, all three had behind them many years of distinguished and self-effacing service for the Cause. We saw them hours before they passed away, though at intervals of about a year between them, hundreds of miles apart. Nevertheless, we had in each case, the same strange and unique experience which we dearly treasure. We both felt in their presence something rare and precious, which we could not understand nor describe.

Two decades later, rereading The Seven Valleys [by Bahá'u'lláh] ... I realized that what struck and fascinated us when looking into the eyes of these three dying men was the rare privilege of a glimpse into the Valley of True Poverty and Absolute Nothingness. [the Seventh Valley]

They were lying helpless, physically broken and spent, some in pain, their earthly strength gone, all desires, possessions and opinions having become meaningless, with no will to live; and yet there was a serenity and lightness about them which put any inkling of despair or hopelessness to shame. Their complete detachment was their true poverty. They were ready and eager for the flight beyond. In each case, when my wife and I said goodbye and left them, we felt enriched and elevated. ...

Bahá'u'lláh writes:

God is as visible as the sun, yet the heedless hunt after tinsel and base metal. ... Until the wayfarer taketh leave of self, and traversed these stages, he shall never reach the ocean of nearness and union.[89]

5

AFRICA AND THE TEN YEAR CRUSADE

IN 1953 the Korean War ended, the Soviet Union exploded a hydrogen bomb and cigarette smoking was, for the first time, reported to cause lung cancer. It was also the year that Elizabeth II was crowned queen, while *I Love Lucy* reigned on television. Meanwhile, Bahá'ís were galvanized by news from Haifa. Shoghi Effendi had launched a momentous Plan: the Ten Year Crusade—to last from 1953 to 1963. [See Glossary] Soon hundreds were leaving their homes and moving to territories and countries around the globe, to help establish the Bahá'í Faith.

Shoghi Effendi wrote:

> The avowed, the primary aim of this Spiritual Crusade is none other than the conquest of the citadels of men's hearts. The theatre of its operations is the entire planet. Its duration a whole decade.[1]

In that same year, the National Spiritual Assembly of Canada was asked to send a representative to an international Bahá'í conference in New Delhi, India and chose Fred Schopflocher. In July, Fred passed away suddenly. Emeric recalls the crisis following his death in July 1953, shortly before the Conference.

> ... John Robarts felt that if no one else could go, he should be the sacrificial lamb. He phoned us long distance from Toronto, as members of the National Assembly, and Rosemary in particular felt strongly that he should go. He told us later that Rosemary's persuasion was the final straw that made him decide to go. None of us realized then that his decision had profound repercussions on the rest of our lives.
>
> After John's return from India we were sitting in his office on November 4th, 1953, at our regular scheduled National Spiritual Assembly meeting. We were all hit like a

bombshell when he announced that within the next few weeks he will leave with his family for Bechuanaland as a pioneer. He learned in New Delhi that we could offer to pioneer. John had been so moved at that Conference that after consulting with his wife Audrey he cabled the Guardian offering to go anywhere.

We were all of course spellbound and deeply moved. Rosemary, sitting across looked at me with longing eyes, and I could see and feel her desire to volunteer also. I too was overwhelmed by the emotion in that room and nodded. With that nod, and without the exchange of any words, our fate was sealed, and we never regretted it.

The day after we cabled the Guardian offering to go anywhere. Two days later we got the answer:

"Suggest Comoros Islands love Shoghi".[2]

Rosemary and Emeric had never heard of these islands. In fact, the Guardian's Crusade turned out to be a huge geography lesson for many Bahá'ís! After locating these four small islands situated in the Indian Ocean, they began gathering as much information as they could. This not-too-helpful reply came from the secretary of the National Spiritual Assembly of the Bahá'ís of India, Pakistan and Burma:

Nov.19, 1953
Many thanks for your letter of 12th instant received today ...
In fact we know very little about Comoro Islands as also about Madagascar with particular reference to the conditions prevailing there. What we know is that these are French territories....[3]

The secretary suggested that they contact others, including Mr. Jalal Nakhjavani in Dar-es-Salaam, Tanganyika, and Emeric wrote, asking these questions:

Nov.26, 1953
We would appreciate any information you could give us about the Islands, electric current, if any, AC-DC, 110 or 220 voltage, and if there are any hotels and in which cities.

We have about 100 books in English, Bahá'í and on related subjects. Would you advise us to ship them along?

We have a six-room house full of possessions. Would it be wise to get rid of most and what should we bring along?"[4]

In my own limited experience in going as a short-term pioneer to Romania in the 1990s, I had the help of pioneer workshops, an office at the National Center in Toronto to contact with any question, addresses of friends in Romania itself. Conditions were first class compared to what early pioneers faced. Here Emeric describes their preparations and subsequent refusal of entry to the Comoros Islands:

We applied for a visa which the Consul submitted to Paris. During the subsequent six months I liquidated my business, we sold our house, brushed up on our French, packed about ten wooden cases, and then we were turned down.

We cabled again to Haifa and were given a choice of Zululand, Madagascar, Rhodesia or Gambia. We applied to South Africa for Zululand and asked for an answer in three months, which was the time required to process an application, to Lourenco Marques [the capital city of] Mozambique by which time we would arrive there. If we were refused, we would have gone to Rhodesia, where we did not require a visa.[5]

It should be remembered that by this time, the Salas were approaching 50 years of age. Their fearlessness is astonishing.

Meanwhile, the Robarts family was setting out for Bechuanaland (now Botswana). While bidding them goodbye in Montreal, Rosemary presented 13-year-old Nina with a large box. In the box were 21 individually and exquisitely wrapped small packages. Rosemary gave firm instructions to open only one gift a day. Nina would obediently wait for high tea which the family had with the captain and chief engineer. All would watch in anticipation as she opened the gift of the day. Included was a photo of Shoghi Effendi at age three, a tiny prayer book of Rúhíyyih Khánum's, a pair of bedroom slippers, a hand-embroidered Hungarian blouse, a box of chocolates, biscuits in a red metal box, a bar of fragrant sandalwood soap... The small gifts were the highlight of the 21-day voyage.[6]

I have a memory of a spring day, the family gathered in our living room at the farm, with Rosemary and Emeric about to depart for Africa. There was a sense of impending change for all. I have a vague recollection of a prayer recited. They left Montreal in May, 1954 on a cargo boat, not knowing to which country they were going. Suddenly they were gone. Their cottage by the lake was empty. I felt the loss.

Rosemary wrote about their four-month long trip to Africa, meeting Bahá'ís along the way. The first stop was Cardiff, Wales.

When we arrived at the chandler's office [upon disembarking] we found a small group of five Bahá'ís there. They had traveled, in such dreary weather on a Sunday morning, and by tramcar, to welcome us. We all traveled back the same way, by tramcar, to Cardiff. All the best restaurants were closed and most of the poorer ones. We found a very unappealing one on a rather miserable side-street. All that could be served us, and rather grudgingly at that, was tea and toast. Then I realized that,...prior to sailing in Montreal ... I had bought some very special pastries and also equally special chocolates. ...I had them in my carry-all! ... And when I brought out the photographs that had been taken of Rúhíyyih Khánum in her Montreal home the year before, joy was complete.

We can never forget this loving gesture of true Bahá'í hospitality of these Welsh friends. It was the beginning of a chain of such greetings, everywhere we went.

Equal hospitality was ours in Oxford [England] where we spent a week-end with the Hofman's. It was for them the sweets had been bought originally! We met the believers, among them Dan Jordan, a student of music at that time. We accompanied the friends to hear a talk by Richard St. Barbe Baker[7] on his recent exploratory journey to the Sahara Desert with some students. After the talk we had coffee together. When he learned that we were on our way to Africa, he showed his delight by sharing with us some of his experiences with the Kikuyus. He could not believe that his beloved Kikuyus, with whom he had worked in a perfect relationship and fellowship on reforestation in East Africa could be involved in the Mau-Mau atrocities. He sang a Kikuyu song for us in a somewhat cracked voice but so full of love and longing for his African friends that our eyes filled with tears.

The deep love he revealed opened our hearts to an anticipation that we too would share in this love when we reached our final destination... Every experience of St.

Barbe Baker we would find realized, within our limitations, during our fourteen years in Africa.[8]

We shared in an unforgettable commemoration of the Báb's Declaration held at the Bahá'í School at Esslingen [Germany]. ... I wish we could have taken a colour photograph of the room. ... The long tables along three walls had lilac blossoms, buttercups and green leaves strewn on the white tablecloths, with bowls of yellow, red and white tulips at each end. ...

We remembered dear Marian Jack [the Canadian pioneer living in Sophia, Bulgaria] who had so often visited the school. It was then we were given the photograph of Marian Jack standing by the door of this school with the beautiful smile on her face. This was sent to the National Spiritual Assembly of Canada and was reproduced in Canadian Bahá'í News.[9]

From Europe, Rosemary and Emeric embarked on what Rosemary referred to as their "Mayflower", the *Kenya Castle*. The ship stopped at various ports as they sailed down the east coast of Africa. They were prepared with addresses of Bahá'ís. Rosemary's collection of anecdotes includes the following:

We had been booked a very nice room on the top deck of this one class boat, but when we got on board we found that passengers getting on in Southampton [England] had been able to change cabins and we found ourselves four decks down in the bowels of the ship with a port hole very difficult to open. To my fresh-air fiend husband, pioneering began at this point.[10]

The Kenya Castle was full of South Africans returning home. It gave us an opportunity of knowing the kind of people we would be associating with, though only casually as we were mindful of the Guardian's instructions not to become too intimate with white South Africans as our teaching was to be directed towards Africans only, except in special circumstances.[11]

Arriving in Cairo, our hearts beat with excitement, thinking of the Master's many visits there and the site of the burial place of Abu'l-Fazl and Lua Getzinger. We visited a curio shop owned by members of the Yazdí family whose great-grandfather had been sent to Egypt by Bahá'u'lláh Himself. While drinking coffee with three of the Bahá'í friends and eagerly speaking (in French) of news of the Faith, a large group of our fellow passengers arrived and gazed at us somewhat curiously as we drank coffee with the darker-skinned friends. Then we realized, that for the sake of the Faith, we would have to curtail our open contact with the Bahá'í friends en route…Our first intimations of what our future life would be![12]

 Arriving at Mombassa we were welcomed so lovingly by Ursula Samandari … and Irene Bennett, another British pioneer was with her. Several African friends accompanied them but they had wisely remained in the background. The white South African [passengers] looked on us with approval being met by two blonde Britishers! …

 When it was learned that the ship would be loading for a week Jalal (brother of Ali Nakjavani) made arrangements that we should take the train to Nairobi to visit [another branch of] the Yazdi family. …

 Aziz [Yazdi] met us on the train as arranged. He had been on a visit to Bahá'ís imprisoned as suspects of the Mau-Mau though the charges could not be proved, so was returning to Nairobi on the same train as we were traveling on. When he met us we saw his face aglow as the result of his visit. He mentioned two most devoted souls whose very contact with other prisoners was conducive to teaching. One of them said, "I begin to teach for it is my duty. I would begin to talk about hygiene (he worked in the hospital) and then the Cause would come out of my mouth." He asked for more declaration cards, nothing for himself. When another pure-hearted believer was praised for his teaching efforts his reply was, "I did not do any work. I'm only a witness to the result of Bahá'u'lláh's words." There were seven declarations in one [detention] camp and again the only thing requested was more declaration cards and prayer books though Aziz had asked if he could send them anything to help relieve the restrictions of prison life. … An LSA had been formed in one camp and permission was given to hold classes. … Aziz remarked, "Love and confidence in the beloved Guardian is the key: he says 'Do it!' and in obedience, the spiritual bounties are poured out.[13]

 June 29, 1954
 …E. and I returned this morning to the boat after visiting Nairobi, 350 miles

inland. We had armoured cars filled with soldiers to protect us! Every male in town carries a pistol or rifle, even some women... We had a heavenly time visiting the Bahá'ís...[14]

July 4, 1954
...We are in Zanzibar! It has been a beautiful approach to the island. ... The wind carries the smell of cloves to us across the green and blue streaked sea.[15]

Zululand

In Mozambique the Salas at last obtained their visas. Zululand was a region in the eastern part of South Africa, the homeland of the Zulu tribes, and today part of Kwazulu-Natal. Here are two descriptions of their arrival. The difference in tone is evident! Rosemary described it this way:

We had left Canada without a visa but happily it was awaiting us in Mozambique permitting us to enter South Africa. Our excitement and eagerness had mounted with every glimpse of that vast continent of Africa. Travelling down the East Coast we had caught so many nuances of smells and sights preparing us for Zululand, our final destination. ...

Our eagerness to reach Zululand made us leave [Durban, South Africa] by bus within three days to travel the dusty ninety-odd miles to Eshowe, the capital city — really a town. Our made-in-Canada bus broke down and we were stranded in the rain on the dirt road to wait for relief. It was dark when we reached the Royal Hotel. One dim light in the hall greeted us while a sweet-faced old Zulu led us to our room and later brought tea and toast. We were in Zululand! This was the first step of a new beginning: now we had to find a business and a home.[16]

While Emeric wrote:

Eight months have passed since our first cable to Shoghi Effendi, offering to pioneer anywhere. And now in June 1954 we are in reach of our goal. Entering Zululand late in the afternoon our bus broke down. Waiting many hours in the cold — since it was winter — and in the dark, we finally arrive about midnight, hungry, at our hotel in Eshowe where the dining room was already closed. We went to bed in a cold, unheated room.[17]

Emeric describes the first months:

> It was winter in Southern Africa. The city [Eshowe] was small, hardly any industries. We were thinking of buying a sugar farm. I was then [close to] 50 years old. I still had to make a living, establish myself somewhere, but it was too expensive for a good sugar farm, and I had no experience either, so we had to give it up after two months, studying it as a possibility. We looked around at lumber yards, other industries or businesses where I could make a living....[18]

> After about four months of investigation and travel throughout Zululand we ... decided on Samungu, a trading post in an African (native) reserve, 17 miles from Eshowe, the nearest police station, doctor and telephone, connected by a very poor earth road, which was not passable after a heavy rain for a week. Since our contact and teaching of the Africans had to be done without arousing the resentment of our white neighbours or the suspicion of the authorities, we bought this store with 18 acres of land, 16 head of cattle, subject to the approval of the Minister of Native Affairs in Pretoria, which we all took for granted. ... The nearest store was five miles from us. We were to sell to about three thousand half-naked, poverty stricken Zulus, corn, bread, tea, sugar, kerosene and other basic necessities. Our store also served as post office and registrar of births and deaths.[19]

Now established at their post thousands of miles from home, correspondence began to flow. Rosemary writes an old Bahá'í friend in Montreal:

> Sept. 19, 1954
> [It] is on a beautiful location almost 2000 ft. above Eshowe, on the edge of the Nkandla forest, in a native reserve. ...
> The store is the usual hole ...It needs windows for light and ventilation — there are none at present. It was packed five deep when we visited, by Zulus "in the raw",

wearing skirts, beshus (men's skirts) and beads. ...[20]

Emeric sent these observations to the Johannesburg Local Spiritual Assembly, entitled "The Mystery of Samungu":

'Abdu'l-Baha [would have] said — If Samungu has nine good qualities and one bad one, overlook the one and see the nine. Anyone living in Samungu who overlooks the bad things lives in Paradise. ...

...the first night it was the rats. They made a terrific noise in the attic and we felt the house was not our own. Well, they are gone. Three cats and our prayers keep them away. I never knew I can love cats that much.

Work from 7 to 5, Saturday until 1, I thought would be too much for a living. I find that I never found work as leisurely and pleasant as now. With no telephone, no pressure, no traffic noise... we prefer this work in Samungu to any holiday resort.

And then the dirt. ... And yet the mountain air is so clean that the collar of my white shirt remains white after a day's work — while in Montreal?

Last Wednesday, returning from Eshowe, I got stuck in the mud of a newly-scraped road three miles short of home. Helping hands put on my Canadian chains for the first time. I like our roads. They are full of curves, often unexpected, up and down, never dull, and then the undescribably beautiful landscape.

Every Wednesday I drive down to Eshowe with about 300 pounds of cash to deposit. I take the Chief or one or two other passengers along, and of course, inevitably, my wife, as bodyguards. But really, there is no danger. I just read that the first Bank of Manhattan had no safe for the first 50 years, and its night watchman had no gun. We of Samungu feel the same way. There is nothing wrong with Samungu, or its people. If there is, it is a mystery.[21]

Here are two of Rosemary's letters to children - this one addressed to me:

Feb. 12, 1955
...I wish you could meet our Zulu friends! ...the children are so bright-eyed, and all, young and old, have radiant smiles. I don't believe I have ever heard a Zulu child —

except a very few young babies — ever cry or fuss. A few of the little girls wear dresses... Most of them wear sugar or potato bags tied around them. No shoes, no socks or stockings. Their hair is oiled ... then plaited into tiny braids, with a few colored beads interwoven here and there... The children come to look at me very solemnly, their eyes peering at me shyly over the edge of the counter. I make them giggle at the funny way I speak Zulu, then we become friends.

One sweet old lady was in the store this morning. We looked deep into one another's eyes, and I felt as though we knew one another very well, this old, very dirty and shabbily dressed Zulu woman and I. She gave me a beautiful smile and I clasped her hand. She spoke in Zulu to Ngotho, our clerk, who was beside me, and told him she wished she could speak to me, to tell me Zulu stories and to have me tell her stories![22]

And a letter to my sister Renée, then 8 years old:

Jan. 24, 1955
The last letter you wrote through your secretary, you said that you were dizzy. I haven't heard from you since to the contrary so I suppose you are still dizzy!

Please forgive me writing to your secretary first. She is older than you, and if I hurt her feelings I might never receive another letter from you. She might refuse to be your secretary. Is she very expensive? What salary do you pay her? Two ice-creams and a bottle of Coca Cola? ...[23]

Emeric recorded his impressions of the Zulu language:

Zulu is an agglutinative language. The stem of a word is taken as a basis. We glue to it pronouns, adverbs, negatives, suffixes and prefixes, until the whole glued word represents an idea. ... In German there are three classes of nouns, in Zulu there are ten ... To pick up Zulu is as easy as to pick up mercury, and the result is just as disastrous. I always tell my Zulu friends that they need no other proof of their high intelligence than the intricacy of their language.[24]

While Rosemary and Emeric were still new to Samungu, customers would come to the trading post to shop and to look them over. Emeric describes one special day:

> One day, when our store was fairly crowded, an old Zulu with a finely chiseled, intelligent face kept on looking at me with startled eyes and amazement. Finally he asked our assistant in Zulu: "Who are these people?" He answered: "Abulungu pecheeeeea". "Abulungu" means white man. "Pechea" means far. If he extends "ea" in Zulu it means very far. If it is extended still farther, "eeea" means it is so very far that it is across the sea, which usually means England or Holland. But in our case, he said, "pecheeeeea"'which means we were white people from much farther than England, across many seas.
>
> When the old man heard this answer his face lighted up, for he now understood. What he meant was this. He has worked for many years in Durban and Johannesburg, and has seen many white men. He has seen in the eyes of these white men arrogance, an expression telling him every hour and every day that he is of the master race. Even the rare missionary he may have met looked upon him with the superior feeling of a father speaking to children, though the native may be twice his age. And now, for the first time in his long life, did he see "abulungu", that is white people, who looked at him and the other Zulus as equals.[25]

This report of Emeric's indicates the racial attitudes of that time in Southern Africa:

> Soon after we were settled down Bishop and Ruth Brown came to visit us urgently from Durban—four hours by car—telling us that they received instructions from our [Bahá'í] center in Johannesburg that we should destroy all our Bahá'í literature, including newsletters, pending secret police investigation. The application we signed for a residence visa stated that we will comply to the South African way of life. This was not defined but we can assume it meant Apartheid. We also knew that under the Act for the Suppression of Communism the Minister of State can deport any foreigner without giving any reason, and without any chance for an appeal. At that time we were unknown to the secret police, and we did not know how they would treat us if and when they investigated us.
>
> Eventually they did investigate some of us, including our literature, and since

we teach brotherly love without violence they decided we are harmless and not subversive, especially since we do not mix in politics.

Most of our customers lived in straw huts with mud floors and spoke only Zulu. We learned a few hundred words for basic communication. Some of our employees and neighbours had worked in the great cities and knew some English. ... We invited our employees and ... new friends for Xmas dinner, and insisted, contrary to custom, that they enter at our front door. Their spokesman told us with great emotion that this is the first time in their lives that they entered a white home at the front door and sat with them at the same table for a meal. It was also standard practice to call their employer "master". It took me a long time to break them from that habit.[26]

Rosemary gives her account of the above-mentioned Christmas dinner:

I decorated the house, prepared turkey and all the extras and a special cake, which we learned afterward was the hit of the party. At the close our "special treasure", Ngotla, spoke in Zulu to the others who nodded in agreement, "This has been an historic evening. This is the first time in Zululand that my people have come as guests through the front door. This occasion will be remembered through all the ages."[27]

A cautiously worded Naw-Rúz greeting sent by Rosemary and Emeric from Zululand, with an image of a Persian print:

March, 1955

How we wish you could visit us now that we are completely at home. We think of you and the friends so often, and especially at this time. We will be here alone on the 21st but will be thinking of you and the Haddens and the other friends down your way ... I will try to write a letter telling of our doings. We are still only two here but hopeful![28]

Edith and Lowell Johnson, two long-time pioneers to South Africa, edited a history of the years 1953-1963 entitled *A Ten Year Crusade Diary for Southern Africa*. This compilation has proved most useful and I have quoted from it extensively. Here is a report about a visit to Samungu by some young Baháʼís:

The Robarts family arrived from their pilgrimage and met immediately with the community. Patrick, instead, climbed into a waiting car with Dale and Kenton Allen, Andrew Mofokeng and Maxwell Ndlovu to go on a teaching trip to Zululand.[29]

Dale Allen described the first fireside:

That evening Rosemary and Emeric invited about six specially selected friends to their first fireside and Emeric spoke in most elegant tones (Max translating). Emeric was an historian and launched into the rise and fall of civilizations pointing out how each had derived its power from one of God's great Messengers. I was spellbound and always wished I had a tape recording. Emeric poured out his heart after not being able to talk about his Faith for all these months. After Emeric spoke, Andrew and Patrick and Max all made contributions. There were many questions, They were on fire with this new Message from God. I explained that Mr. Sala was a very brilliant historian. They replied that they did understand his talk, but truly enjoyed Max and Andrew's talks on Bahá'u'lláh and Progressive Revelation.

(Editor's note: This was the beginning of Emeric's frustration with teaching in Africa; very few in South Africa at that time had the world view which was his approach when he wrote the book *This Earth One Country*.)[30]

This report points out Emeric's challenge in adjusting his teaching methods to a new situation. He had been in great demand as a speaker across the main cities of Canada, and in the U.S. at Green Acre and Louhelen Bahá'í Schools. His lectures in Central and South America created publicity for the Faith, and drew new inquirers. In Africa the requirements differed, with teaching mainly one-to-one or in small groups, never in a lecture hall. One had to make contacts, make friends. There are equivalent challenges for Bahá'ís today (2016) with the focus of regular small-scale gatherings in neighborhoods for study, devotions and activities for children and youth.

At the Salas' first fireside, one of the Bahá'í youth, Andrew Mofokeng noted that among the Zulus there was "some reluctance the cause of which I could not fathom"[31]. Perhaps he felt intuitively the absence of the words of

Bahá'u'lláh, in the native language. He immediately began work on one of the many services he would provide for the Faith. Andrew, in his autobiography, *Tiger*, writes:

> Strangely, it was at Samungu Zululand while at the home of Rosemary and Emeric Sala that some inspiration came my way. It was here that I translated my first prayer from English into Sesotho. ... As we left Samungu for Johannesburg, Rosemary gave me a memento - Prayers and Meditations by Bahá'u'lláh. What a gift! This certainly helped to spur me on with the translation work because it was in Basutoland, during that January 1955 visit or teaching trip that I was able to translate nine more prayers into Sesotho under various headings and Beth Laws was able to put them on stencil and the first ever Sesotho Bahá'í Prayer Book was produced and circulated.[32]

The editors of the *Ten Year Crusade Diary for Southern Africa* included this comment, dated 16 January, 1955: "This first teaching effort in Zululand left a nucleus of interested Zulus which the Salas followed up. About a week later they had their first declaration."

Some years later Andrew Mofokeng, a newly appointed Auxiliary Board Member, visited Rosemary and Emeric in Port Elizabeth. In his biography, he wrote:

> The Salas occupied a very beautiful flat in a modern building overlooking the Indian Ocean ... In the city situation I expected that some arrangement would be made in keeping with the South African way of life at the time. There was none of that. I was welcomed into the flat and shown into my room ...
>
> What I enjoyed the most in Port Elizabeth was to discuss every aspect of our Faith with Rosemary and Emeric. They would come out in real depth and sincerity but all cloaked in a vibrant sense of humour which Emeric had. This made a lasting impression on me.[33]

Finally, after a year's stay in Zululand, the Minister of Native Affairs Dr. Verwoerd, (later Prime Minister) refused to extend the Salas' permit which had expired. Emeric writes:

When the news came that the Minister of Native Affairs would not allow us to remain in Samungu, not being [South African] citizens, it came as a shock ... Our minds were adjusted to stay in Samungu, if necessary, for life. [But] strange is the human mind. When we were forced to see the dark side of Samungu, it looked ominous and foreboding. We suddenly saw the steep grades and deep ruts in the road... the impassability in rainy weather. Our isolation without telephone in an emergency — with a doubtful road, a doubtful car, and a doubtful and reluctant driver in my wife...

Then there was one more reason why we left Samungu. After we signed up all our fortune in this Trading Station we received word from the Guardian that he considered our step unwise and too conspicuous, and this after I made this heroic sacrifice to live among [the Africans] as only a missionary or trader can. I was sure that the Guardian did not know what he was talking about. Now I am sure that he did. What is beyond my understanding is how he knew it. But then there is so much in the Faith beyond our understanding.[34]

Emeric's comments about the Guardian's understanding were based on this letter written in 1954, the year before the Minister's refusal to extend their visa.

> Haifa, Israel,
> May 5, 1954
> Mr. and Mrs. Emeric Sala
> Dear Bahá'í Friends:
> Your letters, one from Mrs. Sala, dated February 20th, and two from Mr. Sala, dated March 25th and April 15th, have been received by the beloved Guardian, and he has instructed me to answer you on his behalf.
> He fully realizes how deep your disappointment has been that you are not able to secure your visa for the Comoro Islands. He himself was deeply disappointed also. However, some of these places are extremely difficult to enter; and he hopes that where you have failed, at least for the time being, someone else will prove successful at a later date.
> He urges you, upon your arrival in Zululand, to find out the status of the Cause in neighbouring places, and, if it is possible for you to settle in one of the

neighbouring countries where the Center is much weaker, and where it is more difficult for people to get established, and there is a better possibility for people like yourselves to build up a business and remain, that you by all means go to the weaker Center, in preference to Zululand, which now has a certain number of pioneers.

He assures you that the example that you and the Robarts have shown has moved him very deeply, and he hopes it will stir the Canadian Community, and impress upon them the advisability of answering the pioneer call now, while the field is open, and the opportunities and the rewards so glorious.

You are often remembered in his prayers in the holy Shrines, and he is supplicating that you may be richly blessed, and meet with success in both your teaching efforts and in your personal affairs.

With warmest Bahá'í love,
R. Rabbani

May the Beloved bless your constant endeavours, remove all obstacles from your path, and enable you to enrich the record of your meritorious services to His Faith.

Your true brother, Shoghi[35]

The Johannesburg Local Spiritual Assembly recommended Port Elizabeth as the next pioneering post.[36]

The trading post was transferred back to the original owner with fair compensation for all the improvements made. Shortly afterwards Emeric met some businessmen who ran a textile wholesale firm and offered him an unusual opportunity in Port Elizabeth. Here Emeric reflects about these seeming coincidences and about leaving Zululand:

When we decided to acquiesce to the Minister's decision and to surrender Samungu without a struggle, Mrs. Ruth Brown told us that she felt that we were now on the "beam". We should just let go, let things slide, and she felt that we will be guided to the right place. ... She was right all along. Things had been moving since, very smoothly, it was almost miraculous. ... It gave me a hint of the inner peace and wonder of those who are always in tune with the Way of God.

When we said goodbye to our Zulu friends, there were several touching scenes. The Zulus ... do not show emotions as visibly as we do, but they were moved. We knew them well enough to read regret in their faces. Some had wet eyes, when they said goodbye to Rosemary, "omama", our mother. Some felt intuitively that they lost more through us than a couple of traders, who were perhaps kinder to them than others. We also regretted that we could not leave them more."[37]

Emeric ended a report on Zululand with a series of questions in 1955 that are still pertinent and could apply to the whole world, as we navigate through these tumultuous early years of the 21st century.

In the meantime, Zululand is waiting for an answer to pressing problems, both economic and social, therefore spiritual. What will happen to the educated Zulu? Who is to develop Zululand's great natural resources and for whom? As the standard of the African approaches that of the European, who is to divide the income of the nation, consistent with justice? As the tribal hold disappears what will be the backbone of Zulu morals? What opportunities are offered to the African in an increasingly industrial society? And last but not least, what culture will they be able to call their own in which they can find their true identity in relation to the rest of mankind?[38]

Port Elizabeth on the Indian Ocean

It was a beautiful ride through the sunlit hills of the Zulu Reserve on our way to Durban. We were carefree and happy. We had no home, no job, no future. We were again wanderers, drifting with the waves of Faith. It was an exhilarating sensation, for we knew that we knew no fear. ...

We attended the Unity Feast of the Durban Assembly. Precious among [the Bahá'ís] was Mrs. Agnes Carey, about 75, an invalid, the oldest Bahá'í in Southern Africa. She was born here and became a Bahá'í through Miss (Fanny) Knobloch about thirty years ago. ... She kept her Faith in all these years, all alone, isolated from the Bahá'í world. What amazes me is the quality of her faith. Though often in pain with arthritis ... almost blind, living alone in the Old Women's Home, yet every time I see her, it is she who cheers me up. She has the same quality of Faith as many of the old Bahá'ís of 'Abdu'l-Bahá's time that I met in the United States.

It was early November, and springtime in the Southern Hemisphere, when we left for Port Elizabeth where we planned to settle. We travelled through East Griquoland and the Transkei, reserves of the Griquas and Xhosas. ... Most of the 600 miles were paved. ... We met about one car in an hour.[39]

I established a wholesale business importing textiles, shoes, clothing, radios, pottery; covering with six salesmen half of South Africa and South West Africa (now Namibia). Our customers were Afrikaner, Jewish, English, Black and Coloured storekeepers. Business here was relaxed, easy going without the pressure and cut-throat competition of Montreal and New York. Our life, once established was pleasant and carefree, were it not for the archaic and unjust treatment of the blacks and the coloured.[40]

New habits and patterns had to be learned to navigate the racial attitudes of government and country, so opposite to the concept of one human family. Emeric writes about the strange laws of South Africa and the related risks:

... most of our African guests entered our apartment through the servants' entrance. We found this very embarrassing, but our friends accepted this humiliation rather than expose us to possible repercussions with the authorities. It was not against the law for whites to entertain Africans in one's home, provided no alcohol was served, but it was not the South African way of life. We pioneers were exposed to the Suppression of Communism Act, under which any alien could be deported at short notice, without any explanation or opportunity for appeal. Shortly after our arrival, a young rabbi, a former Rhodes Scholar, was given two weeks notice to leave the country. The only explanation his friends could give us was that he had entertained African and Coloured intellectuals in his home and that his sermons were outspoken. As Bahá'ís, we had to obey the law of the country, but we also wanted to speak about our Faith. To reconcile the two meant to walk on a tightrope.

Eventually, we were investigated by the secret police. Since we were found to be genuinely religious, nonpolitical, nonviolent and law-abiding, we were allowed to remain. Nevertheless, we were watched and at times followed...[41]

The website of the Bahá'ís of South Africa casts light on this time of apartheid:

> During this period of gestation, the Bahá'í Faith was being watched continually by the security police. Both the individual Bahá'í and the administrative bodies were under police investigation and surveillance. However, although the believers never compromised the principles of the Faith and gradually developed racially integrated Bahá'í communities, the numbers were too small and peaceful to be considered a threat to the apartheid regime.[42]

Rosemary depicts life in South Africa as a fantasy tale:

> May 15, ca. 1959
> This country becomes more Alice-in-Wonderlandish. These new flats ... have maid's rooms, but after the 1st of June no African maids are to be permitted to sleep here! They must be headed back into their locations at night, ... eleven miles from here and costs $9 a month bus fare. We may have Colored maids sleeping in but not Africans. This means the African women will be unemployed. I suppose the government hopes to force them back into the reserves which as yet cannot support them except on a meager diet of mealies (corn).[43]

Many white South Africans disagreed with their government's racial policies. The Glennies and Norman Bailey were examples. Here is how they became Bahá'ís, before the Salas had a chance to digest the policy, coming from the Guardian, to concentrate on teaching Africans. Rosemary writes:

> We also had an exciting time with Sheila and Bourne Glennie. While in Johannesburg we met that precious soul, "the father of South Africa", for he had remained faithful to his belief even though isolated from Bahá'ís and news of the Faith. Reg Turvey said he would send us the address of his niece Sheila as he used to speak to her of the Faith and he was sure she would be interested. When the address came it was found to be next door to our flat! Bill Sears was visiting us (before he became a Hand of the Cause) so we invited Sheila and Bourne ... We three arranged before that we would not mention the Faith but wait to see if she wished to speak of it — you remember the Guardian's

instructions about certain restrictions in teaching? Sheila and Bourne came and we fell in love with them ... We chatted about this and that for about twenty minutes until Sheila sat up straight and said, "I didn't come here to just talk. I want to learn about the Bahá'í Faith". We looked at one another laughing in joy and asked who would speak first! In two days, Sheila signed her card. Bourne took a little longer. All this took place during the first few months in Port Elizabeth and this reconciled me for leaving beloved Zululand.[44]

Norman Bailey, a student of theology and later a renowned opera singer, became the first European male Bahá'í to enroll in South Africa. He had been introduced to the Faith by Bahá'í Sylvia Benatar while in Salisbury, Rhodesia.[45] Sylvia gave him Rosemary and Emeric's address in Port Elizabeth. Here Rosemary describes the eventful meeting:

Remember Norman Bailey? We have just received a British magazine with an article on him saying he is the best Wotan (Wagnerian character) of today! It was so exciting the day we met him, when we were living in Matopos Flats up on the hill opposite the park. Emeric came in one evening and said to me, 'I have just seen a beautiful young man to whom I longed to speak of the Faith — he should be a Bahá'í'. We were about to sit down to supper when the doorbell rang and there stood the beautiful young man! He was then studying for the ministry. .... He asked me one question: to explain a verse in the Bible that puzzled him in relation to the Cause. I said a silent prayer for assistance — the answer came — and immediately Norman said, "Yes, that is it".[46]

In this excerpt from the *Ten Year Crusade Diary*, Norman Bailey reflects:

Few members of the Christian community were prepared to accept racial integration, and even the clergy were divided as to if, or how hard, they should try to convince their church members to accept other races into their churches. In this respect, the Bahá'í Faith was leading the way for generations to come and to me, the Bahá'í Faith was like a breath of fresh air in a racially stifling atmosphere.[47]

Emeric and Rosemary received some advice about teaching in South

Africa, from a "seasoned" pioneer and long-time friend Bahiyyeh Ford Winckler who was later appointed to the Continental Board of Counsellors for Africa:

> I read in your letters the question about teaching white people and a flood of memories came over me. Do you recall that when we came [to South Africa] Harry had a class of over ten, and all was in a flourishing condition? All this very soon after we arrived. Then came the day when we received the message to teach only the Africans. It was a real blow. We stopped everything and even offended some. But then began the heart-rending job of trying to find the first soul to teach. We drove for hours thru the locations praying, praying. Well you know that first soul was found and then another and another. We look back and see the God guiding wisdom in all that happened. The white souls as radiant as they seemed, could not, or would not, we have realized, been able to take the words of the Guardian. The Faith was established on a firm foundation <u>because it was in African hearts!</u> There is no question about this. The Guardian has said that the day will come when we can teach the whites but not yet.⁴⁸

In a letter to Bahá'í friends in South Africa, Rosemary refers to the request to focus the teaching work on Africans rather than whites.

> June 28, 1956
> (Sheila and I) could join the Red Cross group or some similar one, or the American and Canadian Women's Club for me, but this step I have avoided. I understood that the fewer connections we had with European groups the better.⁴⁹

The Library Project

Not long after moving to Port Elizabeth, Rosemary met the wife of the Dutch Consul who had just received a permit to establish a library in a nearby African township school. (Townships were areas in which the Africans and colored people lived a segregated life.) She offered to help. Within a few months the Consul and wife were transferred to Capetown. Rosemary continued with the work in New Brighton Township for the next 11 years.

To build up a collection, Rosemary would visit bookstores, libraries, consulates and contacts asking for discarded books and magazines, as well as shelving, nails and paint with which to build up the library. For additional stock, she appealed to friends and relatives in Canada to collect suitable books; a ship's captain whom she knew, transported these free of charge to Port Elizabeth. She would write with detailed instructions.

> Aug. 27, 1964
> The important thing to remember is that there must be no Bill of Lading: the books should be packed (depending on size) 100 to a carton and should be in charge of the captain or an officer. They can be addressed to me and labeled 'for under-privileged children' — not African children as before. ...
> I've just phoned the Holland-Africa Line. Mr. Van Hattum is on leave and will be back in September. I'll get in touch with him then. That will give you time to appeal for more books, perhaps from Shelley and her friends. Can she beg from her whole school? No school textbooks - unless attractive class readers or gaily colored science books.[50]

In Montreal, Sala and Gillies relatives were busily collecting books wherever possible. Rosemary's nephew Malcolm and I worked together, packing a large wooden crate and following the detailed instructions to get it to South Africa.

A young Cowan Secondary School student confirmed the positive effect of the project. He wrote the following letter to Rosemary's friend, Amine DeMille, who had sent some books:

> 19 Aug., 1958
> Dear Mrs. De Mille,
> I am very grateful indeed for the five books you sent us. I read two of them [by] George Washington Carver. I found them very very interesting indeed. I was even boasting to my school mates that I am the first and luckiest boy to read such books. Every child in our school enjoys your books. As soon as I had finished reading George Washington Carver, I was requested by ten boys to hand the book over

to them, because I told them how interesting the books were. I think you are really interested in us. These books are of the world's best.

May God bless you and keep you in everlasting good health.

Yours faithfully,

Douglas Ngesi (Prefect)"[51]

Years later, Rosemary was interviewed by Louise Baker who was collecting information about her mother, Hand of the Cause Dorothy Baker. Rosemary recalled that Dorothy Baker had once met George Washington Carver. "...he said to her, in his little, thin, quavering, old voice, 'Oh, tell the world, Mrs. Baker, that George Washington Carver thinks very highly of the Bahá'í Faith."[52]

In the following excerpts, Rosemary writes to friends and family about her project and in a subtle way provides hints about life in the South Africa of that time:

Dec. 17, 1957

I'm cleaning papers off my desk as I'm expecting three girls from Cowan School at 9:30 a.m. ... to help me mark, cover and catalogue over a hundred books from the Canadian shipment. I'm taking a chance at having Africans here. It is Xmas and I think our neighbours will be not too unsympathetic. Tomorrow, Mrs. Quinta (principal's wife) and her five children come for a Xmas party, and to play in the park, the section for African children. ...

This weekend we had fresh strawberries, grapes, peaches, plums, apricots, oranges, bananas, mangoes, pawpaws, and apples and pineapples! What a fabulous country, in physical beauty at least.[53]

I went to visit my pet school for the first time this year, owing to my illness. Such a warm welcome I received from all! Hannah (my treasure) had baked a caramel cake and I iced it to bring as a celebration. The teachers loved it. Everything was very quiet and peaceful but I will not go to the location (like a reservation) during Republic Week, as demonstrations are expected. A woman had offered to help me with three schools, but when I telephoned yesterday, she said she had been asked not to go to the African location. People are so afraid!

(The principal's wife) is such a precious believer—exceptionally fine. I had offered to send her to Convention but she left things too late and hasn't got a permit yet. I spend my rent money (received for summer cottage at Rivière Beaudette) on such things, as well as helping to educate my two Xhosa daughters and two sons. One girl is in training for a nurse, the other wants to be a doctor. They wrote that they would care for me in all future illnesses, bless them. Of course things would have to change as they wouldn't be permitted to at present.[54]

Nov. 2, 1960
The school library work has been extended. I have begun working in four additional schools this year. Two South African (white) women have offered to share the work and will each take three schools. One of the newspapers is going to do a write-up on the need of and eagerness of teachers and students for a library which it is hoped will stimulate people to donate books. Naturally, none of us will have our names mentioned! The more impersonal the better, these days and in this country.[55]

In another article in 1964, a Port Elizabeth newspaper with the headline "Books Bring A New Life" describes the school library project and a talk Rosemary gave to the Port Elizabeth branch of the National Council of Women (NCW). At the top of the clipping Rosemary added a note:

I have always refused to give talks for publication on my work but the NCW has been so kind in making yearly collections that I consented to speak. ... I told the NCW that as a result of their efforts during the past six years and efforts of others, the keenness of teachers has forced the Govt. to take recognition of this need—this year for the 1st time. [The Bantu Education authorities had built up a fund to be spent by regional inspectors to buy library books.][56]

Robert Mazibuko was a student at Cowan School. He became a "son" to Rosemary and Emeric, and in turn, they became his "Mamacita and Papacita". After Emeric's death in 1990, Robert and I began corresponding, first by letter, then by email. He sent vivid descriptions of his relationship with them that began with the library project. He has recently published his autobiography, *This Side Up*, which is dedicated to Rosemary and Emeric. Robert's first meeting with Rosemary occurred in the library:

> The library seemed to be run by a white lady who was very kind. She was able to remember the likes and preferences of some students and help them make choices of books, while in the library. She soon noticed that I loved books on adventure and that I preferred books about "Biggles".[57]

Rosemary loaned Robert a special "Biggles" book which was promptly absconded with by another avid fan. Robert returned nervously the following library day. Rosemary was strict and decided on a consequence: "My punishment was that after school, I was to stay in the library and help cover and catalogue books for the school."[58] And thus began a friendship.

Robert provides a close-up account of Rosemary's courage and inadvertently, of his own:

> In 1957 when I met Rosemary, there had just been very destructive riots in Port Elizabeth when a Jewish cinema owner was killed and several Jewish shops ... were burnt down. ... So, it was an act of great bravery for Rosemary to board a bus full of Africans in New Brighton at the time, but she proved she was there to stay, at least for a while...[59]

> ... There were four of us helping in the library: Angelina, Eunice, Daniel and I. What we did was cover books, label and register them and catalogue new books. This would happen after school between 2:00 pm and 4:00 pm. We did not have to worry about lunch as Rosemary Sala would bring sandwiches and soda. Usually a ride came and picked her up. The driver would most of the time be Abdul, an Indian clerk at Emeric's (business) Sala and Company.
> One day the ride failed to pick Rosemary up and she had to get out of New Brighton before nightfall. She called the office a number of times and found out the car was possibly out of town. She then said she would go home by bus and asked me to come along. We were all frightened for her as the political situation did not permit this at all. Five years ago there had been such terrible riots that left many buildings gaping black ash into the sky. ... The final statement was that ... [word left out] were no longer welcome in the township and were not too popular.

I prepared myself for whatever might have to happen ... I carried nothing with me having left my books at school and Rosemary carried a bag with her working tools like paper, scissors, plastic and some paper clippings.

We got out of the schoolyard into the street. That part was not so difficult as everybody on that part of the street knew Rosemary. We did not rush and did not talk. For some reason I trusted Rosemary knew what she was doing. We turned the corner and headed for the bus route. Everybody was watching this strange sight: a young boy walking with a tall respectable-looking lady. We did not stop or outwardly flinch. No audible comments were made. We went down Funde Road to Mendi Road and crossed the road to stand at the bus stop.

It was strange, no friends passed by to say hello though there were many students from Cowan in that area. This used to be the busy part of New Brighton. Today it was very quiet. This was the critical part: How long would we wait? Would somebody come and want to talk to Rosemary? Would the bus refuse her entry? We stood there in the sun, not talking and not looking at each other but I was ready to follow any cue. The bus arrived. We entered. The conductor looked curiously at Rosemary and allowed us to sit side by side next to the door. Rosemary paid for both of us. There were no events on the bus but the subdued conversation.

We got to the city and had to transfer to the Summerstrand bus. In this bus things were different. I deliberately went upstairs as the bus was marked on bottom floor WHITES ONLY and upstairs ALL CLASSES. As I passed Rosemary she winked. When the bus inspector came my way I told him my ticket had already been paid for ... and he believed me. We got off the bus near the sea and only then did we attempt to talk. It was a relief to get to her apartment and be able to really talk. However, she showed no signs of stress but continued as if that was what life was meant to be. This did not matter to me at the time and now years later I understand. Later Rosemary gave me bus fare to go back and I had no problem going home.[60]

Rosemary's involvement in an African school did not go unnoticed by officials. An entry in *A Ten Year Crusade Diary for Southern Africa* states:

Rosemary and Emeric Sala were visited at their flat by the secret police who wanted to know what Rosemary was doing at Cowan School in New

Brighton township so many hours a week and who the Africans were who were visiting them.[61]

Robert takes us into Rosemary and Emeric's home:

> The home of the Salas was the first White home that I entered not as a servant but as a visitor. In this home was a room we used for working on books. Rosemary called it "The Horrors". In the Horrors you would find boxes of books: some from the American Consulate, from the Canadian Embassy, from the Public Library and from friends overseas. You would also find parcels to be delivered to needy friends she had. Most of these boxes had clothing. Some of this clothing was for the "library helpers" to fit and take home. ... Besides clothing, you would find musical records. Once I found a box of books I liked and Rosemary asked me to buy them from her. I could only afford to pay a tickey each time I met her. After about four tickeys [South African threepenny coin] I was asked to stop payments!
>
> In one corner of the room was a curtained off area and there Rosemary kept many things. Some of these were projects. Some of the projects were making clippings from magazines which she mounted for the schools. I do know that sometimes when we asked a difficult question she would go to the corner and dig in and find something that would illustrate that better.
>
> Against one wall was a bed which Rosemary used when her phlebitis was causing her some discomfort. This is where she would lay down. Away from the bed she would put a foldaway table. The four of us would then sit there and work and chat and inquire...It is in this room that I met the Bahá'í Faith. It is where I shed many tears because of the sadness in some of the prayers of the Faith.
>
> At lunchtime when Emeric arrived, Rosemary would ask us to go to the bathroom and wash face and hands before going to eat with Emeric ... Rosemary never sat for long. She would be up serving everybody and fetching food and things from the kitchen. If I came alone to visit she would serve me in the "Horrors" so we could talk. ...
>
> In the Horrors I discovered there was a bookshelf and on that shelf were a number of Bahá'í books. Here I was deepened. It was also here that I found a second mother.

Rosemary would say that in the next world she would find a room like the Horrors where we could visit.[62]

I found this draft of a letter to the Guardian in Rosemary's files. She rejoices in the entry into the Faith of the first African in Port Elizabeth.

Beloved Guardian,
We have not written you for some time as we felt we should not take up your time, or give ourselves this great joy until we could report some worthwhile result of our pioneering. Today we are very happy as we have accepted the first African in this city into the ranks of Baha'u'llah's community. He is Xhosa, and may be the first of his tribe. He has worked for us for a little less than a year.[63]

A Ten Year Crusade Diary for Southern Africa records that development:

Frederick Gqola, an employee of the Salas in their business, enrolled as the first Xhosa believer there. ... He told us he had one interested contact but that he had been disappointed to learn that he was a member of the ANC [African National Congress], so he has the point of our attitude toward politics clear. (Editor's note: Fred was an active Bahá'í with many contacts for many years, then he became impatient with the seeming inability of the Bahá'í Faith to make changes in South African society, turned to the ANC himself, became an active member, and subsequently was arrested and served time on Robben Island. He was eventually released and settled with his Bahá'í wife in Transkei.)[64]

Rosemary persevered with her work and in the next ten years placed over 10,000 books in 11 schools. An editorial note by Edith and Lowell Johnson in their Ten Year Crusade Diaries states: "This library project at the Cowan School in New Brighton, Port Elizabeth was probably the first standard-setting Bahá'í socio-economic project in southern Africa, although performed on the basis of individual initiative."[65]

Years later, in 2003, the Bahá'ís of the Nelson Mandela Metropolitan Municipality dedicated a plaque at Cowan High School library in remembrance of Rosemary Sala. This was part of their celebrations of the 50th anniversary of the Bahá'í Faith in South Africa. Here is part of a report by Ian Sogoni, former principal of Cowan School:

> She got involved with Cowan High School when it was building a room as a library...She donated lots of books, some collected in South Africa and some brought from overseas. ... She was not only involved in Cowan High School, she helped in other schools as well... Newell High School... Kwakakhele Secondary School and Ithembelihle Technical School.
>
> She established a Sala Prize which was to honour a student who showed leadership qualities. The student did not necessarily have to be academically gifted. He/she had to be someone diligent, assisting teachers without being asked, exemplary to other students and also respected. ... She suggested a Xhosa name for this prize and Imbalasane(kazi)[66] was adopted."[67]

Years before this, in 1958, as the project was becoming recognized, Emeric wrote to the National Spiritual Assembly of Canada about Rosemary's accomplishments and his pride in her:

> Yesterday, Saturday afternoon, we went to New Brighton, an African location, to the school closing of Cowan Secondary School. There were over 400 students, 100 parents, the staff of about 10 teachers, 2 African ministers, a white Government official, the American Consul's wife who presented the prizes, the General Manager of the Morning and Evening Paper (English), a City Councilor and a few other European sympathizers.
>
> The Principal announced that two years ago the staff room was turned over to Mrs. Sala and through her efforts the school library has increased from 80 to 4,000 books, and if she would not have been so selective for quality they would have over 5,000 by now. The desire for books among the students has constantly increased.
>
> After the closing speech by a prominent industrialist, and after all the prizes were given, the Principal presented Rosemary with a wooden tray depicting a Xhosa. He read the inscription: "From the staff and students to our Mother and dearest friend the school has ever had."
>
> There were tears in my eyes and if that was the only purpose of my coming

to Africa I am satisfied.⁶⁸

While serving on the National Spiritual Assembly of Canada, Emeric witnessed the incorporation of the Faith in that country. The Canadian national body was in fact the first in the world to be formally incorporated. This happened in 1949 by a special Act of the Canadian Parliament. It may have been because of this that Emeric encouraged the National Spiritual Assembly to acquire greater legal status for the Faith in South Africa. These two entries in the Ten Year Crusade Diaries describe his efforts:

Emeric Sala received a letter from John Ferraby answering his request to the British Assembly asking how to approach colonial governments about registration of the Faith. (Editor's note: This detailed document gives the history of how the Faith was registered in Nairobi and, thanks to Emeric, was later used by the National Assembly in assisting Assemblies in the Region, notably the Rhodesias, to register their Assemblies under British colonial conditions.)⁶⁹

Following up on Emeric Sala's prodding, the Assembly asked Fred Schechter to check on the laws governing religious bodies and the registration of missionaries in South Africa. (Editor's note: He spent many hours in the J.W. Jagger Library at the University of Cape Town and many weekends at home in the search, but found nothing definitive.)⁷⁰

Robert Mazibuko contributes additional glimpses of Emeric, of his restraint in teaching, and the impact of the few talks he gave. As already mentioned, Emeric's strong point had been in speaking before the public. In South Africa, because of the system of apartheid, Africans and whites could not meet in public together. Public gatherings were out of the question. Thus, while Rosemary would discuss the Faith with her contacts one or two at a time, Emeric would stand aside, silently teaching by example.

Rosemary would tell me sometimes that she could not answer me until she consulted with Emeric. Silence was the teaching method Emeric used. One time I was saying a very short prayer and was repeating it many times in Rosemary's presence when I heard Emeric come in. I opened my eyes after a while and he was standing there looking at me. He stood for a minute, smiled kindly, and left.[71]

Rosemary always said Emeric was being 'sainted' but did not explain to me what she really meant except to say that he used to give talks in many languages in the Americas.[72]

He was a man of quiet habits, a great reader and a Bahá'í scholar. His measured speech and systematic method of tackling a subject thrilled me even as a teenager. I know when William Masehla visited our community, probably round about 1962, I heard Emeric speak for the first time and I found I could not resist bursting out: 'Keep talking Mr. Sala! Keep talking!' and immediately felt so embarrassed for everybody stopped listening and looked at me![73]

The *Ten Year Crusade Diary* records that:

During the day the National History and Archives Committee reviewed the tape of the 1958 Convention, at the request of the National Assembly, and recommended that only Emeric Sala's talk be saved. The rest of the tape could be used for other purposes.[74]

Robert describes how Emeric managed his business:

Emeric had many customers in the African community because he sold many items Africans could afford to buy. Many African salesmen came to his office to buy in bulk. In the Traanskei, one of his customers was a paramount chief who later became a prime minister of that Homeland state. The chief took many items on credit, promising Emeric he would pay later. Emeric never forgot the debt and kept after him until the full amount was paid. As a result Emeric was not popular in the Transkei. This is how Emeric wanted Africans to own up.[75]

On his staff, at Sala and Company, he had a Hindu, two Moslems and about three Africans but there was no problem. He worked well with all these people and they respected him very much... You could mention that Emeric knew all the exploitation that was going on in the country at the time, but offered his workers a deal they did not take advantage of. He proposed that they put in a little money into the company and he would give them shares which was very unusual in South Africa in any job! They would have benefited when he sold the company in 1968... Emeric never handed money around to create an advantage but believed that anybody who bought things from him had to pay. He became unacceptable in some quarters when he followed up on monies owed ... to his company, even if they were African.[76]

There were many Jewish businessmen in Port Elizabeth, in fact the Mayor was Jewish, but Emeric never used his own Jewish background for any gain. None of the Africans knew that he was Jewish. Instead, Rosemary, because of her philanthropic activities was suspected of being Jewish. Nobody knew that Emeric lost relatives in the Holocaust. There might have been sympathy from the Africans.[77]

I have a great respect for Emeric as a person. Perhaps it is because of the way he talks and conserves words and weighs them before he uses them at all. If he had nothing to say, then he would say nothing! ... I know he wanted me to be an "independent" person and free to make my own decisions and evaluations of the Faith without his interference. He always said I should be exposed more to life and that Rosemary was over-protective of me! ...

When I got to the US your uncle told me to find a job but every winter sent me $500 so that I could survive. ... That was your uncle, my hero as a Bahá'í![78]

Rosemary and Emeric did not have children of their own. Rosemary used to tell this story, related to her by May Maxwell. "It seems that Lua [Getsinger] longed for physical children and begged 'Abdu'l-Bahá several times to grant her wish. One day he took her to look upon a cat and her kittens saying that physical birth was a function shared by the animal world but that His prayer was that she would be blessed with spiritual children."[79]

From his own life, Robert Mazibuko provides an illustration to the story:

When I had my first child, Rosemary and Emeric were both in Mexico's Guadalajara. I sent them a cable that "Emeric Husayn Bonga Mazibuko" had been born. I did not hear from them for a while. I then received ... a letter from Emeric. He said he knew I wanted a girl so that I could call her "Rosemary" and that he was second choice. He went on to explain that Emeric had been "Emerich" before and had been Russian, German, Hungarian and had become French later and that it had a meaning. The meaning is "Valiant". ... To me Emeric is my spiritual father — period![80]

Emeric did not keep quiet when he perceived an injustice. A letter had been written by the National Spiritual Assembly of South Africa about non-participation in party politics. This entry from *A Ten Year Crusade Diary* tells the story:

Emeric Sala read the National Assembly's letter to Joseph Musole concerning non-participation in party politics which was published in the Bahá'í newsletter as a warning to everyone. One paragraph in particular upset him and one of the well-educated new Bahá'ís in Port Elizabeth, Grace Qunta. As a result Grace wrote to the National Assembly asking to have her Bahá'í membership suspended.

Emeric wrote a cover letter to her request as follows:

After discussing your August insert (in Bahá'í News) about politics with a few other pioneers who did not like it, it was suggested that I write you. Several of your statements we thought to be un-Bahá'í. I have never in my life written a letter of criticism to an N.S.A. and had no desire to start one now.

But when Grace Qunta's letter arrived, of which I enclose a copy, which confirms the damage which was anticipated, her letter expresses the feelings of the educated African much better than I could. To condemn all their [African] leaders was, to say the least, unkind. From what I have read about [Albert] Luthuli and judging from statements he has made to the press (which we Bahá'ís are expected to read) he has the makings of a Gandhi.

I appreciate your desire to protect the Faith. Your methods are probably best suited for the masses who are uneducated. But, if we are to attract the Africans of capacity could we not evolve an approach which will appeal to all?"[81]

Lowell and Edith Johnson, in their *Ten Year Crusade Diary*, provided this clarification:

> The phrases in the [NSA] letter to Joseph Musole which raised the strongest objection were probably the following: "If the African leaders could perfect their lives and show themselves to be the well-wishers of ALL MANKIND rather than falling into the pattern of dirty politics with an aim to enhancing their position personally, by stirring up hatreds and sedition, and when opportunity offers become the oppressors..."[82]

And from Grace Qunta's letter of resignation:

> I am sorry you have not had the opportunity of meeting some of those would-be seekers of power. I'm sure that even the N.S.A. would change their opinion about them. I believe they must get their impression of men like Chief Luthuli, Professor Matthews and [Oliver] Tambo only from the press. These men I consider martyrs for their people. We are not so clever as to be able to predict the future, but all that I can see that awaits these men is hardship. All in all I do not agree that these people have selfish aims.
> I think I should suspend my membership, study more the holy Teachings, pray that I may fall wholly under the guidance of Bahá'u'lláh.[83]

The National Spiritual Assembly considered Emeric's letter:

> Emeric Sala's letter stimulated a healthy discussion on the Assembly's attitude toward politics and politicians. In consultation with the Assembly, Val answered Emeric's objection to the statement on politics and political leaders ...: "Perhaps sometimes because of too oft repetition we may become a little too

strong in our statements. Such letters as yours makes us pause and re-evaluate our own attitudes and approaches to the problems arising in the Region".[84]

The National Spiritual Assembly drafted a letter to appear in the next issue of Bahá'í News [of South Africa]. Here is an excerpt:

When the unfortunate term "dirty politics" was used we did not mean that all politics are dirty, but referred to the violent, abusive, revolutionary type. This letter was written to one individual in answer to specific questions and therefore easily misunderstood when published without the original letter.

We also want to correct the impression that all African political leaders are self-seeking and are only interested in gaining personal power. We know that many men in politics are God-fearing and righteous men. We believe that African political leaders are like political leaders everywhere else. Some are motivated by high ideals; others are not.

The chief reason why Bahá'ís cannot join a political party is because each political party represents the interest of only a part of mankind. A Bahá'í heart — having accepted Bahá'u'lláh — belongs to all mankind. It is inconsistent with our conscience to swear loyalty to a part — that is, a particular political party — when we know that the salvation of every group, tribe or nation, is inescapably tied together with the salvation of the human race."[85]

The year that Emeric wrote the letter to the South African National Spiritual Assembly, I took part in a march to protest the racist laws of South Africa. There had been a demonstration in Sharpeville, a South African township, which turned deadly. Police opened fire and killed 69 people who had been demonstrating against 'pass laws'. McGill University students in Montreal protested what would become known as the Sharpeville Massacre.

My activism continued during my university years. The Bahá'ís disappointed me, with their seeming silence in the face of the injustices of racism and nuclear proliferation. What were the Bahá'ís doing about it? Only later did I come to realize how many ways there can be to promote justice and peace, and how much the Bahá'ís were doing. A friend of the family, Milly Rena Gordon told me in later years about her time in Atlanta, Georgia, helping the Bahá'í cause. That was during the harsh days of segregation. She told of Bahá'í gatherings in homes with police appearing suddenly at the door. Neighbours had objected to the mixed races inside. I wish I had heard her courageous stories during my youth.

From Emeric in South Africa I received encouragement for my ideals. Following the anti-apartheid activities, I became involved in the Student Campaign for Nuclear Disarmament. Here is what he wrote me in the 1960s:

> I like your joining a movement for Nuclear Disarmament. Whether it is right or wrong is not important, for truth is relative and it can be judged only if measured against an up to date Divine Standard. What is important is that the pattern you follow is right. You are fighting for an ideal, greater than any sectional interest. Morally you are greater than anyone who opposes you to protect national or vested interest. You can measure the moral good of any ideal to the extent it does the greatest good for the greatest number.
>
> At first everything looks to you black or white. As you learn in discernment you will see that they are really grey. There is good in everything incl. Communism. But is it good enough? The critical student will be disillusioned unless he can observe and perhaps judge from the standard of the Most Good or the Greatest Good that is an up-to-date Divine Standard. Otherwise the road of the intellectual ends in doubt, cynicism and disillusionment.
>
> McGill will open your mind but not your heart (or soul). McGill is not sure about the soul — or things of the spirit. It can't ignore it, for without the Spirit in Man there would be no civilization. Yet modern science is confused on the subject of the soul. Therefore the universities of today do not produce wise men, only knowledgeable men.
>
> But you ... will want more than knowledge. Try to get this from men of wisdom, from men who can blend mind and soul, knowledge and intuition, will and spirit.
>
> Is there a Baha'i Youth Group in Montreal? ... Such a group might give you the balance [that] McGill cannot give. This is just an idea for 1961.[87]

To my knowledge there was no youth group at McGill in the early 1960s. By the end of the decade a Baha'i Club existed and a good friend, Violet States, would invite me to meetings in the basement of the old Student Union building. One meeting I remember well. I was thrilled to learn that an elderly man was coming who had actually been in the presence of Bahá'u'lláh. I felt the significance and made a point of going to hear Hand of the Cause, Mr. Samandari. In spite of my various dissatisfactions with the Faith, I sensed the significance of its Founder and wished to set eyes on one who had met Him.

On a different note, I must have written Rosemary and Emeric about a favorite book at the time, the well known novel, J.D. Salinger's *Catcher in the Rye*. In this reply, Emeric gives his analysis with his own delightful versions of the author's name and the book's title:

Dec. 19, 1963
I read recently Salzinger's 'Green is the rye', or similar. I liked the frankness of his style. It is the story of a boy in search of his soul. Since most of us are in that search we could often identify ourselves with that boy. What was sad in a way is that to the end he did not come one iota nearer to his goal. Many contemporary writers of Europe write in the same vein. They do not help except to remind the reader that he is in the dark valley of search.[88]

News came in October, 1957, and Rosemary writes exuberantly to old friend John Robarts:

October 13, 1957
I read the letter first and, having no phone, was bursting to tell Emeric. When I asked him to tell me who were the two Hands of the Cause for Southern Africa, he guessed so easily!
Dear John, memories of our giving the news to Sutherland Maxwell, then the moving account from Leroy of his own experience, of Dorothy's, Horace's crowd my mind. You belong in exalted company, and how rightly - The beloved Guardian knows so well who are his specially devoted, dedicated assistants. ... As for the Canadian friends, I think I can hear their shouts of joy in my ears! I must write Laura, for we both anticipated the

Guardian's choice, in whispers to each other.

Emeric adds these words in his inimitable way:

Dear John, Now you've had it. You are in. That is, in the Inner Circle. It has its joys and responsibilities like life itself. Now we have to love you more, if that is possible.[89]

And John Robarts answered:

October 26, 1957
Your letter and telegram were more appreciated than you could ever know - a typical Sala letter, so wonderful to come at this time.
Yes, I too, recall the experiences of Leroy, Horace, Dorothy, Fred, Sutherland. Good old Freddie remained calm, cool and collected, didn't he? I have tried to emulate his way of accepting that appointment, but it doesn't work with me.[90]

6

AFRICA — SHIFTING OF GEARS

At the end of 1957, a shock jolted the Bahá'í world. The beloved Guardian had passed away, following a short illness. In one letter Rosemary writes:

> Emeric and I recalled our Feast that night of November 3rd in our apartment in Port Elizabeth. ... For some strange reason, after we had dispersed, I suddenly said, "Why we did not say the prayer for the Guardian!" Somehow, our prayer seemed to be said with more feeling, as, unknown to us, the beloved Guardian was passing from this world to the next. It is the prayer which he himself composed and asked us all to say for him:
> "O God, bestow upon Shoghi Effendi all the strength and vigor that will enable him to pursue, over a long and unbroken period of strenuous labor, the supreme task of achieving, in collaboration with the friends in every land, the mighty triumph of the Cause of Bahá'u'lláh."[1]
> Then his appeal, linking us so intimately with him and his efforts:
> "Gracious Master, overlook our weaknesses and failings and make us worthier and better servants of thine."[2]
> This last appeal truly reflects the divine humility of the beloved Guardian making us one with him in his efforts, our "true brother".[3]

Among Rosemary's papers is a moving document sent to the pioneers. It consists of notes taken at a meeting held by the Hands of the Cause in London, in the days after the Guardian's passing.

> You have no idea how you, the pioneers, have thrilled and assured us by your wonderful response. So many of you have expressed a redoubled dedication to the goals of the Crusade, and your loyalty to the Hands of the Cause.
> We believe you would also like to have a few notes taken at the meeting held by the Hands of the Cause in London, on November 10th (1957). Crowded into the rooms

of the Hazirat'ul-Quds were Bahá'ís from many countries, united in their common grief. Here are some of the things that were said.

Tarazullah Samandari chanted a tablet revealed by 'Abdu'l-Bahá three years after Bahá'u'lláh's death, full of precepts to be always united ...

After moving us to tears by accounts of some of his last talks with the Guardian about the Guardian's tremendous load of work and about the amount the Bahá'ís could do "if they would have the strength and the power to release themselves", Leroy Ioas asked for such a rededication as would enable us to excel the goals of the Crusade ...

General Shu'a'u'lláh Ala'i reminded us that unity can never be had except under the Bahá'í institutions, and advised us to abide by these institutions, the "achievement of which was the life-work of the beloved Guardian." ...

For our consolation, Dhrikru'llah Khadem quoted from ... an early tablet of the Guardian's on the passing of the Master: "When the clouds pass from the face of the sun, the sun gives more light. The clouds are nothing but the physical temple of the Master." Mr. Khadem said, "We will witness even greater victories in the days to come." Along this line, Mr. Ioas said, "The power of a great soul after passing is a thousand times greater than when on earth."

The climax of the meeting was the entrance of Rúhíyyih Khánum, rising above her own supreme bereavement to comfort the grief of others. She described the last days and the death of Shoghi Effendi, an official account of which we will all have in time. Before anointing us with attar of rose, she pleaded with us for love and unity. "The Cause is not based on rules and regulations, but on unity, on the love Bahá'ís have toward each other. Except in a few instances, we have never had unity. Go out and unite the Bahá'ís, comfort the Bahá'ís, love the Bahá'ís."[4]

Rosemary writes of visiting the Roberts family, and hearing Hand of the Cause, John Roberts talk about the time after the passing of the Guardian.

John told us about the Bahjí Conference. There were 23 Hands present. Horace Holley has left the States and will live in Haifa. He is old, but so wise says John. Alice Kidder (remember?—Elizabeth Ober's twin sister) lives with Rúhíyyih Khánum in the Master's home, where the Guardian lived. They eat their meals together and invite the other Hands over for dinner in turns. John says Alice has helped Rúhíyyih Khánum and Paul and

Marjorie Haney, Leroy and Millie with her wonderful osteopathic treatments. John told us that Rúhíyyih Khánum felt so shocked and depressed after the Guardian's death, that the fine Jewish doctor who attended the Guardian and came to examine her asked, "Madame Rabbani, are you a Bahá'í of your own conviction or because your husband was one?" That made her realize that depression had no place in [her] life! ... John is more wonderful than ever! He and the mantle of a Hand are one.⁵

In January 1961, Rosemary and Emeric attended the dedication of the first House of Worship on the African continent—in Kampala, Uganda.

> Nov. 2, 1960
> Emeric and I have been arranging our itinerary for Kampala in January. It will be such a joy to meet whom we want, go where we wish without fear and restrictions!⁶

In this article on the Kampala Conference Rosemary writes about the Temple, the Guardian's travels in Africa, the story of Enoch Olinga, and finally, the gift of a spear:

> The Temple rests serene and lovely on its hilltop, the blue green of its dome taking colour from and adding colour to the sky and trees around it. The open doors, the latticed stone walls, the spaces filled with delicate green, blue and lemon glass add to the airy spaciousness and light which the sight of the Temple gives. Therein is space, immense space in which the soul of man can reach out and stretch up towards God. ...
> That afternoon, the Conference began. Rúhíyyih Khánum spoke, thrilling the friends with the announcement that the Guardian, with her, had travelled the whole length of Africa from Cape Town to Cairo. It happened that they were stranded in Europe in 1940, at the beginning of the war and had had to take a boat to Cape Town, then travel up Africa to reach Haifa! They were in Cape Town, Durban, Johannesburg, Pretoria, Mafeking, Bulawayo, Livingstone to visit the Victoria Falls, Stanleyville. Then Shoghi Effendi had hired a car to drive to the source of the Nile to take a boat up the Nile to Cairo. We all clapped at this announcement and the Teso believers burst into song with the nine-fold "Bahá'u'lláh" in their beautiful resonant voices. ...

At the close of this session, Musa Banani, our beloved first Hand of the Cause in Africa ... moved to the front and spoke simply and movingly about Enoch Olinga. Enoch Olinga was not present because of the unrest in the British Cameroons. This was a great disappointment to us all, so Mr. Banani tried to console us with the following stories:

Mr. Banani related that on his pilgrimage to Haifa in 1953, after spending a year in Africa, the Guardian asked him how many African believers there were in East Africa. Mr. Banani replied, "Two". The Guardian then said that they both must pray at the Shrines for more declarations. This they did.

The next day a cable came saying that the third believer had been confirmed. His name was Enoch Olinga. He had been raised up through the prayers of the Guardian, though his future station as a Hand of the Cause was not to be revealed until four years later.

The following is that story: In 1957, Enoch Olinga arrived on a teaching visit to Kampala ... All his clothes had been stolen from him. The friends were able to provide him with shirts, but nowhere could he get trousers large enough to fit him. At last Mr. Banani suggested he wear a pair of his trousers ... Enoch Olinga was shocked at the suggestion that he should wear a garment worn by a Hand of the Cause, he felt too unworthy. A few days later came the cable from the Guardian announcing Enoch Olinga as a Hand of the Cause.

Enoch read it silently, went into his bedroom and locked the door. The friends could hear the great sobs which issued from the room. For three days Enoch Olinga remained secluded and then appeared among them, another being. ...

A moving incident took place. One of the many Teso believers present came forward, carrying an eight-foot spear upright in his hand. He spoke in Teso thus:

"In my country we have a saying that a youth does not become a man until he has made a spear with which he can protect his home. This spear is a symbol of the protection of the word of God. The Teso people would like to know more of this Word of Bahá'u'lláh through more translations so that they will have greater protection. The Teso people wish to give this spear to Rúhíyyih Khánum as a sign that we wish the protection of Bahá'u'lláh to go with her wherever she may be."

As the believer turned to give the spear to Rúhíyyih Khánum and she arose to receive it, the whole audience, truly one great family, arose also, clapping their hands. Rúhíyyih Khánum unpinned the red and white carnation she was wearing on her dress, (taken from the silver vases on the table at the Temple Dedication) and pinned them onto the khaki shirt of the gift-bearer. We all sat down, then Rúhíyyih Khánum spoke very movingly of the past gifts she had received from the African friends, and how much she treasured them, especially the drum she had received in 1958. She described how in harassed or troubled moments she would go to her room, beat upon the drum and hear in its voice the love of the friends of Africa, and be comforted. Her voice broke and trembled, while we all sat silent, tears in our eyes. ... It was a moment of great love and unity. Translations did not disturb, the spirit was so perfect.

As there was no successor to the Guardian, in the years following his passing the Hands of the Cause directed the affairs of the Bahá'í world. In 1963, the Ten Year Crusade ended victoriously, reinforced by many new members. All goals had been won or surpassed, with hundreds of new territories now open to the Faith. The number of national administrative bodies—National Spiritual Assemblies—had multiplied from 12 at the beginning of the Crusade, to 56 at its end. The time had come for the birth of the institution ordained by Bahá'u'lláh—the Universal House of Justice. The election took place in the home of 'Abdu'l-Bahá in Haifa. Immediately, the Hands of the Cause relinquished their custodianship of the Bahá'í community to the newly elected institution of the Universal House of Justice.

Months before, Rosemary wrote a friend about the events to take place during Ridván, 1963—the election of the Universal House of Justice in Haifa, which would be followed by the First World Congress in London, England.

April 26, 1962
Will we be seeing you in London this time next year? What an experience that will be! Though it will bring in the Universal House of Justice, I feel akin to the believers who passed from the days of the Master to the days of the Guardian. There is no division in the world of reality but there is a shifting of gear, a line of transition which makes me conscious of the new phase. Thank God there is a new generation growing up to adapt itself wholeheartedly to this phase which will include oldsters like myself. We are all part of the whole but inevitably we move from the hub to the perimeter. The exciting and fascinating process of life.[7]

Words similar to Rosemary's could be uttered today as "old-timers" watch the youth adapt wholeheartedly to new phases in the expanding Bahá'í community. As I write this, a small number of young Bahá'ís are visiting people in one of Montreal's neighbourhoods, sharing with those who are interested the various activities taking place nearby—gatherings for devotions, classes of spiritual education for children, regular meetings of young adolescents, meetings for spiritual study. Youth in their 20s are at the forefront of supervising and planning. A new phase, a shift of gear has again taken place. The youth are moment-to-moment in touch with their new friends and with each other by cellphone, text and social media. We "oldsters"'stand back somewhat in awe, helping as much as we can, as we move to the perimeter.

In 1963, from 28 April to 2 May, some 6000 Bahá'ís gathered at Royal Albert Hall in London, England for the first Bahá'í World Congress. They came from around the world to commemorate Bahá'u'lláh's announcement of His mission 100 years before, to rejoice in the victories of the Ten Year Crusade and to welcome the newly elected Universal House of Justice. En route to the Congress, Emeric met a friend who had news about one of his relatives.

> At the London airport we met an old friend, Gertrude Bloom, pioneer in the Solomon Islands in the South Pacific who told me that in Sydney a relative of mine had become a Bahá'í. I knew of no Australian relatives.[8]

> After the conference, Rosemary and Emeric visited Emeric's cousin, Feri Steiner, who had lost nearly all his family in the Holocaust. Only a sister and a niece survived. That niece, Eva, along with her husband, Fred Grant, had joined the Bahá'í Faith. They had done so halfway around the world in Australia, not knowing that a branch of the family in Canada had also become Bahá'ís. At a joyful moment during the 2nd Bahá'í World Congress in New York City nearly 30 years later, Eva, her son John and I met for the first time. Her husband, Fred Grant, had passed away a few years before. With the wonders of the computer age, we remain in close contact.

Other meetings took place at that first Congress. Rosemary made a note that this postcard was sent in 1964, not in regular mail, but through friends. It came from Bahá'ís in Baghdad, Iraq.

My dear Bahá'í sister and brother

It is one year past to our meeting from Congress of Bahá'í in London ... It was best gift from Bahá'u'lláh to give us these meetings after hundred year, how can we thank this valuable gift. My family and I sending for you and your kind husband our warm congratulations for the coming of Riḍván for both of you.

Your sister

"G—"

There were opportunities to travel. One trip was described in *A Ten Year Crusade Diary for Southern Africa*:

Rosemary Sala informed her husband, Emeric, that she was going on a teaching trip to the Islands next June whether he goes or not. That afternoon he told his friend Mrs. Tate that he would be visiting the Islands soon. (Editor's note: Emeric was so immersed in his import-export business that sometimes Rosemary had to use shock tactics to break through his concentration, but he was very good natured about it when it happened — he would smile, make a mental note of it and carry on.)"[9]

Emeric reported on that 1962 visit to several islands in the Indian Ocean:

There were 400 Bahá'ís on Mauritius, of Indian, Moslem, Chinese, Creole and French extraction. We stayed in the house of Pouva Murday one night. Their hospitality was disarming. On our last night the friends organized a farewell party—sumptuous supper, calypso songs, music, dance, specially composed songs for the occasion ...

(In Reunion) we made friends with Abdoul Gangate, an Indian Moslem, 22, native of Reunion. All he has of this earth is his island of 30 by 40 miles, and Mauritius, which is still smaller. He speaks only French and some Arabic. His schooling was sketchy. And yet at 22, he appeared to me at least as wise and mature as I am (which is not much) at 56, in spite of my world travels. We discussed the finer points of the Faith, life and death, marriage and business, and I was amazed at his perception. We spoke to each other as I would to an old Bahá'í of my age. He had only been attracted to the Faith. Now, he said, he is going to sign his card.[10]

At last, Rosemary and Emeric had the opportunity to visit the Comoro Islands, the original goal suggested by Shoghi Effendi which had been impossible for them achieve. Emeric continues his report:

...we got into a DC3 which was to take us to the islands of Dzaudzi, Majotte, Anjuan and Grand Comore, which was our final destination. About half of the plane's seats were removed and used for cargo. The passengers were Comoriennes, some in Arab costumes, some women veiled...The flight was bumpy and uncomfortable in this small, old, and not too clean two-engined plane. But we were to see our Comoro Islands.

... Finally, after 4 hours, we landed in Moroni, the only town of the four islands. ... a very charming Malgache Bahá'í, who works in the Bank — there is only one — drove us through the town. It consists of two streets, paved, and a few narrow alleys. ... It has two mosques, a port where a large steamer arrived every three months, a hospital with one French and two Malgache doctors. There is only one dentist who stays on each island 3 months only of each year. ...

The next day we met a Frenchman ... who after an 8-year contract in the Comoros, returned to France for good. He could not stand Paris and its materialism and tensions. He decided to return. He is employed by one of the companies, bought a house 4 km out of Moroni—in a palm forest—got engaged to a Creole girl, and appeared very happy with the idea to remain in Moroni for the rest of his life. After that I looked at the island with different eyes and admit that if we were meant to settle there we could have made it. But I thank Providence for being in Port Elizabeth.[11]

A few years later, in 1966, Emeric went alone on a three-week journey through five countries of West Africa.

Leaving Johannesburg on a Pan-American jet I found four Africans sitting in front of me. They were students on scholarship from Swaziland on their way to America. Since the Allens were very successful teachers amongst the Swazis, I asked the group if they had heard of the Bahá'í Faith. The face of one lit up when he said, "I am a Bahá'í".
... At our next stop, Kinshasa (Leopoldville), we met the Congo's pioneer Ola Pawlowska. In spite of every setback and hardship, [she] called the Congo since eight years her home, its people her friends, and sees a brilliant future for this sorely tried country ...[12]

Elsewhere, Emeric describes time spent in Bathurst, Gambia.

> I met there a young Californian who had two-thousand dollars to spare and decided to spend two years in Gambia to teach the Faith. He lived in a small but clean native house where chickens walked outside his door. The other pioneer at that time was from Sri Lanka, whose height was under five feet but his name was about a yard long.... He was a very devoted Bahá'í of Buddhist background who had a deep longing to teach in Africa ... One day we three drove ... to a Moslem village to proclaim the Faith. On a porch in front of the post office we spoke to a group of about thirty young Moslems. Towards the end of our talk we told them that one of us came from America of a Christian background, the other from Asia who was formerly a Buddhist, and the third came from Europe, of a Jewish background, and now we are all professing and teaching the Bahá'í Faith to Moslems in Africa. We did not need a more impressive demonstration of the effectiveness of our Faith. ...
>
> One night, after midnight, I arrived at the airport in Monrovia, Liberia, and was greeted by a group of Bahá'ís. One of them told me that he had heard me talk at a public meeting in Kingston, Jamaica, 20 years before. The last sentence of my talk made him decide to become a Bahá'í. Now he was pioneering in Africa. In those days, I had always closed my talks with the words of Bahá'u'lláh: "This earth is but one country and mankind its citizens."[13]

The Salas returned a few times to Canada for visits. On one such occasion, Rosemary traveled to the Maritime Provinces to visit the Bahá'í communities she knew so well. Here she writes about Ken and Celia Bolton, steadfast pioneers to Halifax and describes another one of those incidents illustrating the smallness of our world:

> August 1, 1965
> How much I admire Ken and Celia and others in the Maritimes, but especially these two as they have moved from place to place to suit the needs of the Cause ... The Boltons' live in a basement flat (which can't be good for Celia) no rug on the living room floor. They are just making ends meet but doing it with such a relaxed spirit. Canada's wealth has not reached the Maritimes as a whole.

We met at Fran's. ...Present as Bahá'ís were a young couple from South Africa eager to hear news and corroborating much that I said. ... After the talk, a young African entered, a Dalhousie student. I asked him where he was from. "Basutoland" he replied. Which city? "Maseru". Said I, "I'm not full-witted at the moment and can't remember names but do you know the Mohapis?" The young man really looked at me and replied, "He is my uncle!" ... So I said "Chadwick Mohapi and his wife were the first Bahá'ís in Basutoland." Everyone looked too stunned for words. Said the young man, "To think I had to travel 10,000 miles to learn that my people were Bahá'ís!" He had been educated in the Transvaal and away from home so he hadn't heard of the Faith in Africa but was attending classes in Halifax. This incident made a most impressive impact on the group needless to say![14]

Rosemary relates ominous news to an old friend in St. Lambert:

June, 1967
Last year on May 10th my permit to enter the African Townships was refused! The past two weeks I was asked to be present at two prize-giving functions, one to be speaker, and permission to enter even for a few hours was refused! It is a natural development of course, a logical step in the process but none the less sad. I am now teaching art to two classes, one of youngsters, the other of teenage girls, in a coloured township (negroes) so as to get to know that group. At present, no permit is required though that will come. So sad! Separated though we be, here we stay.

As regards the Faith, teaching grows more difficult. As separation continues more adamantly, suspicion arises on the part of the majority. Of course, this throwing the Africans on their own resources, meager, pitifully meager though they are financially, will develop ingenuity etc. and will serve the Cause well in the future.[15]

Rosemary now had administrative responsibilities, having been elected to serve on the National Spiritual Assembly of South and West Africa in 1967-68. A few years later she wrote to Robert Mazibuko, just elected to the same body.

> I trust...that you are finding a reward in spite of the, at times, heavy burden of administrative duties. There are times when one feels one is a bricklayer as the spirit may seem so far from our deliberations! Remember the Guardian said that we are not yet fully born administratively speaking—but tiny efforts performed for Bahá'u'lláh's sake have an ocean of power in intensity! It is always a joy to have contact with the Bahá'í work throughout the country when one serves on a National Spiritual Assembly.[16]

In 1968, as a member of the National Spiritual Assembly of South and West Africa, Rosemary attended the second International Convention in Haifa. These conventions are held every five years to elect the Universal House of Justice. She shares an experience at the Shrine of Bahá'u'lláh, and meditates on her view of the process of Bahá'í election:

> I was in such a state of joyous excitement by the time of the Ridván Feast and all the delegates sat around the perimeter of the Qiblih [the resting-place of Bahá'u'lláh] waiting for the Hands of the Cause to arrive. Suddenly I felt the whole place was transported — the Qiblih, the gardens, the Bahá'ís were floating in space above the world just under the shadow of the Supreme Concourse. I was so lost that only the touch of Rúhíyyih Khánum's hand on mine as she passed me awoke me to the realization that everyone was standing as the Hands passed by! ... But what a bounty! It was woven into me by the thoughts crowding my heart and mind: that the vote of every Bahá'í, first appointing regional delegates to the National Convention; then regional delegates [electing] the National Spiritual Assembly, then the National Spiritual Assembly delegates by their voting attracting the power of infallibility to the Universal House of Justice. ... Isn't it exciting?[17]

Rosemary used to send special bookmarks as gifts. She made these herself using dried petals from the thresholds of the resting places of the Báb and Bahá'u'lláh, enclosing them in tiny cellophane envelopes and sewing the envelopes to velvet fabric with gold thread. Here we learn of the origins of those bookmarks as she writes to friends working at the World Centre:

Dear Janet, dear Forsyth,

I can still say "Two months ago I was in Haifa!" How blessed we all were, and how blessed to have had that last day with you both, caring for us so lovingly.

... And if you should have any more packets of petals how I'd love some! I enclose a book-mark I made for our NSA members plus others and I was able to make 75 tiny packets tied with gold and silver cord for each of our delegates so you can see I used them all to give some of the joy you gave us to others.[18]

On my first pilgrimage in 1984, the 40 pilgrims all received a small bag filled with these dried petals. When I returned years later, each of the approximately 300 pilgrims could select nine petals out of a bowl. We are told that in the future there will be so many pilgrims that we will not enter the Shrines of the Báb and Bahá'u'lláh, but rather circumambulate these sacred spots.

In 1966 Hand of the Cause John Robarts and his wife Audrey, at the request of the Universal House of Justice, left Africa to devote themselves to Bahá'í work in Canada. Here is an extract of Emeric's letter:

One month from today you are to leave Africa. Leaving behind 4 children, 4 grandchildren, and all your spiritual children, and their children! It is a wrench.

You made a great sacrifice when you left Canada. Now returning you are doing it again—Is that how great souls are born?[19]

The time came two years later for the Salas to follow the path of the Robarts, and to leave Africa for Canada. It ended with a dream, as Emeric explains:

In April, 1968, while Rosemary [as member of the National Spiritual Assembly] was at the International Convention in Haifa, I had a very vivid dream—the kind one may have only once in a lifetime. Somebody appeared at the foot of my bed and told me: "Go home, go home, go home." Neither Rosemary nor I had any desire to "go home". We had no other home than South Africa and were reconciled and happy to remain there for the rest of our lives. Anyhow, I was disturbed and unsettled, and after one month, having consulted my wife, we decided to liquidate the business within the next three years. By then I would be 65 — then return to Canada for a visit before retiring to Mexico.

I wrote to [my brothers] accordingly. Ernest answered me in June that to qualify for [Canadian] old age pension, I would have to be a resident of Canada for at least one year prior to retirement. Furthermore, he knew of a unique opportunity to take over an agency of some Chinese textiles ... which would give us a nice living for the next three years. I would, however, have to reach Montreal within the next few months.[20]

The ease with which the business in Port Elizabeth sold, the chance meeting with a friend that resulted in facilitating the release of their funds from South Africa, normally a complicated procedure, all appeared as positive confirmations that it was time to leave. In a letter to friends at the World Centre, Rosemary expresses her feelings:

Please say a prayer for us. Just a few days ago Emeric received a business proposition from his brother which has made us (or E.) decide to return to Canada. Emeric, as a naturalized Canadian would have had to return in two years time to re-establish his Canadian citizenship in any case. Now he must try to sell his business (wholesale) or liquidate it—probably at a loss. If you could both spare a moment to pray for the right guidance and Bahá'u'lláh's solution to our problems it would be a comfort I know. My heart aches at leaving a task uncompleted.[21]

In the following letter the National Spiritual Assembly of South and West Africa expressed its gratitude to Emeric and Rosemary:

Dearly loved friends,
The National Spiritual Assembly has received information that you dear ones will soon be on your way back to Canada, leaving our Region with all the wonderful memories that we will share with future generations of Bahá'ís.
Believers in the Region will always remember you as the Pioneers who, with

nothing to sustain them but their faith in Bahá'u'lláh, arrived in Zululand to be [among] the first Bahá'ís to set foot on this wonderful land of the great King Chaka of the Zulu Nation.

Your patience during those difficult days of July 1954 is indeed a great tribute to your wisdom under the circumstances that could have tried other beyond their ability to withstand the trials of this strange land. However, your dedication to the Cause, backed with your singleness of purpose when you arrived there, made it possible for you to lay the foundation that has today produced more than 12 Local Spiritual Assemblies. ...[22]

This list of items left by Rosemary and Emeric for Robert Mazibuko is reminiscent of the gifts Rosemary prepared for young Nina Robarts in 1953 when the journey to Africa began.

These are some of the things left with me by Emeric and Rosemary on their departure from Port Elizabeth, South Africa:
A list of the old Bahá'ís with instructions to locate them.
A picture of the Master with the writings of the Guardian in which he exhorts Bahá'ís to internalize the teachings in their private lives.
A 10 inch 78 rpm record of the message of the Guardian to Bahá'ís gathered during the dedication of the temple in Wilmette (now in the archives in U.S.A. National Center), recorded by Kelsey Studios.
2 Twelve inch 78 rpm recordings of programs called Words for the World (selections from the Writings), recorded by Kelsey Studios.
A copy of An Early Pilgrimage [by May Maxwell].
A copy of All Things Made New [by John Ferraby].
A box full of newsletters and clippings.
Many pictures of Japanese art work.[23]

Emeric reflects on the years in Africa:

When we arrived in Africa in 1954, there were only three independent nations:

Egypt, Ethiopia and Liberia. When we left fourteen years later there were forty. [The Bahá'ís] attempt to conquer Africa spiritually coincided with its political emancipation. ... Future historians will probably elaborate how these two parallel events have had a complementary effect. In these fourteen years we felt the wind of change and heard the insistent rumbling of independence. We could also witness that the lifting of colonial domination did not realize the long-cherished dream of peace and prosperity.[24]

In October, 1968, Rosemary and Emeric left South Africa. We recall the beginning of their pioneer journey and their meeting with Richard St. Barbe Baker in England, some fourteen years before. He had sung for them a Kikuyu song "so full of love and longing". Their journey ended as it began, with song.

[The township schools] were allowed to come to the airport once a year to see how it operated, so the teachers had decided to save this day for our departure. They came hurrying down to the white section, to tell us to please come upstairs where the African children were. They were all assembled, and they sang, "Sikalele Africa", which is 'God Bless Africa', and then "The Lord is My Shepherd". So that was our farewell.[25]

Time has a way of coming full circle. More than 40 years had passed since Rosemary and Emeric left South Africa. A Bahá'í, Suzanne Schuurman, who had known them in the early days, wrote of the following experience during her pilgrimage:

While on pilgrimage we sat beside a couple from South Africa and chatted. I asked the man how he had become a Bahá'í. Emeric and Rosemary Sala had taught his father the Faith. That has become one of the most poignant memories from the pilgrimage because it shows the circle of pioneering harvests.
I can still so vividly recall visiting with the Salas the first time in Beaulac when I was 17. They were such an enormously attractive couple, warm, engaging and elegant in more than the fashion sense. When they decided to pioneer in Africa, they were the first Bahá'ís I knew to do such a thing and again I was impressed by their dedication and full

of wonder at the totally foreign world they had entered.

 Theoretically we know that all our efforts bear fruit but sitting beside that South African couple waiting for the members of the House to welcome us I was overwhelmed by the realization that beside me sat a man who might never have been beside me if the Salas had not left everything and gone to Africa in response to the Guardian's call.[26]

Rúhíyyih Khánum and Amelia Collins at the Maxwell home, April, 1953.

Rúhíyyih Khánum and Emeric at the grave of Sutherland Maxwell, May 1953.

The grave of May Maxwell in Quilmes, Buenos Aires, Argentina.

Rosemary and Emeric arrive at the border of Zululand.

Rosemary fording one of the rivers, Zululand.

Above: Travel teachers at the Salas' home in Zululand.
Back row: Dale Allen, Emeric, Patrick Robarts
Front row: Andrew Mofokeng, Ken Allen, Maxwell Ndlovu, and Rosemary.

A visit from the Robarts family in Zululand.

Left to right: Emeric, Audrey, Rosemary, Nina and John.

Rosemary at the Cowan School library with three helpers.

Rosemary and the library helpers taking a break on the balcony of the Sala's apartment.

Left to right: Eunice, Rosemary, Robert Mazibuko, and Angelina.

Emeric before his talk at the Salisbury Convention.

Above: Rosemary with friends from the schools bidding farewell at the airport, September 1968.

Below: Rosemary and friends at the Martha Root Institute, Yucatán, Mexico, 1974.

At Green Acre.

Left to right: Emeric, Rosemary, Mildred Mottahedeh, Hand of the Cause William Sears, Marguerite Sears, and Gertrude Blum.

Emeric in Lisbon with Counsellor Erik Blumenthal and Anna Costa, member of Portuguese NSA.

Emeric and Rosemary in their home near Guadalajara, Mexico

7

MONTREAL—GUADALAJARA

Rosemary and Emeric returned to Montreal in October, 1968. From their apartment in Town of Mount Royal, a small municipality within the city of Montreal, they looked out on buildings, rather than on the Indian Ocean. It was autumn, and a Canadian winter lay ahead. My sister was with the family at the airport to welcome them. As they drove into the city, she recalls Emeric saying, "I will have to get used to driving in this traffic and all the new roads." He writes:

> Gone were the restful sunny days of Africa with its pure air washed by the Indian Ocean. Now we were to be closed in a metropolis full of stones and windows, surrounded and chased by an unceasing menace of cars and more cars, emitting suffocating gases and causing unending noise and pressure to our unaccustomed nerves....[1]
>
> ... the joy of meeting old friends was sometimes dulled by our inability to communicate and share our new experiences. ... The people seemed less friendly, and we experienced a stronger culture shock in reverse, than when we left at the outset.[2]

Rosemary reflects on the return to Canada:

> I never felt culture shock in Africa. It was too exciting and too fascinating. Something new to learn every day ... I was growing my own vegetables and early in the morning I would go out and walk among my eggplants growing from seed, green peppers from seed. I had never done this in Canada and I could really feel, "Oh God, I'm working with you." ...
> Coming back ... where the darling Bahá'ís were preoccupied with whether they needed a second or third television set ... whether they needed a new car, a new carpet, and one remembered the Africans. It was very trying here ... 'Abdu'l-Bahá is reported to

have said that the time will come when a Bahá'í will not be able to sleep or eat if anyone in the remotest corner of the world had no place to lay his head or go to sleep with an empty stomach. How can we gorge ourselves? We haven't arrived at the sensitivity of consciousness...[3]

Not long after arriving in Montreal, Rosemary had a small accident that prevented her from writing. This must have been agony, to be unable to communicate with friends in Africa. Eventually, she was able to resume correspondence.

Dear Friends, dear, dear friends,
How constantly we have thought of you! I longed to write but the accident to my right hand necessitated a splint and stitches, preventing me from writing. I seemed to receive little haunting thoughts from you about our apparent neglect ... But truly, each one of you is so imbedded in my soul or unconscious if you prefer—that snatches of voices I hear or glimpses of faces, or people's very walk, will make your names and faces and voices bubble up to the surface to give me joy at the vivid memory of you. Don't dismiss this as one of Rosemary's romantic expressions. I feel, with Tennyson, that "I am a part of all I have met" and I rejoice that you are all a part of me, and like it or not, I'm a part of you! ...
We are settled in a pleasant flat (lacking the Indian Ocean, alas!) in a city suburb of Montreal, ... the Town of Mount Royal. The tree-lined streets ramble around crescents which make it confusing for motorists to find their way ... A train two blocks east takes us underground to the center of the best shopping district in Montreal, in eight minutes. ... In fact once one is on the transport, one need not walk outside on the street unless one wishes—which, on a bold or rainy day, can be quite agreeable as the enclosed shopping plazas are very elegant. We were astonished at the increase in the number of these shopping plazas and, in contrast, sadly disappointed when we passed through the slums of fifteen years ago, to find that they still remain — a very sad commentary on this so-called second richest country in the world! ...
I'll be a little sad to say "good bye" to 1968 as it will bring the memory of our sudden and unexpected departure from South Africa close to us. But dates of days,

months, and years have no reality in the world of the spirit to which world our relationship with each other belongs.

Much love and best wishes for happy holidays to all.[4]

In the following excerpts of letters to Robert Mazibuko in South Africa, and to other friends Rosemary uses words like "lethargy", "nervous shock". She refers to homesickness and nostalgia for the past. Today we might call this depression.

February 4, 1969
Though I haven't written I've thought of you and the other friends all month. It has been difficult for me to adjust to the climate as I have been ill since I arrived, off and on, kept indoors for weeks on end — very strange. And too lethargic to write ...[5]

September 2, 1969
I've been reading the American Newsletter and seeing the faces of the Bahá'ís of Southern Africa made me weep with longing to be in that part of the world again. ... I had a "nervous shock", delayed reaction to being torn from Africa and hurled into the speed and noise and polluted air of this great city so I spent two weeks all alone by myself at our cottage on the Lake. There were only the birds, the fish and wild ducks to listen to and talk to, besides my inner communings with Bahá'u'lláh and His helpers in this world and the next. I felt so refreshed and as though my soul had at last caught up with my body.[6]

I left all this information at the Beaulac School which is now closed. I am so feather-brained now. Still confused with the speed of life in North America and too many Bahá'í activities for my time or energy. (Oh dear — I'm haunted by that phrase, "No capacity is limited when led by the power? spirit? of God.")[7]

September 14, 1969
This great city is like a ghost town — so few of the old believers of our day here.[8]

Emeric would have been busy at work each day; and was not one to dwell on his feelings. He enjoyed renewing ties with his family:

> We looked forward to the weekends on the farm to meet the family and get reacquainted with our nieces and nephews who had grown up in the meantime.[9]

These nieces and nephews reflected the 1960s. Those of us with curly hair now sported afros; those with straight hair wore it long—outward signs of a reaction to the conservative 1950s in which we had grown up. There were anti-war demonstrations, civil rights protests; experiments with transcendental meditation and with drugs. Montreal had been transformed the year before by Expo 67, a World's Fair. The "Quiet Revolution" sweeping over Quebec brought about deep changes, loosening the grip of government and church.

I remember those days well. I was happy that my exotic aunt and uncle were back, living nearby. However, we were not as connected as before. My childhood interest in religion, enthralled by Rosemary's stories, had faded. While discarding the proprieties of "bourgeois" life, I had cast out faith as well, impatient with Bahá'ís and what appeared to me their lack of involvement in the issues of the day. At the same time, I was proud of Rosemary and Emeric's years in Africa, and their contributions. I just could not see the long-term impact. I had tumbled into the Sixties counterculture, believing it to be a movement of peace and brotherhood, oblivious of the cracks in the foundation—or the lack of foundation.

Years before, Rosemary wrote to me when they had just returned to South Africa after a visit to Canada. She refers to our time together in the art deco restaurant on the 9th floor of Eaton's department store.

> Two weeks ago at this time I had just left you after our happy luncheon. ... When a Bahá'í can share what he or she loves so deeply with another, then we have a real meeting on the level of the soul. ... I wish you could have seen your own face while we talked—it glowed like a pearl. You must look like that to God! I am not saying that lightly. Bahá'u'lláh said that our souls were mostly veiled from each other, otherwise we couldn't bear to see the glory God put in each soul—it would be too strong for us. But 'Abdu'l-Bahá told us that God gave us these precious glimpses which were a "real meeting", and

that when such a "real meeting" occurred it would last throughout eternity, no matter what physical separation took place.[10]

In 1968, I was no longer that person and regret that I must have contributed to the culture shock of their return.

Gradually, Rosemary and Emeric developed new interests. One July day in 1969, the first man was about to walk on the moon. My husband Marty and I drove hurriedly to the farm in our Volkswagen Beetle to watch the landing. We found Rosemary and Emeric there, and the television on. It would be some time before the landing would take place. Emeric was tired and went to bed, but Rosemary, caught up in the excitement of this historic event, stayed up with us as we saw those first tentative small steps. It was unbelievable to look up at the moon that clear night, and think that there were human beings on it.

Rosemary was ever interested in the world around her. My sister Renée remembers Rosemary leafing through a copy of The Whole Earth Catalog, a back-to-the-land catalog of that time. She watched as Rosemary came across some photos of nude pregnant women, with new types of cushions to sleep in comfort, wondering how she would react. Rosemary's unexpected response: "What a great idea".

We would see Rosemary and Emeric from time to time. Dinners at their apartment were unique. Rosemary prepared delicious salads, rolls of fresh bread, her trademark little dishes of butter, cut in small squares, sprinkled with parsley, all set on a beautifully laid table. Emeric contributed by picking up the main course, a bucket of Kentucky Fried Chicken. Ever pragmatic, with Rosemary spending less time in the kitchen, yet still maintaining her decorative touches!

Emeric used to join us on cross-country skiing ventures. One such expedition to the mountains of Vermont was memorable for me. We went with a group of friends, and that evening, shared a pot-luck meal. Someone had brought wine. I knew very well the Bahá'í law against consumption of alcohol and wondered what Emeric would do as our friend offered him some. After an initial protest, with the greatest courtesy, he allowed a little to be poured in his glass. I watched him take a sip. In this gesture I sensed Emeric's sacrifice to courtesy and felt an upwelling of love for my uncle. Rosemary did not take part in these skiing outings, and I wonder what she would have done. Both were sensitive to the "seeker"—in this case, though I did not realize it, me. I never felt pushed by them to attend Bahá'í gatherings. In fact, when I think of it, I was not generally invited by them to talks or firesides! They certainly did not proselytize.

A highlight for both in those years in Montreal was a trip to the Orient. Emeric's business trip included an early venture into 1969 China. Rosemary went along and jotted down her perceptions:

> Happily our first night in Tokyo coincided with a 19 Day Feast. We were guided to the Bahá'í Centre by an American pioneer whom we had first met at Green Acre forty years ago. As always, it was a revelation to listen to the Bahá'í prayers read in another language so different from one's own, yet to recognize the same spirit created when one listens with the heart to words read with devotion. And this happens always in every Feast in every country. ...
>
> Arriving early one morning at a Temple where no bus loads of tourists are permitted, we saw the temple sweepers, men and women, enter to kneel and pray before the day's work. We knelt also on the spotless floor mat to say a Bahá'í prayer, that the renewed spirit of Buddha might find recognition in the hearts. The symmetry of line and form, ... the subtlety of the color tones in wood and stone and nature gives the ... visitor an awareness of how religion has affected the soul of the people.[11]

In his unpublished manuscript, "Two Worlds", Emeric gives his impressions of China in the days of Mao Tse-Tung. So much has changed in today's China.

> A business trip took us to Canton for one week in the fall of 1969. It was not very successful since the Communist export executives are hard men to deal with. The impression, however, created by these poor, honest and industrious people was overwhelming.
>
> The first thing that strikes the visitor is cleanliness and order. Coming by train

from Hong Kong, the contrast was very evident. The fields looked well-tended and neat like gardens. We saw hundreds of field workers bent over their task, none were loafing, though they were all working for the state. Canton, an industrial city of four million people, had hardly any smog. The reason was obvious. There were very few cars on the cleanly swept streets. Transportation was on foot, by bicycle or bus. ...

The people were all poor, dressed alike in grey or blue cotton uniforms, whether it was the boy who brought us tea or the department chief from the Peking head office. Although we were dealing with large amounts, there was no feeling of greed or envy. The average annual income in China was at that time under one hundred dollars per person. The Chinese did not create that depressed, dejected atmosphere we often experience among the very poor. They appeared eager, confident and busy, without that exhausted, tired look we often associate with our competitive, industrial world.

We made friends with several contacts and three interpreters. One evening five of them were in my room, talking for hours comparing their world with the West. They appeared so naive, honest, unsophisticated and, of course, brainwashed, that too much knowledge of the West might only confuse and contaminate them. I spoke to them about our Baha'i objectives to which, at this point in time, they could give only polite attention. ...

Within twelve years after taking over the country, the Communists built 46 dams, much of it by hand labor, for lack of machinery ... and have had no famine since 1961. This collective effort, for the benefit of all, seems to have given the people a feeling of togetherness, assurance and satisfaction, which to a Bahá'í observer was very revealing. Here was a poor country, the most populous in the world, with no apparent greed or corruption, no rich people and no one hungry. It had no inflation nor unemployment, no beggars, no drugs, no vice, nor crimes. ... It could not have been a perfect state, but we could feel and see that some Bahá'í principles ... were in operation here. ...

When I left China I felt a deep affection for its people, which was not sentimental and which I cannot describe. I have also felt that they have grasped and applied some of the principles of Bahá'u'lláh, and if they can continue to progress in peace, they may discover the Source of the Power of the New Age and will then have an unimaginably glorious future.[12]

It should be pointed out that during this time period in China, the

"Cultural Revolution" was in full swing, with its attendant injustices and human rights violations. All this would have been hidden from the eyes of foreign visitors. While Emeric did business in China, Rosemary traveled on her own to Cambodia. There was increasing unrest in that small country, a neighbour to Vietnam where war raged. Rosemary was adamant about seeing the ancient temples of Angkor Wat.

> The visit to Angkor Wat enthralled me: to witness the magnificent ruins kings had built to the glory of Khrishna and Buddha. On the chief gate of the Angkor Thom temple, a monumental head of the 'future compassionate Buddha' was carved in relief. Associated with every temple were libraries; every tower and courtyard, even the moat surrounding the Temple had its relation to a concept of Heaven.[13]
> I went on to Cambodia by myself ... I couldn't find the Bahá'ís and it was dangerous to search. I was stranded in Phnom-Penn through some error in the air transport office, but was able to speak of the Faith to about six young Cambodian men of Buddhist, Hindu and Catholic background. I told them I was going to pray to Buddha, Krishna, Christ and Bahá'u'lláh to assist me out of my difficulties and told them why. They were very sweet and when I left they called out, "Au-revoir, adieu chère grand-mère!"[14]

Rosemary had petals from the threshold of the Tomb of Bahá'u'lláh. While seated in a park in Phnom-Penh, she carefully made a dent in the ground and buried the petals in the earth with a prayer.[15] She could not have dreamed as she sat there, that years later, in 2012, another city in Cambodia, Battambang, would be designated by the Universal House of Justice as the site of one of the first Bahá'í local houses of worship in the world.

Back in Montreal Rosemary writes:

> Emeric and I attended the Winter School at the Bahá'í property [Beaulac] in the mountains. There were 50 people there, Emeric and I being the oldest.... All the rest were youth, from 23 years to 15 years of age—some Bahá'ís of only a few days. All long-haired, with a most beautiful spirit. I became Bahá'í "grandmother" to many of them. I gave talks on the early days of the Faith in Canada and told stories of the early believers.[16]

During these years in Montreal, Rosemary served with a committee of local Bahá'ís in taking care of the Maxwell family home which was now a Shrine. She worked persistently on albums describing the early days of the Montreal Bahá'í community. Scribbled on the back of an envelope would be a last minute request: "Dear, do you have any photos of Anne, Elizabeth, or any others? Please send." Rosemary wrote to a friend whose mother took care of the house in the 1940s, following Mr. Maxwell's departure for Haifa:

> Being on the Shrine committee has been my greatest joy—how I wish you were here to consult about things! Rúhíyyih Khánum was very helpful but she too had to have her memory jogged. She was so shocked at the condition of the house furnishings that she took them to Haifa. This was after your mother left. The friends could never understand your mother's nervous prostration whenever the friends were careless about cigarettes, ashes, etc...
>
> Lorne MacBean is coming this afternoon to bring me a picture of Martha. Dear, have you any photographs of old time Bahá'ís and events of Montreal? I must get it all organized before we leave [for Mexico] in eight months—Somehow, I feel I came back to Canada to do this work![17]
>
> So many memories we share dear Dorothy, of the Maxwell days. I'm sure we'll relive them in the other world and find their real meaning. How proud May and Sutherland — not to mention 'Abdu'l-Bahá and the beloved Guardian must be of Rúhíyyih Khánum! Didn't you thrill at the African Safari stories written up in American Bahá'í News? I remember Rúhíyyih Khánum writing me after her marriage saying, "Who am I, little Mary Maxwell, to be so blest?" ... And how blest we all were dear to live in Montreal with the Maxwells, dear Anne, precious Martha and Freddie and Eddie and Elizabeth Cowles—a litany of names ... What wonderful times we'll have dear, on my little pink cloud![18]

In a letter to Robert Mazibuko in Port Elizabeth, Rosemary wrote about praying in 'Abdu'l-Bahá's room in the Shrine:

> Those precious souls—Bahá'ís and non-Bahá'ís—I yearn and pray ever so often, whenever I am in our Bahá'í Shrine, the only place so designated by the Guardian in all North and South America. I ... circle the whole world with prayer while faces and names

pour from my heart to my mind and are uttered by my lips in that blessed spot. So your name has been uttered and is imbedded in the atmosphere of the room in which the Master slept. ...[19]

I currently serve as a guide to the Shrine, one evening a month. Friends come, sometimes parents stop here with their newborn, a first visit on their way home from the hospital. Visitors to Canada make special stops in Montreal just to visit the Shrine. For years, Rosemary's albums had a place in one of the upstairs rooms, where one could sit in a cozy leather chair and quietly leaf through them. They served their purpose and the albums have since been removed.

Russell Kerr, who worked at the National Center in Toronto in the 1970s, describes one of Rosemary's visits to the national office.

I came into the main building for my coffee break and chatted with Rosemary Sala, who was busy sorting and documenting gifts to the NSA archives (working on a large ping pong table in the main room). She picked up an alabaster box and said, "Isn't this lovely?" She handed it to me and as I opened it, she said those are rose petals from Shoghi Effendi's wedding. She said May Maxwell had given it (the box with the roses) to her. I handed it back to her and went on with my coffee break. It wasn't until later that I learned that the wedding of the Guardian had not been a traditional one, but very private and that these petals were from the Shrine of Bahá'u'lláh and given to May Maxwell by the Guardian.[20]

Those petals in the alabaster box now can be found, along with other precious objects, in the Council Chamber of the National Spiritual Assembly of the Bahá'ís of Canada.

Avocado Orchard in Mexico

In November 1971, Rosemary and Emeric, newly retired, left Montreal for their final pioneer post, Guadalajara, Mexico. Rosemary writes about the journey, the new house, and their first weeks in that country. Her letters are again filled with exuberance and a sense of adventure.

>It is three weeks today that we left Rivière Beaudette to get caught in a blizzard in Toronto. [We] received news of a teaching campaign in Waco, Texas. This we attended for a few hours, meeting all the radiant youth and several oldsters like ourselves dividing themselves into mixed groups of five, armed with literature, to find those precious gems Bahá'u'lláh speaks of. Five had been found in the morning, and more were hoped for that afternoon. Paul Petitt, the Auxiliary Board Member ... was there to tell us how exciting this process was, all started in America by precious Pouva Murday of Mauritius Island, off Africa! Paul told us that he had set out with a group on a rare snowy day to walk down a street empty of all inhabitants. Then, suddenly, as the friends proceeded down the street, one person and then another would come out on to their porch to greet them. When the story was told, one would say, "I think my neighbour at number 36 would like to see and hear you" and would send a child to ring that neighbour's door. Pamphlets would be given and followed up in a few days or within a week. ...
>
>Passing the border and into Mexico, we would cry out to one another "Basutoland", "Swaziland", "Zululand", "Nongoma", "Transkei", so you in our beloved South Africa may know how our thoughts were closely tied to you, as we began this new pioneer journey. ...
>
>Prayers have certainly been raised up... for we had the promise of a house on the ninth day after our arrival! And a new house, at such a low rental, furnished! ... Our to-be landlord ... owns an avocado farm of 150 acres, situated at the bottom of a mountain range, and the little house he decided to build "on a whim" because the base of the old, torn-down adobe house was too good to waste. We have pure spring water tapped into the house, beautifully made closets and cabinets .... A Mexican village is nearby. ...[21]

Wherever Rosemary lived, something was growing. I remember the window boxes at the cottage in Rivière Beaudette overflowing with red and pink geraniums and deep blue lobelia. In the house in St. Lambert I recall a long copper container filled with houseplants — the copper and green colors vividly complementing each other. Some delicate houseplants in Port Elizabeth, Rosemary once laughingly confided, were actually marijuana plants.

When she learned this, she sadly discarded them. Now in Guadalajara a beautiful rose garden provided the home with fragrant bouquets. Emeric would return from his mountain hikes with wild orchids which he would attach to trees so that they could continue to grow.

Emeric loved the outdoors. In his youth in Romania, he hiked in the Carpathians. In South Africa he regularly went climbing. And after all, was it not the mountain at its center that had attracted him to Montreal? In a report to a local Guadalajara English newspaper, he writes not just of the mountain but of his climbing companions:

> Cerro Viejo rises to about 10,000 feet elevation, near the village of El Molino about 20 miles south of Guadalajara...
>
> I am not a young man and there were only two reasons that I could reach the summit. One was the overcast sky, which kept the temperature bearable and the other was our guide, Juan. He is 60 and lame. His foot was injured in an accident many years ago and he still can't bend his toes. He was told to exercise and took up mountaineering and fell in love with it. He made his way up Orizaba and all the highest peaks of Mexico...
>
> Cerro Viejo, like all our other mountains, has no markers, nor signposts, nor maps to guide the wanderer. There are only cowpaths, often crisscrossing each other....
>
> Juan led us unerringly, mostly by instinct, or was it a sixth sense? His pace was steady and his patient determined limping on and on, and up and up, could not but prevail on most of us to carry on for six and one-half hours to the summit...
>
> By the time we reached the summit the sun had come out and the view was breathtaking. Lake Chapala, between ranges of green mountains, intertwined with other smaller lakes, with an interplay of clouds and shades, delighted the eye...
>
> We had a great day, a satisfying adventure and we knew a growing comradeship with our Mexican hosts which we will not easily lose.[22]

Rosemary ventured forth in her unique way, by bus:

January, 1972
I went exploring this week.... Emeric is really very helpful, and eager to be my chauffeur but our wishes regarding places in which to linger do not always coincide. So I

took a bus and travelled about 15 miles for the vast sum of three cents to the end of the line and came back again. I took notes of places I wished to visit en route. I plan to explore each quarter of the city in the same way. ... I had successful chatty visits with quite a number of my seat companions, especially when the bus reached the poorer sections and outlying districts. One very sophisticated senorita was quite haughty but one darling old woman gave me her address and invited me to call on her.²³

Also unique was Rosemary's method of practicing Spanish. She watched Mexican soap operas on television in the afternoons.

Rosemary and Emeric continued to travel, to visit Bahá'ís and attend conferences. Emeric describes two special events in the spring of 1972:

May 15, 1972
[In Mexico City] we attended the National Bahá'í Convention which had many touching scenes. A Maya Indian from the Yucatan, a cobbler, had settled as a pioneer more than 1,000 miles from his home to teach the Faith to the Yaquis. Two such Yaqui Indians—whose ancestors were cannibals—were there as delegates, living on bread and tea, until we could supplement their budget. The new National Spiritual Assembly consists of six Mexicans, one Austrian, one Spaniard and one North American, showing great strength and confidence.

Eighteen Bahá'ís boarded the plane ... and we were joined by others in Guatemala. At the Panama airport we read [a sign with] big lettering "Bienvenida A La Conferencia Bahá'í". A welcome committee whisked us through customs ... and arranged our transport. The next day, local papers reported that 3000 Bahá'ís arrived from all continents, some on charter planes from Iran, Germany, and many US points. ... It was to inaugurate Latin America's only House of Worship, symbolizing the uniting point of North and South and the Atlantic and the Pacific. ...

When we visited Panama [in the 1940s] there were only three Bahá'ís. They had obtained a hall at the University and three column excellent publicity with picture on the front page for a public meeting, to which no one else came. Now there were many thousands at a superbly programmed public meeting in Panama's largest hall. ...

We met old friends we had not seen for 25 years or more. The available minutes were not enough to bridge the gap of time, but since we were tied by eternal laws, it did not detract from our joy of seeing each other. Problems and worry, sickness and sorrow of these 25 years were swept away as inconsequential, and all we saw in each other's eyes was growth of soul and character. And when we parted with the words: 'Until we meet again in this world or the next', we understood with no sadness what Rosemary meant."[24]

Around the time that Rosemary and Emeric left for Mexico, I set out on a different adventure. When an opportunity arose to travel to Israel, I took it, "to check out my Jewish and Bahá'í roots". Eventually I reached Haifa. Here I had the good fortune to meet Mrs. Margaret Ruhe outside the Shrine of the Bab. When she asked me how I had heard of the Faith, I explained the family connection. She remembered Rosemary and Emeric fondly from her youth. In the next days I had the opportunity to join Mrs. Ruhe on a visit to Bahjí, the resting place of Bahá'u'lláh. Her husband was Dr. David Ruhe, a member of the Universal House of Justice. I sensed vaguely that this was significant. One time, he asked me if there had been a young Sala who had died young. I felt my heart beat. He was referring here, half the world away, to my cousin Norma who had died during childbirth. Perhaps this concept of humanity as one family could actually be true. I was deeply touched.

And so it was, a few months later, that I made the decision to sign a Bahá'í declaration card, intending to try the Faith out as an experiment for three months. Three months turned into six, and the six turned into ...

Rosemary sometimes awoke early and, propped up in bed with a cup of tea she would communicate by letter with friends and relatives far away.

November 14, 1972

What happiness your letter of Oct. 28 brought us! I read it to Emeric this afternoon in the car, the first letter I opened. There were tears in my eyes when I read that momentous first paragraph. ....

There may be moments when you may feel as though you have been thrust onto a lonely mountain peak, the winds of the world swirling about you, and in the valley people moving about in their cosy familiar traditional worlds. But the adventurers, whether physical or spiritual, break away from familiar patterns only to find that there is a unitary principle that leads like a mounting spiral from the old to the new—so that there is no beginning and no end! A wonderful, wonderful adventure. As long as we cling to that pivotal point of faith in Bahá'u'lláh as our point of reference, infinite worlds of experience are before each one.

One of my first thoughts on learning of your decision was to say to myself, "Now I have one of the younger generation to whom I can leave my Bahá'í treasures!"[25]

The door had re-opened to that little girl who once sat on the swing, enthralled by Rosemary's stories. "Treasures" started coming almost immediately. Rosemary would send assorted articles, stories, photographs related to the Faith. For example, this fragment of a pilgrim note:

If we make an effort to the best of our ability and apparently fail, it is not a failure in the world of the spirit. It lays a foundation for a second attempt; any act, deed, done in love of Bahá'u'lláh ... was a "princely deed".[26]

Emeric's skills as a speaker were once again put to use. In the summer of 1975, he was invited to give a course at Green Acre. Rosemary's letters describe this happy time:

Emeric has been asked to give a course at Green Acre this summer so we go there in August for a week, then to Canada for another week. ... I'm so happy Emeric accepted. It will be the first course he has given since we left for Africa over 20 years ago. Do please, please dear Doris say a prayer for him! It rejoices my heart to see him studying to prepare himself and I'm asking for assistance from many sources. I remember the days when Genevieve Coy told me of two Bahá'í speakers she would cross the continent to hear: Horace Holley and Emeric Sala as they always had a new approach. Ah, the days of our youth! But each age brings its compensations even though it also brings awareness of one's imperfections. I daren't die yet I've got so much more to learn and yet at the same time I seem to seek out all the prayers and quotations about the mercy of God."[27]

September 16, 1975
"It was wonderful to see Emeric on the Bahá'í beam again — his six talks were enthusiastically received and so many came to tell me so. At the last talk, those present made him promise to write a book — a sequel to "This Earth One Country"...[28]

Emeric did work on a book which he called *Two Worlds*, based in part on the courses he gave at Green Acre and Bosch summer schools. In the book he emphasizes approaching the Faith through social justice. He shows how "the non-Bahá'í world, following its uncertain collision course, runs parallel with the Bahá'í world which has a chartered course projecting into a distant and certain future." It remains unpublished.

October 13, 1975

It is 6:15 a.m. and I have just ended my prayers. It is still dark outside but early morning sounds are emerging out of the night-quiet. A lovely feeling—to be bathed in the power of the prayers inwardly and outwardly by the tears which they evoke.

The best way to use up this power is to use it … some of it immediately, while it is still pure, not yet intermingled with the criss-cross pattern of the "vain imaginings and idle fancies" that come as the day progresses—I usually end with the healing prayer 19 times for ourselves … others, such as Rúhíyyih <u>Kh</u>ánum, yourself, etc., etc., then ask the scattering angels Bahá'u'lláh mentions to shower the healing on those He wills! After that long pre-amble, I'll now begin our news.

The summer was wonderful! The joy was to see the "real" Emeric emerge at Green Acre. … It is amazing—up to a hundred every week, and at times 150. And so many young—the majority from early twenties to late thirties …

The children were adorable! One morning as I was sitting in the Master's room, just absorbing the atmosphere and recapturing memories of other days, a class of about eight 4-to-6 year-old children came in with bouquets of wild flowers clutched in their hands. Their teacher directed them to place them in the flower vases in the room and it was so sweet to see them, so earnest and happy, no pushing, no shoving, do so. Then they settled down and each said a line of a prayer or a prayer. I thought of 'Abdu'l-Bahá saying—children's prayers are always answered! …

I must confess I went to very few classes … I used the time in remembering, praying and rejoicing to be there again—thinking of Elizabeth Greenleaf, Harry Randall, Agnes Alexander, Martha Root, May Maxwell, Anne Savage, Harlan and Grace Ober, Genevieve Coy—oh so many of that galaxy who had known 'Abdu'l-Bahá! I was supposed to have spoken on those early days—1927-1933—but got such a mighty cold and cough that I couldn't speak. …

Emeric was always being taken off by small groups to discuss points of his talks. His main theme was the stream of political action and thought touching on the increasing influence of the movements of the left, moving horizontally with the spiritual stream of the Bahá'í Faith; impelled forward to become worldwide through the impact of the Divine Plan as initiated step by step by the Guardian and the Universal House of Justice. His reference from the teachings of the social implications of the Faith were very powerful and he intimated that the advance of the "movement of the left" the Master spoke of was partly due to the Bahá'ís not responding more wholly to the Faith. He devoted one whole talk—very powerfully, I was told, on pioneering—and ended with the Seven Valleys! Several young people told him they wanted to prepare themselves to pioneer and to forget the more lucrative professions, as a result of his talks.

Oh my dear … One doddering old dear (whose name I could not recall) came up to me saying that her one summer visit to Green Acre from 100 miles away was purposely made to see me again!! Inside me, I had been feeling just like the Rosemary of almost 50 years past and now here I was thrust against reality—one old dodderer to another. She was so sweet, so deeply a Bahá'í! I thought of the words quoted so often by Genevieve Coy, "Patient lives of active service give life to the world". She remembered a National Convention held there in 1925 when Sutherland helped make salads and to serve the guests at the tables. …

We visited Stanwood Cobb—94 years of age with a mind more alert, more aware of the changes in the world and the forces of the Cause moving them, than many half his years. The cottage is tumble-down, the chairs on the porch where so often we had wonderful tea-parties with Juliet and May and Grace, were somewhat old with broken springs, but the atmosphere was new as tomorrow. He told us he had dreamed in which he was told he would live to be a hundred if he stood steadfast. I teasingly said that we would all have to pray earnestly for his soul if he died before! He laughed and said his precious wife would protect him as his guardian angel.[29]

Stanwood Cobb died, as it turned out, at the age of 101. Many years before, he had been on pilgrimage in the time of 'Abdu'l-Bahá. He wrote:

'Abdu'l-Bahá spoke of the need for loving patience in the face of aggravating behavior on the part of others. One might say, "Well, I will endure such-and-such a person so long as he is endurable." But Bahá'ís must endure people even when they are unendurable. Three extraordinary qualities which characterized all of 'Abdu'l-Bahá's utterances were to be found in these... conversations: His supreme logic; His delightful sense of humor; and the inspiring buoyancy with which He gave forth solemn pronouncements.

For instance, when He said, "But Bahá'ís must endure people even when they are unendurable", He did not look at us solemnly as if appointing us to an arduous and difficult task. Rather, He beamed upon us delightfully, as if to suggest what a joy to us it would be to act in this way![30]

Emeric was asked by the International Goals Committee, responsible for arranging Bahá'í speakers, to travel to Spain and Portugal. On his month long trip, in the spring of 1976, he gave 25 talks and held many informal meetings with the friends. Unfortunately, health problems prevented Rosemary from going. Emeric's thoughts on the social and humanitarian teachings in the Faith are outlined in this report:

> On May 1st and 2nd, I attended the National Convention [of Portugal]. I had the privilege to meet many of the devoted and hard working believers. Most of them were young. The proceedings were as usual in other countries. The emphasis was on what was to be accomplished. Little time was spent on how to do it. Through a delegate I asked for permission to address the floor for five to ten minutes on the subject of a suggested new method for teaching the Faith. Since there was no response I assumed that the request was rejected, until ... the second day, when the chairman announced that the Convention closes at 5:30... and that at 6:00 p.m. I will propose some suggestions to those who can remain. ...
>
> As I found my audience interested, they encouraged me to continue for about 25 minutes. Then they refused to go home. They all stayed and kept on asking me questions until after 8 p.m. A synopsis of what I said would be something like this:
>
> Our teachings have two parts—the personal or spiritual teachings and the social or administrative and humanitarian teachings. Although Shoghi Effendi told us that to separate the two is a mutilation of our Faith, we have done so for the last seventy years. Three reasons were given.

First, the early believers' Christian background attracted them only to the personal or spiritual teachings, with no understanding or appreciation of the social.

Second, the audience they spoke to were of the same background and inclination.

Third, the implications of our social teachings were unwelcome, and in some cases, intolerable, in the political environment in which we lived. This was especially true in Portugal until two years ago. [The "Carnation Revolution" of 1974 put an end to five decades of dictatorship.] That many of 'Abdu'l-Bahá's and Shoghi Effendi's published statements are in sympathy, and in many cases in accordance with the aspirations and stated objectives of the leftist and socialist movements, we have, in the past, for the above reason, either forgotten or ignored, or hidden in our subconscious.

The suggestion was made that perhaps our traditional, unbalanced presentation of the Faith produced unrooted believers, which could be one reason why so many left or are "inactive". Since the majority of Portugal's population is left-oriented, especially the new generation, the suggestion was made, not only to give a balanced presentation, but to approach the public first with the social teachings of Bahá'u'lláh, and only after having gained their confidence, and in some cases their friendship, to present them the personal or spiritual teachings. The suggestion is to reverse our method, giving ultimately equal emphasis to both aspects.

If this idea has any merit, we have to study the historical background, ideals and method of the leftist movements; especially where they coincide with our own, just as we did study [Christianity], Islam and Judaism, if we wanted to teach their followers.

The response of the attendance, which included about two-third of the National Spiritual Assembly ... was as far as I could see and hear, much more favorable than I expected. Architect Imani, the Auxiliary Board Member, supported the idea and stated that in Italy many ex-Communists are now believers, and some of them are among the most active European Bahá'ís. It was also noted that more than half of this earth's population is now left-oriented, while our teaching method and emphasis is out of alignment in respect to this important sector, which will continue to increase in importance during this century.[31]

From the report on Spain:

Here in Madrid the Youth Committee told me that the youth of Spain do not want to listen to religious talks. After a phone call from La Coruna, [a city in northern Spain] they were anxious to hear my social approach, and arranged a meeting .... I had an ... audience of about 30, some of whom complained why they did not know about my visit, why I was not used in Madrid and Barcelona, and that they could have used me for their University contacts.[32]

Such travels take their toll. On his return to Mexico, Emeric wrote the family:

Back three days and I am still recovering. It was an exciting but tiring six weeks. The Committee wanted me to go on to Luxembourg, France and Corsica for another ten weeks, but I had to say no. ...
Mildred [Mottahedeh] wants me to make more trips like the above, and that we should settle in Portugal, or somewhere in Southern Europe. I have no such desire. No place like Mexico.[33]

Both Rosemary and Emeric kept up their visits at home. These were a beautiful illustration of guidance that would come from the Universal House of Justice many years later:

As they call on one another in their homes and pay visits to families, friends and acquaintances, they enter into purposeful discussion on themes of spiritual import ...and welcome increasing numbers to join them in a mighty spiritual enterprise.[34]

Last week Emeric and I with a Mexican friend went to visit a new community and LSA at a pueblo (town) four hours drive from here, near the sea. ... We arrived about 11 am and went around to homes and places of work to invite the believers to meet with us in the evening at 5 p.m. We arrived at a house up a steep road, partly cobbled with stones, partly rough trenches cut away by the rains. The house had dirt floors; the room where we met, one double bed, four stools, two chairs and one long table where the great-grandfather of 75 stood mixing dough ... He apologized for working but said he couldn't afford to waste the wood-heated stove. The grandmother (his daughter) apologized as she had to go to the weekly cinema to try to sell the cakes that had been baked. But the great-grandmother, the grandson (a man of 50) and the great-granddaughter (21) and two others were present. One neighbour—Bahá'í—refused to come as she said she was warned someone always died after Bahá'ís met! So we have superstitions here too.

But the spirit was beautiful. When the young secretary said that they weren't going to elect a delegate as the community—had no money to send anyone to the convention, Emeric gave a beautiful little talk. He said for the first time in religious history, the people, humble folk from a tiny village or learned ones from a great city could participate in a great spiritual movement, going up step by step to create an infallible body; to be part of this through electing first their Local Spiritual Assembly, then their delegate who represented them in electing the National body, and that National body, this year, acting still as representatives of every tiny village, town and city, every single believer, illiterate or learned, in electing the Universal House of Justice. So that every believer through their representatives and through their prayers would be present in spirit in the Holy Land at the great moment of electing the Universal House of Justice!

I wish I could express it as clearly as he did! My dear husband loves the Spanish language and speaks it so well.

When the meeting ended (I spoke on the power of Faith) the precious great-grandfather took both my hands in his and said, "Every word spoken here went right up to the Divine Kingdom." He cannot read or write, but he has the wisdom, the language of the heart, a force greater than all book learning. It was a rich experience.[35]

Rosemary would follow the advice of 'Abdu'l-Bahá who wrote:

We should all visit the sick. When they are in sorrow and suffering, it is a real help and benefit to have a friend come. Happiness is a great healer to those who are ill... This has greater effect than the remedy itself. You must always have this thought of love and affection when you visit the ailing and afflicted.[36]

When friends were ill, Rosemary called on them regularly. The few weeks spent each summer in Montreal would always include visiting her long-time friend Hedda Rakovsky, afflicted with Parkinson's disease. I would be enlisted to drive her the long distance to the east end of Sherbrooke Street, to see Hedda. Hedda could not talk clearly; she communicated through the light in her eyes, the beauty of her smile. Rosemary wrote about the days of her youth, and how she learned from Martha MacBean, an early Montreal Bahá'í.

> Martha was the epitome of gentleness though she had many difficulties in her private life with a brilliant but erratic husband living on a very limited income. She was the one who obeyed the Master's injunction to visit the ill, the unhappy and despondent. I went with her once to visit a believer who lived in the slum district of Montreal. Though dirt and noise existed on the streets, Martha passed through them undisturbed into the tiny spotless room where the Bahá'í sat weeping. She was going through an experience of such unhappiness and almost degradation which I had never known, but Martha spread such loving comfort around that soul. She had brought a few flowers, tea and cookies out of her own meager substance. I had felt at first an intruder but Martha's gentle spirit drew me into the magic circle of her compassion. She was a true example of the Master's words in regard to visiting to bring comfort to the sick.[37]

Rosemary writes of personal difficulties with ego, backbiting—seeing them as "soul-purifying".

> ...I think she felt that Emeric and I were not as good pioneers as they were, as she kept telling about all they did for the Cause. ... each one works differently. I do admit, my halo slipped; I grew defensive and began to use too many 'I's in trying to counter with what 'we' did. But I am always embarrassed remembering how 'Abdu'l-Bahá said, "I, me, my, mine are the swear words of the future!"
> You spoke of "levels of meeting"—Oh, there are so many levels—one is childish, mature, babyish and wise all in one hour![38]
>
> We left ... exhausted by our dear hostess! She is so devoted but is a compulsive talker poor dear. Emeric could escape at times with ... but I was left to listen. I can understand she suffers isolation from the stream of Bahá'í activity ... Forgive my criticism—I can understand the patterns of talk ... but I was too weak to blank out my mind! As Emeric said we did not in any way show any discourtesy so we get one pale gold star.[39]

> I have thought of you so much since Panama, for through you I have gone through a soul purifying purgatory! Now I can write for I can truly say I have gone through over six months of having no desire to say "one unkind word about another". Did you ever hear Genevieve say that a soul can only be cured when it shocks itself into a realization of its illness? So it was with me: I thought I had cured myself, but the spirit of Panama probed and dug—I hope, I hope!—the very roots of backbiting. And your re-action was soul-healthy but made me weep for weeks. It was such a shock to me to find I could make such a snide remark about one of my most devoted friends. I have defended her against so many for whom her honest directness was a strain—and then to … fail because my little ego was hurt![40]

In a letter to John Robarts, Rosemary expands on Emeric's perceptions of ritual in the Faith and how he disliked the custom of audiences rising to their feet for a Hand of the Cause or Counsellor:

> John, you are one of the few who listen to Emeric patiently, attentively and lovingly as he exposes those edges which to so many seem rough, uncouth and worse, un-Bahá'í! He used to be able to talk freely with Glen Shook, Kenneth Christian, Genevieve Coy and Horace Holley—there seems no one now of his generation—and I am so grateful for this true detachment, pure humility of yours that permits you to listen! … One of the questions Emeric (and those like him, a Persian doctor of architecture to whom he spoke) asks is what form apart from a ritual, should this respect take? When we saw Stanwood Cobb, 94 years of age attending Marziah Gail's talk on "Bahá'í Memories" Emeric asked "Is he expected to stand up for a Hand or Counsellor?" At breakfast Emeric asked Jamshid and two other Persians about this question of ritual or respect. Jamshid said something interesting, that when a well-mannered Persian child even enters and greets an older person (a guest) politely, the guest rises to return the greeting! It is a question of culture. Emeric still fights the rigidity of Austrian-Hungarian manners! Can you see him clicking his heels and bending over a lady's hand now? Yet this is what he used to do when he first arrived in Canada! He was delighted to learn that this was not necessary in Canada![41]

In all the times I have attended talks given by Hands of the Cause, the audience has always risen on their arrival. What I have observed is that not once did a member of that institution seem to revel or delight in the acknowledgement. Often, with downcast eyes, they would quickly motion for everyone to sit down. Their body language told the story of their humility.

⊛ ⁕ ⊛

Amine DeMille, her husband John, and family were longtime friends of the Salas from the early days in Montreal. (Amine was the lady who had donated that much sought-after book on George Washington Carver while Rosemary was working on the library project in South Africa.) Following John's death, Amine returned to Little Rock, Arkansas, her hometown. It is interesting that in the early days in Montreal, one of the difficulties Amine had with the Faith had to do with the concept of mankind as one, racial equality. From her upbringing, she had trouble accepting blacks as equals.[42] She obviously overcame this test. Rosemary describes Amine's struggles when she moved to Little Rock:

> Alas, her influential relatives (one of whom had assisted in establishing the town library), refused to give any except very minor assistance when they learned she was mixing with the Negro Bahá'ís! It was the time of the uprisings and the graduating class in the Negro high school were refused help with schooling. Daisy Bates, the remarkable Negro organizer appealed for volunteer teachers to help the students to graduate and go on to college. Amine offered (though she had a very small salary as an assistant librarian) to teach in her spare time. Because of this, Mrs. Bates was so grateful that she procured a scholarship for Joyce, Amine's daughter, (together with the same for Negro students) to enter college to prepare for medicine![43]

Some years later, Amine, with her daughter Joyce, moved to Panama. In a letter to mutual friends, Rosemary described her visit to Panama early in 1977, months before Amine's death:

> I had been planning to keep my promise to visit Amine. We arranged dates for last fall; Amine's operation prevented a visit. Then the urge came that I must go in January—so off I went. Joyce met me at the airport—Amine was not well enough to come. So

we had a chat in private together. Joyce told me then that the doctor had said her span would be six months to a year! ... Joyce has certainly been raised up by Bahá'u'lláh to be the support and treasure her mother needed at this time ...

Amine met me at the door of the apartment looking so beautiful, all softly aglow to greet me ... It was as though the years had been swept away, and two old ladies had become again the young women they were when first they met! ...

The next morning, Sunday, Joyce drove us to the Temple. It looks so beautiful, on the top of the hill, standing there alone with a view of the surrounding valley, another hilltop on one side and the ocean circling around a distance away on the other ... The service that Sunday was to commemorate World Religion Day, and much to Amine's delight, Joyce had been asked to read and had consented to do so. Amine and I sat close together on a bench. It was a beautiful experience to renew our bond in such a place! After the service, so many friends clustered around Amine as it was her first appearance since her operation. ... It was such a joy—to see Amine in full bloom one might say, relaxed and happy as a flower in the sun, accepting the bounty of the love of the friends as a flower accepts the sun. ...

It was a wrench to leave Amine and Panama, knowing well that the stream of letters flowing between Mexico and Panama would cease soon, but I set my face resolutely towards the Merida Conference where I was to meet Emeric. During this whole visit, we never spoke of "last times" just let each day slip by as though it would continue so forever. We'll be picking up the threads again sometime in the Kingdom.[44]

This letter from Guadalajara was written by Rosemary to Amine, just around the time that Amine died.

April 17, 1977

I was awakened early this morning by a touch on my shoulder from someone standing behind me so I couldn't see who it was. I fell asleep again and awoke saying the Healing Prayer for us both, and as usual, in that lovely blue-white translucent light that at times comes with prayer when I "hit the target". You seemed to stand in the center and I on the fringes of the circle. It seemed to me quite natural that this should be so with all your spiritual gifts and capacity so much greater than mine. So here am I writing you to let you know. But I'm not sure whether you touched my shoulder or not! Let me know![45]

During that same visit to Amine before her death, Rosemary said prayers for many at the House of Worship in Panama. This response came from a young friend in northern Canada.

> Rosemary—I feel compelled to write. For 3 years Andy and I have been inactive—several weeks ago we developed an inexplicable spiritual yearning—and turned towards the Faith. Then came your postcard—you had been busily intoning our names in the Temple in Panama. Your prayers were effective and I want to thank you for your patient abiding love and conviction, and hope![46]

In the years since that time, Andy and Susanne Tamas have served, and continue to serve in countless ways, nationally and internationally.

Rosemary and Emeric would travel from Mexico to Canada every summer and visit family and friends. Rosemary describes one of the family gatherings held at Lake St. Francis Farm, home of my parents, Paul and Ida Sala.

> ... Lillian spent the night and worked so quickly and efficiently next morning with your mother and me—I did the "plebeian" jobs cutting up tomatoes and cucumbers and making salad dressing. Everyone came—all forty guests ...
> The farmhouse glowed with that special warmth, everyone mingling together, if not affinities at least accepting each other. I told Sheila what a tremendous experience it has been for me from a Scottish-Presbyterian background to be hurled into such a living vortex for which the Faith prepared me of course ...
> There just has to be a replica of the spirit of this farmhouse in one of the other worlds of God for it has meant so much to so many people that the waves of warm feelings which have touched so many lives will go on as immutable and eternal as energy itself.[47]

Rosemary loved children and they responded. She would peer into their little faces with complete attention, or tease them, or play games. Rosemary and Emeric did not have children of their own, but they maintained warm relations with so many scattered far and wide.

Hurry up and send a photo of the new baby Renée! I have just framed a photo of 'Abdu'l-Bahá. Below this photo are mounted your infants, Bill's Norsola, plus others, mounted on colored photos of flowers, and above these words that He wrote:[48]

"These children are neither oriental nor occidental, neither Asiatic nor American, neither European or African, but they are of the Kingdom. Their Native Land is Heaven and their home the Kingdom of Abhá."[49]

A letter to a great-niece — age 5

Dear, very dear Leida,
Your Opa sent us a photograph of you at the farm.. You were smiling so happily that I wished that my arms were long enough to stretch all the way from Mexico to Newfoundland to give you a tight squeeze! Remember the beautiful messes I made in our bedroom at the farm? And how I was always saying: Where are my glasses? Where are my earrings? Where is my pencil? And you told how clever Jennifer is at finding things.

Do you look up at the stars at night? I blow a kiss at the stars I have named Leida, Elin, Jennifer and send a loving thought (a prayer) for each of you.[50]

Rosemary's loving attention was scattered far and wide through her letters. When Angus Cowan was appointed to the Continental Board of Counsellors, Rosemary sent her congratulations.

Years ago, after a Convention in Vancouver in the fifties, you were kind enough to write me a loving appreciative letter about a talk I gave. I have never forgotten this and at moments when I feel that my efforts for the Cause of God have been written in water, your loving gesture has been among the memories Bahá'u'lláh has given me to refresh my soul!

So now it is my turn: When the Canadian Bahá'í News arrived with your photo as a newly appointed Counsellor, I felt as though my own personal hidden thoughts had been realized.[51]

Rosemary would share bits of news that inspired or touched her— such as this letter conveying news from the Bahá'í World Centre:

Then another letter from Haifa from a worker there (secretary) who was with us in South Africa. ... She wrote that the architect of the proposed temple for India was in Haifa with a model. It is a representation of a lotus flower and, she wrote, will look as though it was made of cemented moonbeams!

And in an added postscript to that same letter:

Oh Doris [the friend in Haifa] said that the Bahá'ís working there had been given a tour of the Seat of the Universal House of Justice—the outer shell as yet, but that the view will be magnificent. Imagine seeing the "Ark" Bahá'u'lláh mentions, sailing on Mount Carmel! My heart leaps at the thought.[52]

Rosemary would have loved to visit the Lotus Temple of India and the Seat of the House of Justice. This was not to be.

❧ 8 ☙

THE BEAUTIFUL PROCESS OF DETACHING

IN her final years, Rosemary maintained her routine of visiting, nurturing friendships, being helpful whenever she could, and of course, letter-writing. She also kept working on the photographs and documents of the early history of the Faith in Montreal, verifying information, collecting and organizing the material. This project begun in the early 1970's, was nearing completion. It was indeed a labor of love.

Two close Bahá'í friends, twin sisters, had retired to Guadalajara. They were Elizabeth (Kidder) Ober and Alice Kidder, both retired osteopathic doctors. They had lived in South Africa as pioneers. Elizabeth had married Harlan Ober after the death of his first wife Grace Robarts. John Robarts and family maintained a close relationship with Elizabeth and Alice, due to the connection to John's aunt, Grace. In her letters, Rosemary describes the move of the twin sisters into a nursing home, and the visit of the Robarts family. She refers to "the beautiful process of detaching". It is a process we all go through; indeed from the moment we are born. It is with age that some become more aware of it, and even see its beauty.

> March 8, 1979
> So now they had to be persuaded to give up their little home and settle in a nursing home. ... The wonderful young Bahá'ís, with the help of us and Emeric's brother and wife, arranged for an auction of the household effects. First, all the trunks and suitcases of fifty years of living had to be unpacked and sorted out! I was given seven large files to examine, guard the treasures and dispose of the rest. ...
> They even had a dream that [Elizabeth] traveled to the Kingdom and Alice followed after. When she told her dream to Alice, Alice was delighted and promised to follow her as soon as possible, at once, if God permitted! So the beautiful process of detaching is taking place — one feels it in the room more deeply each time one visits.[1]

May 17, 1979
Dearly beloved friends of South Africa,
It is so beautiful to witness within the past few weeks, the clarity, the luminous purity in Elizabeth's eyes as she approaches the transfer from this stage of existence to the next. When visiting her, in spite of her pain, her fragile body, all sadness is wiped away by the triumph of the spirit. She is wonderfully prepared for her flight.[2]

April 5, 1979
I have just finished the task of going through ten albums and boxes of photos and papers, nostalgically moving at times. ... Mountains of stuff had to be thrown away. As soon as I am rested, I must go through our papers. John told us that Millie burned all her letters. And I am constantly reminded of what Dr. Susan Moody said when asked to write of her own work and experiences, "Let it all pass into eternity". All the worth of our little doings in the Cause go into a vast pool of resources from which future generations of Bahá'ís may draw: the yeast, perhaps, of which Bahá'u'lláh writes. This I believe. Recording our little doings are of no moment usually.[3]

Rosemary fortunately did not succeed in discarding all her letters and papers. In the months before her death, she received this letter from author Gloria Faizi.

July 14, 1979
Thank you so much for the reference to the story about 'Abdu'l-Bahá. ... In the meantime, I wonder if you would be so kind as to send me any stories you might have among your notes. I have often thought of collecting these wonderful stories about 'Abdu'l-Bahá, but there never seems to be enough time to do all the things we want to. After reading your letter, I thought I would at least make a start by writing to one or two people to see if they will let me have stories they have heard.
My husband joins me in sending you and Mr. Sala our warm greetings. Mr. Sala's book, "This Earth, One Country" was one of the first Bahá'í books I read and I loved it. I take this opportunity to thank him for writing the book.[4]

Mrs. Faizi wrote several books, including *The Bahá'í Faith: An Introduction*, in print since 1971. She did go on to compile *Stories about 'Abdu'l-Bahá*, published by the Bahá'í Publishing Trust of India.

A new mood enters Rosemary's letters. Iran was being shaken by revolution. On September 8th, the House of the Báb in Shiraz, Iran was destroyed. A week later came the news of the murder of Hand of the Cause Enoch Olinga and his family in Kampala, Uganda.

October 17, 1979
We first learned of the Olinga family when spending a night with the McHenry's in Albuquerque [en route back to Guadalajara] but they told us that Enoch had been saved. Only a few weeks ago at a reunion of Bahá'ís here we learned the awful truth. I was so shocked I was useless and speechless...[5]

A wave of persecution of Iranian Bahá'ís had begun. Rosemary received this letter from her friend Doris Ballard:

November 14, 1979
Things are going from bad to worse in Iran; thank goodness I don't know any terrible details to relate in this awful letter full of bad news. One of the darling Persian women ... says she dreads to answer the phone for fear of bad news, more bad news.[6]

There is a thoughtful tone in Rosemary's reply:

November 27, 1979
...I wonder why I unburden myself? Perhaps because life seems so transitory. One never really knows when one does something, sees someone for the last time ... I spent two and a half hours with Alice [Kidder] a few days ago. We both recited prayers - Healing for Rúhíyyih Khánum, you, plus others, Removers [of Difficulty] for Iran, and the world, Departed for Enoch [Olinga] and family, and Elizabeth [Ober] ...[7]

One of Rosemary's last letters was to my sister Renée in St. John's, Newfoundland:

January 10, 1980
The experience living in Toronto last year must have been an enriching one, but the home life in Newfoundland goes deeper. Something like the stability of your life on the farm and my own life in Montreal. Even though we lived in a big city, our home life was quiet and warm and our long summers on Hamilton's Island, crossing the lake in a row boat (later a motor attached), hunting for Indian artifacts on other islands, picking strawberries (wild) and wild raspberries, learning the names of wildflowers and birds have been experiences knitted or woven into me. …

We were delighted to learn of your increasing success in your vocation [weaving]. I wish we could be nearby to visit one of your exhibitions but I'll have to wait until I can look on you from my little pink cloud some day! And how splendid that Duncan is happy and contented in his new field. Altogether, with the girls, it gives a picture of a happy family.

Much love to all of you.[8]

And from her last letter to me.

January 12, 1980
And at the end of life, dear Ilona, the only quality of worth remaining is how we have loved, with a sacrifice of ego to achieve a more eternal end."
Much love dear—as always—Aunt Rosemary.[9]

The last time I saw Rosemary was that summer of 1979. Just as she and Emeric were leaving, I gave her one of those rainbow-making crystals to hang in a window. I remember a profound sadness that I could not understand, but felt comfort at giving that small gift.

January, 1980: A crackly long-distance phone call from my parents who were spending the winter in Guadalajara. Rosemary was in a coma following a stroke. Later, my father, Paul, wrote:

February 11, 1980
It is now the third week and Rosemary still holds on. The doctors can't understand, it is so unusual. …

Rosemary suffered a stroke ... and affected both sides of the brain. That is why she is fully paralyzed ... Some days she can open her eyes, but can not express recognition. It is eerie and very hard to say if and how much understanding and consciousness is left.

We go daily to the nursing home and Emeric comes there too. He stays a little longer, and then we have dinner at our place.

Emeric is holding his own, in the first days the shock was great—now with time, he settles in to the inevitable and tries to adapt and accept a new phase of life.

Without the Faith and the spiritual support of it—it would be unspeakably hard ...[10]

From my mother Ida:

January 28, 1980
I can assure you, Rosemary is very well prepared and her Bahá'í Faith helped her. A few days before this happened, she said to us, "I am ready to leave this world at any time."[11]

And Emeric's words:

In January 1980 we made our usual winter visit to Manzanillo on the Pacific Coast, meeting our Bahá'í friends, which for Rosemary was always a special joy. Returning home, on January 24th, we had our meal and went to bed tired ... That night, Rosemary suffered a massive stroke and never regained consciousness until she passed away on February 20th.[12]

From the Bahá'ís of the Montreal area gathered to elect delegates to the National Convention, flowers and a cable were sent. Nina Robarts Tinnion wrote Emeric:

February 4, 1980
Immediately after the names of the 11 delegates were announced, and the very first comment to open the consultation was Dr. Ghadirian's loving sug-

gestion that the Convention send you a cable; followed immediately by Raymond Flournoy telling of Rosemary's letters always containing a fragrant few petals and his suggestion that flowers accompany the cable — both these motions were immediately and wholeheartedly accepted. Eric Frost drew up the cable, Lucille Maloney ordered the flowers, and many people asked for further news...[13]

Rosemary died on February 20. A few days after, in a letter to friends around the world, Emeric wrote:

> February 26, 1980
> Rosemary often told me that when the end came she wanted it to be quick, and she also said again and again that she wanted to die before me. She also longed to be buried as a pioneer at a pioneer post. All her desires were fulfilled. ...
> Rosemary had several premonitions which I ignored. One of her greatest joys these last years were the preparation of the albums for the Shrine in Montreal. While working on an album last month she said this is my last one. She also said that she was getting old and tired. She was 78. In Manzanillo she said, without context, "my Bahá'í work in Mexico is coming to an end."
> After the Afghanistan invasion [by the Soviet Union] she said: "I do not want to live through another period of violence."[14]

It would have been soothing to Emeric to receive many letters of condolence. From them, he created a compilation, and here are a few excerpts:

> What I found so incredible is that a person was dying in Mexico, the news was not broadcast over the media and yet within 2-3 days Bahá'ís all over the world were saying prayers for her.

> The wave of love and prayers around the world for Rosemary has so much significance—they are like bouquets of flowers given to an actress after a superb performance. She has received the equivalent, widespread attention that a noted world figure might receive at their passing. But different, because the love and prayers, telegrams and phone calls welled up from peoples' hearts...

I have never lost a mother, and I never knew what it was like. Now I know. I have lost my defender in times of trouble, my adviser in times of hardship and my protector in times of need.[15]

March 20, 1980
I recall one Sunday last year after a sumptuous vegetarian lunch with you and Rosemary and Paul and Ida, perhaps also Dad, that you and I were walking ahead of the others back to the cars, and we stopped and turned to watch them crossing the street towards us. The sun was glinting on Rosemary's silver hair, and you turned to me and said: "Just look at my Rosemary. Isn't she beautiful?" And she was![16]

Amatu'l-Bahá Rúhíyyih Khánum wrote this about Rosemary:

She was a remarkable woman, a very sweet one, and her devotion to the Faith was truly exemplary. It never flagged but went on year after year to the very last breath. May we all die as she did, with the good pleasure of Bahá'u'lláh. She was also a devoted friend and a loyal one, and I shall miss very much receiving her letters ... Rosemary will certainly go down as one of Canada's outstanding Bahá'ís as the Canadian community emerged and grew in stature and strength.[17]

Rosemary died as she had wanted: suddenly, before Emeric, and at her pioneer post. In Guadalajara among Mexican graves, is a simple stone:

ROSEMARY SALA
PIONERO DE LA FE BAHÁI

The Universal House of Justice sent this cable:

EXPRESS OUR PROFOUND SORROW PASSING ROSEMARY SALA DEDICATED VETERAN SERVANT BAHAULLAH PIONEER TEACHING FIELDS AFRICA AMERICAS MEMBER FIRST NATIONAL ASSEMBLY CANADA TIRELESS

EFFECTIVE DEVOTED BAHAI TEACHER THROUGHOUT LONG BAHAI LIFE. ASSURE PRAYERS HOLIEST SHRINES PROGRESS HER SOUL WORLDS GOD

9

FINAL JOURNEYS

The loss of Rosemary after 46 years of marriage was a tremendous shock. Emeric decided in the spring to make the trip that he and Rosemary had originally planned together, through the southern United States to Florida. He also accepted an invitation to visit Rowland and Vivian Estall in Antigua, and Edith and Al Segen in Dominica.

On my return flight I had to wait in Antigua for a change of planes. It was a hot day and there was no air-conditioning in the airport. I entered the bar and asked for a tomato juice. The bartender answered that he could sell it only with alcohol... I then asked for orange juice, but before the bartender could answer, a young man, sitting next to me at the counter, gave $2 to the waiter and told him to give me what I wanted.

I protested, of course, but the man insisted. He was from Georgia ... now was studying at the medical school in St. Thomas as he wanted to become a doctor. As I was finishing my very small glass of tomato juice, he again gave the bartender another $2 for another glass. Now I was really embarrassed since he would not let me pay. Then, out of the blue, without any relation to what we have discussed, he said as a very positive statement: "You have lost your wife recently." I was, of course, nonplussed and asked him how did he know. He only smiled and then said: "Your wife wants you to be very happy." His plane was then called and he left.

I never experienced anything like this before. Whatever the source of his information, that was the kind of message, I knew, Rosemary would have wanted to send me. This experience had a deep and lasting effect on me.

One month after my return to Guadalajara, Priscilla Blake brought a friend of hers, Donya Vroclava Knox, to her first Bahá'í study class. I was speaking... We exchanged afterwards, inevitably, a few words. The next day, I was to speak in another home in Spanish. Since Donya had shown interest in the Faith, I hoped she would come. Priscilla brought her again. After my talk we had an interesting conversation, and as she had to leave, Donya invited me to her house to continue our conversation. She told me afterwards that she had no other idea in her mind than to get more information about the

Bahá'í Faith from this man, who seemed to know what he was talking about.¹

On September 27th, 1980, Donya and Emeric were married and shared an eventful ten years together. First they hosted Rúhíyyih Khánum on her 1981 trip to Guadalajara. Then Donya was initiated into the rigours of travel teaching across Canada. Later, they made several trips abroad.

Emeric describes the trip across Canada:

> After attending the National Convention in Montreal, we made a tour across Canada giving 44 lectures. Donya spoke about the Montessori system, having owned and directed a Montessori school [for many years]. The Canadian Bahá'ís who had known Rosemary and me for so many years, looked at Donya at first as a strange phenomenon; but they warmed up to her rapidly and embraced her with that love which had the unmistakable Bahá'í stamp on it.²

I was nervous meeting Donya for the first time, but she immediately charmed me, as she did the whole family. She had an assertive personality, tempered with understanding and humour. She lived life with zest, and was a perfect companion for Emeric's last years. The strange story of the student from Georgia helped me to think of Donya as a gift from Rosemary.

A 1982 voyage overseas included meetings with old friends, first during a stop in New York City, then in Bucharest.

> While waiting in line on Times Square for a ticket, a lady in front of me told me that the only play she wanted to see is "Master Harold and the Boys". It was about Africa but she did not know which country nor the name of the playwright. I then asked, "Could it be Athol Fugard?"...My guess was right besides Fugard was directing the play. I then bought tickets for the play ... and after [the performance] went back stage and met Athol Fugard, whom I had known in Port Elizabeth, and with whom I did some mountain climbing. The rejoicing after 15 years was great.³

> ...In Bucharest we visited my old friend Josef Tumureanu whom I had not seen for 55 years. We had been corresponding with each other all these years, that is more years than with any other member of my family. During the war years we lost track of

each other. [Some years later] the indomitable Josef sent me a letter c/o the Bahá'ís of Canada, Toronto. This letter was delivered to the Bahá'í National Office, which was in Toronto, and they reforwarded it to me in South Africa.[4]

On April 21, I had to give a talk in Spanish in Guadalajara. There were about 40, including children, not one North American. I told them that 12 years before, there were six pioneers of whom only two spoke a little Spanish, about six Mexicans, mostly old people who could not read. All activities were arranged only by the Gringos, generally talks and prayers were in English. … [Now] the Mexicans arrange everything with some assistance from two Persian families. This is progress.

I feel increasingly that my days of giving talks are coming to an end. I rejoice leaving this to the younger generation with their new ideas and fresh approach.[5]

1990

There were other adventures, a trip to China, attendance at the dedication of the Indian Bahá'í Temple, a last visit to the Holy Land. By the spring of 1990, because of health factors, Donya and Emeric moved to Victoria, British Columbia. Donya had been ill and her condition worsened. In hope of better care she went to a health clinic operated by a relative in Florida. It was here that she passed away in early August, 1990. In a copy that Emeric kept of a last letter to his friend, Rúhíyyih Khánum, he wrote:

August 26, 1990

I am very sad to have to inform you that Donya passed away on August the third, nineteen days before her eightieth birthday…

Donya loved Rosemary's prayer books with her markings and drawings of flowers, and used them to the end. We both felt ten years ago that she brought us together. She often spoke of Rosemary, sometimes in desperation, for not having made a better man out of me. Nina Tinnian Robarts writes to me: "Can imagine Rosemary and Donya up there having a wonderful time sharing their great love for you, and—smoothing your path now, you are certainly going to be well looked after."

> When I said goodbye to your Mother over fifty years ago in New York (having been the last Canadian Bahá'í to have seen her alive) she asked me to pray for her. After her passing I said a prayer for her every morning for the last fifty years. When my niece Norma died at childbirth I included her name in the same prayer. When Rosemary passed away I added her name. Now it is Donya. ...
> Next summer I might go to Hungary and Rumania, besides British Columbia. I find world events very encouraging and inspiring.[6]

Not long after Donya's passing, Emeric attended a fireside given by two young Canadian pioneers to Romania. He was deeply moved by the recent development of the Faith in his homeland. As he listened for the first time to a Bahá'í prayer being recited in Romanian, he leaned forward, asking, "Please say it louder." He did not want to miss one word. Immediately, he made the commitment to visit Romania the following spring.

Robert Mazibuko writes about contacting Emeric who happened to be visiting his brother Ernest, in Ontario:

> In the beginning of August I again felt worried that I was not hearing enough [from Emeric]. I ... called my old friend, Ernest, on whom I could rely in finding Emeric! Ernest replied that Emeric was with him at his home and asked me to hold on! Emeric's first question was "How did you know I was here?"—there was pleasure in his voice. I told him I had not known but had decided to call his brother to find out. He then reassured me things were fine. I then told him to please look after himself and for the first time Emeric replied so obediently with, "Yes Robert, I will!" It really sounded like a son and his father when the father had got on in years – which was the case![7]

Emeric's life was punctuated by dreams. One day, while visiting with Harry and Giselle Liedtke, he described a recent dream. A radiant figure dressed in white was calling him, using a childhood nickname: "Imre, come..." Soon after, there were complications following a minor operation, and on September 5, 1990, he died.

The news spread quickly. A group of Canadian Bahá'ís travelling in what was still then the Soviet Union heard the sad news. Several members had known and loved him. I think it would have pleased him that on a train moving through the sunlit Russian countryside, prayers were said for this valiant soldier of Bahá'u'lláh.

The morning of the funeral I went to pick up my father. I found him quietly weeping. Later at the gravesite, a native friend chanted with a drum as an eagle circled in the blue sky overhead.

Years before, as Shoghi Effendi's Ten Year Crusade was being launched, Emeric wrote to Jamie and Gail Bond who had recently pioneered to Keewatin in Canada's far north. Emeric and Rosemary had just decided to go to Africa on the other side of the earth. Emeric concluded the letter with these words:

November 23, 1953
We are planning to sail from New York February 18th and will many a day pray for a cool breeze from the Arctic Bay.
This is a grand world. It may look large to some, but it is a small place and we live on it only once for a short while.
With love from both of us[8]

From the Universal House of Justice came this message:

HEARTS GRIEVED PASSING VETERAN TEACHER PROMOTER FAITH EMERIC SALA. HIS WORLDWIDE TRAVELS, HIS HISTORIC EFFORTS IN REARING ADMINISTRATIVE STRUCTURE CANADIAN BAHA'I COMMUNITY, HIS SCHOLARLY WORK, HIS ENTHUSIASM, ARDOUR AND STEADFASTNESS WILL ALWAYS BE REMEMBERED. PRAYING HOLY SHRINES PROGRESS HIS NOBLE SOUL. CONVEY FAMILY FRIENDS DEEPEST LOVING SYMPATHY. UNIVERSAL HOUSE OF JUSTICE

APPENDIX A

Twelve New Principles

Three days before He left America, 'Abdu'l-Bahá gave a talk in the home of Mr. and Mrs. Edward Kinney in New York City. He outlined new teachings of Bahá'u'lláh that were not found in the sacred writings of past religions. Here they are, in condensed form:

1. A fundamental teaching of Bahá'u'lláh is the oneness of the world of humanity.
2. Another new principle revealed by Bahá'u'lláh is the injunction to investigate truth.
3. Bahá'u'lláh has announced that the foundation of all the religions of God is one… This teaching is new and specialized to this Manifestation.
4. He sets forth a new principle for this day in the announcement that religion must be the cause of unity, harmony and agreement among mankind.
5. Furthermore, He proclaims that religion must be in harmony with science and reason…The harmony of religious belief with reason is a new vista which Baha'u'llah has opened for the soul of man.
6. He establishes the equality of man and woman. This is peculiar to the teachings of Bahá'u'lláh, for all other religions have placed man above woman.
7. A new religious principle is that prejudice and fanaticism—whether sectarian, denominational, patriotic or political—are destructive to the foundation of human solidarity.
8. Universal peace is assured by Bahá'u'lláh as a fundamental accomplishment of the religion of God—that peace shall prevail among nations, governments and peoples, among religions, races and all conditions of mankind. This is one of the special characteristics of the Word of God revealed in this Manifestation.
9. Bahá'u'lláh declares that all mankind should attain knowledge and acquire an education. This is a necessary principle of religious belief and obser-

vance, characteristically new in this dispensation.

10. He has set forth the solution and provided the remedy for the economic question. No religious Books of the past Prophets speak of this important human problem.

11. He has ordained and established the House of Justice. This international House of Justice shall be appointed and organized from the Houses of Justice of the whole world.

12. A specific teaching not given by any of the Prophets of the past… is the ordination and appointment of the Center of the Covenant. By this appointment and provision He has safeguarded and protected the religion of God against differences and schisms, making it impossible for anyone to create a new sect or faction of belief.[1]

APPENDIX B

Memories of 'Abdu'l-Bahá and of some Hands of the Cause of God

Less than 20 years after 'Abdu'l-Bahá came to North America, Rosemary became a Bahá'í. She met many early believers, absorbed their stories and made notes. As the years went by she would be asked again and again to tell these stories.

Memories of 'Abdu'l-Bahá - 1912

Anne Savage

In the Maxwell home, we can see a letter that Mrs. Maxwell wrote to Anne Savage, one of the earliest Bahá'ís of the city, about the momentous forthcoming visit to Montreal of 'Abdu'l-Bahá. We can imagine her joy as she wrote:

Now He is coming and will be here about the middle of next week, and I hope that nothing in this world will prevent your being here![1]

Rosemary would spend time with Anne, listening to her stories. Here are some of her experiences, "written down verbatim just as Anne told me, or as close as possible"

I saw the Master four times. The first three occasions were in the Kinneys' beautiful home [in New York City]. The first time I went, the drawing rooms, the upper and lower halls, the stairway were crowded with people waiting for the Master to appear. When He came, every eye was as if imprisoned in His glance—I cannot describe Him.
The Master walked up and down the small space left free for Him by the large crowd. I sat on the floor near the door. As he walked, His cream colored aba would swing

with His stride. I said to myself, filled with longing, "If only 'Abdu'l-Bahá would stand before me for just a moment so that I could touch the hem of His robe". The Master walked towards me, still talking and stood for a moment directly in front of me... I don't want to be reminded of my stupidity! I dreaded to make myself conspicuous by stretching out my hand!

On another occasion, the Master walked up to me in the room crowded with people, took my hand in His and spoke to me while tears ran down my face. May asked me eagerly, "What did He say?"—I had to reply "I did not know!" His kindness was overwhelming. I was not on earth.

At another time, the Master left the gathering to walk outside to a waiting carriage. We crowded to the door to see Him. I put my hand on Ahmad Sohrab's arm and asked, "Oh, is He going away?" Ahmad followed the Master to the carriage. 'Abdu'l-Bahá sent him back with a bunch of violets to give to me and to tell me that the Master wished me to come to Him. The people made a pathway for me. I felt like a princess, but again I felt that I could not go before all those people. The Master asked Ahmad a question, and I saw Ahmad nod his head.

The third time I saw Him, He was seated in a bay window. When I went into the room, He beckoned to me to come to Him. I sat there beside Him, looking and looking at Him. He glanced at me with such a loving smile and said, 'You do the easy things and leave the difficult things to God". I thought He meant me to go, so I rose and left at once.

Every time I entejured His presence, He gave me flowers, beautiful yellow roses at one time. He always wore a deep fawn aba and a white, white turban.

The last time I saw 'Abdu'l-Bahá was at a large supper. Before the supper was served, He went around anointing each head with attar of rose from a small vial, though there were over a hundred people present. At our table were six or eight women: May, Juliet, Rhoda Nicholls, myself and others. When He came to me I turned and faced Him looking up into His face while He anointed my head. The bottle which held the attar of rose was just as full when He was finished as it was when He began.

On the train going home, I was overcome by my stupidity which prevented me from accepting all the bounties the Master had offered me. I prayed, and as I prayed His presence became so real to me, as real as any meeting.[2]

Grace Robarts

This story was sent to me by Rosemary at a time in my life when I was working as an over-qualified (so I thought) waitress. In the letter that went with this story, Rosemary wrote, "It is a good experience to be probed by the forces of life to learn to accept the real meaning of democracy, equality and that all work done in a spirit of service is as worship."

Grace Robarts was a gifted artist, a graduate of Pratt Institute. Before she became a Bahá'í, her foremost conviction and her greatest pride was her acceptance of the fact that honest labour makes the garbage collector one with the professor. When she met 'Abdu'l-Bahá as a young Bahá'í she was an art teacher. The Master asked her to be His hostess, greeting His guests, arranging the affairs of the household while in New York. This service Grace was happy and well-qualified to give—a rare privilege. She would greet the guests that flocked to meet 'Abdu'l-Bahá, arrange for the meals he wished to serve, with the Persian Bahá'í cook.

One evening as the Master and His guests prepared to leave to attend a meeting, Grace went upstairs to get her evening wrap. As she came downstairs, the Master said to her, "Grace, you will remain here tonight and do the work of the cook while the cook comes with us."

Too stunned with shock to say anything, Grace stood immobile, unable to move for anger, until 'Abdu'l-Bahá and His guests had left. Furious, saying to herself over and over again, "How could the Master insult me so!", she changed from her evening dress into something more appropriate, then came downstairs to attack her task. (In telling me this story, I remember the laughter in her voice as she said that scalding hot tears that poured down her cheeks were almost sufficient to wash the pile of greasy plates and pots and pans.) Driven by fury, her task at last completed, she went upstairs to her room and flung herself on her bed, consumed by the thought, "Why, oh why had "Abdu"l-Bahá so deeply insulted me?"

All energy gone, she at last lay quiet. Suddenly, there came to her the warning words of a friend: "Remember the Master always tests one on what one thinks is one's strongest virtue." With this memory came her conviction in regards to honest labour. She said to herself, "What a fool I am! Why should the service of the cook be considered as degrading, worth less than my services?" With this thought, she prayed for humility, and the healing tears came effortlessly.

Suddenly, at this moment, there came a knock on the door. When she opened it, there stood one of the Master"s secretaries. 'Abdu'l-Bahá had sent him to escort her to the meeting.[3]

Grace Robarts eventually taught her nephew about the Faith. His name was John Robarts, and he went on to serve on the first National Spiritual Assembly of Canada, to pioneer to Africa, and to be appointed a Hand of the Cause.

Millie Rena Gordon and Mrs. Guilaroff

Millie Rena Gordon was a professional comedienne, and would delight gatherings with her skits and stories. She was a friend of our family, and we adored her. Millie Rena Gordon became a Bahá'í in Montreal in the 1930s. 'I'm no angel,' Millie remarked to May Maxwell when she was contemplating making her declaration of belief. 'If the Bahá'ís expect me to be an angel they've got another think coming,' … Mrs. Maxwell said, with a smile, 'I don't think Rena you will sprout wings.'"[4]

Some years ago I was able to interview Millie and record some of her experiences. (In later years, she used the name Millie, but in the early days in Montreal, she was known as Rena). I take the liberty to include this story in which we encounter Millie's good friend and neighbour, Vera Guilaroff Raginsky and Vera's mother.

Vera had crossed the street from her house in Montreal to attend a fireside in the nearby home of Millie Rena Gordon. The hours passed swiftly and when it was time to leave, the friends milled about at the door, among them, Eddie Elliot, the first Black Bahá'í of Canada. The friends were all gone, and Rena was picking up the cups and saucers, when the phone rang. It was Vera. "Oh Rena! My mother is so upset. She saw Eddie and is furious that I attended a mixed gathering. She is on her way to give you a piece of her mind!" Rena was devastated and did not know what to do. There was a loud knock at the door.

It was Mrs. Guillaroff, obviously in a foul mood. Before she could open her mouth, Rena invited her in to have a cup of tea, and dashed out to the kitchen before the angry mother could say a word. As she prepared the tea, she noticed that there was silence in the living room, and was surprised.

When she returned with the tea, there was Mrs. Guillaroff next to the fireplace mantle, gazing at a picture of 'Abdu'l-Bahá. "What a wonderful man!" she said. "I know

Him." Rena was stunned. "How do you know Him?" she asked. Then Mrs. Guillaroff explained that she and her husband, when they were younger, would go to all types of public lectures in the city, anything that seemed of interest. So it was that they had heard 'Abdu'l-Bahá speak at the Unitarian Church, long ago in 1912, during His visit to Montreal. She had never forgotten Him.

Rena showed her a framed list of Bahá'í principles [see Appendix A] and said, "This is what He was teaching, and these principles are what we discuss here during my fireside gatherings." Mrs. Guillaroff was enthralled; had her tea, and went home. Vera continued to attend Rena's firesides, and became one of the early Bahá'ís of Montreal.[5]

Carrie Kinney

Emeric sometimes had to go to New York City on business and Rosemary would go along, meeting Bahá'ís and listening to their stories of 'Abdu'l-Bahá.

Carrie (Kinney) went with 'Abdu'l-Bahá who wished to travel by subway on this occasion to visit a Bahá'í friend. A group of nuns were waiting near them for the train. 'Abdu'l-Bahá noted them, then said to Carrie, "Go to them and tell them their Lord has appeared!" Long since had Carrie lost the inhibitions of her upbringing; obediently she approached the Mother Superior and gave her the message from the Master. The Mother Superior, bowed her head, inclining it towards the Master and replied, "Yes, I know it!"[7] "The Master then told Carrie that many in the convents and monasteries knew of and had inwardly accepted the Faith but the time was not yet ripe for them to leave.[8]

STORIES OF SOME HANDS OF THE CAUSE OF GOD

Hands of the Cause were a unique group of men and women appointed by Bahá'u'lláh, 'Abdu'l-Bahá and later by the Guardian to help protect and propagate the Faith. There were fifty Hands of the Cause in all, four named by Bahá'u'lláh, four by 'Abdu'l-Bahá and forty-two by Shoghi Effendi. In the 1950's, Shoghi Effendi appointed three contingents of Hands of the Cause. Emeric and Rosemary had personal contact with several and in later years,

Rosemary would often be asked to tell stories about them.

Fred Schopflocher

Mr. Schopflocher immigrated to Canada from Germany. Here, he built up a successful chemical business. His help with the building of the Bahá'í House of Worship in Wilmette caused the Guardian to call him "The Temple Builder".

Now when you see a picture of Freddie Schopflocher before he became a Bahá'í, you see the face of a man who was a hard-headed businessman. A mouth like a steel trap across his face. Hard, cold eyes... Then he married a young woman, very adventurous... she was always interested in esoteric movements. She joined one after the other. Freddie, being very impatient over this, but as a man in love, listened to her tolerantly as she told of Theosophy, of Christian Science etc. And then she heard of the Bahá'í Faith. He said, "Laurel, haven't you learned yet that these people are just after your money?" But Laurel didn't listen... While in Green Acre she had heard that the Source of All Knowledge was 'Abdu'l-Bahá and that He was in Haifa, so she said to Freddie, "I"m going to see Him in Haifa." Freddie decided that he was going to go too. So they went but he went protesting all the way. They arrived in Haifa just after 'Abdu'l-Bahá's passing. The family was too prostrate to pay any attention to them, but courteously welcomed them.

Laurel was up in their bedroom one day shortly after their arrival looking into the garden when suddenly she saw her hard-headed, difficult-to-persuade husband weeping great sobs in the arms of Fujita, the Japanese gardener.

Then Freddie became this marvelous person who ended up a Hand of the Cause. His devotion to the Guardian was such that I don't think I have ever seen it excelled anywhere. His whole life was pinpointed into that of service to the Guardian. ...

He was so generous. The Guardian called him the "Temple builder".[9]

Long afterwards, on another trip to Haifa, Mr. Schopflocher was told personally by the Guardian of his appointment as Hand of the Cause:

He happened to speak at the Ridván Feast after he arrived home ... At the end of his talk he said, "And the Guardian ...", and then he broke down weeping, and the tears were rolling down his cheeks. And that whole hall was filled with that unmistakable feeling of the devotion of a Hand of the Cause. It was something indescribable. ...

You see, we were very privileged; it was a bounty to belong to that age when we saw these people as our co-workers and co-sharers, working together with them, and even saying, "Oh Freddie, you're talking nonsense!" Then suddenly to see the mantle of this station fall on the shoulders of these people, and having them express fully the essence of their devotion....[10]

Mr. Schopflocher died not long after this appointment. He is buried on Mount Royal, very close to the grave of another Hand of the Cause, Sutherland Maxwell.

Dorothy Baker

A renowned and well-loved Bahá'í from the United States was Dorothy Baker, appointed as a Hand of the Cause by Shoghi Effendi. Here are a few of Rosemary's recollections:

Dorothy Baker once asked me at Summer School to go with her up a hillside and we would say the Long Obligatory Prayer together, but each to himself. I knew it by heart but I was so caught up in Dorothy's complete concentration I just stood - or sat - immovable and speechless. I was as yet not able to abandon myself (the Scot in me!) with another. As we walked down the hill together, she told me some of her thoughts regarding this prayer, that it is like the ocean from which we spring, symbolizing that ... Most Great Ocean of which Baha'u'llah speaks and in which all life is involved. That in the prayer, the soul ebbs and flows, advancing and retreating in its approach to God until at last it overcomes the consciousness of its own frailty and abandons itself to the mercy of God ... After saying it, I tell myself that anymore lingering on one's own frailties is pure egotism ... that one's powers must be turned to creative impulses, not negative even of oneself, that is not humility.[11]

I said once, "Dorothy, with all the adulation that surrounds you, how can you keep your balance? How can you keep so sincerely humble? Has anyone in particular helped you?" She thought for a moment and said, "Louis Gregory," and she told how she had been driving, and her car turned over. She wasn't seriously injured. She was telling about it during an NSA meeting, and the others said, "Oh Dorothy, how dreadful! But of course nothing could happen to you. Bahá'u'lláh would certainly protect you." But Louis just looked at her and said, "Were you driving too fast, Dorothy?" ...

Two months before Dorothy's death I had the following dream, which I didn't understand. I dreamed that she was standing on a distant shore; very brilliant - wonderful - and I was standing on the earth's shore. In between us was the ocean. Suddenly, the waves of the ocean turned into Arabic writing, and that became a bridge between us. It was very beautiful. I felt this wonderful smile of hers coming over those wonderful waves. ... It took me a few months to understand it, that the connection is eternal through the words of Bahá'u'lláh. [12]

In January, 1954, Dorothy was among the passengers of a plane that crashed into the Mediterranean Sea. No one survived.

Louis Gregory

Louis Gregory was one of the first African American Bahá'ís. The Guardian appointed him a Hand of the Cause and called him "noble-minded, golden-hearted". Rosemary writes about visiting him and his wife Louise in their home where she saw for the first time a photograph of the sister of 'Abdu'l-Bahá.

I was given a photo of the Greatest Holy Leaf by Louis and Louise Gregory given to them by her. They had invited me to have lunch with them in their home in Portsmouth. I saw on the mantlepiece this photo in a brass oriental frame and burst into tears! These precious darlings - so little endowed with worldly goods, took it and put it into my hands. I was overcome and sat at the table with it before me. Someone robbed me of it - or perhaps having the same reaction as I did, couldn't resist its appeal. But the thought of the immediate loving reaction of Louis is an imperishable bounty and brings tears so often to my eyes.[13]

Leroy Ioas

Appointed a Hand of the Cause in 1951, Leroy Ioas served for many years at the World Centre in Haifa.

Leroy Ioas came to consult with the Canadian National Spiritual Assembly in regard to our joint activities ... He started out so bravely saying, "The most embarrassing thing about meeting with you is this question of the Hands of the Cause." His business-like tone faltered a little, then he went on, "I've always thought of the Hands as saintly souls, appointed after their death, not stumbling, fumbling, inefficient—". Here his voice broke entirely. He covered his eyes with his hand while tears ran down his cheeks. We all sat in silence, feeling that spirit of utter humility fill the room, and I think all of us had tears in our eyes ... Finally, Leroy wiped his face and glasses and continued, "When the cable came, I took to bed for two days – the shock was so great."[14]

Amelia Collins

Amelia Collins, known as Millie, was an American Bahá'í who served for years in Haifa as Shoghi Effendi's secretary. She was appointed a Hand of the Cause in 1951. During a visit, she told Rosemary many stories.

Millie told us of the austerity in Haifa, the severe food rationing. There had been no heat all winter, no hot water. ... She told me how she longed for a cup of hot, strong coffee, but it was always so weak and lukewarm. ...
She told ... that never in her long years of service to the Cause had she ever had so little time to pray and meditate as in Haifa, serving the Guardian. She then said that through constant service, a drop, a brief moment of prayer becomes an ocean in its intensity!
The Guardian had given her 'Abdu'l-Bahá's room in His house. ... Shoghi Effendi told her when she no longer needed the room, it would never again be occupied by another![15]

John Robarts

Born in Toronto, Ontario, John learned of the Faith from his aunt, Grace Robarts Ober. He and his wife Audrey were close friends of Rosemary and Emeric, and had a deep influence on their lives.

John always was John, but of course with the station of the Hand, and his devotion, he had been raised to the purest essence and degree of what John was meant to be. But you got a glimmering of this in the very beginning.

I remember ... at some public meeting his sister came. I [asked] his sister, "Was John always like this? Was he always a catalyzer? Did he always bring people together?" ... She said yes, he was always like that, even as a young boy. I was very happy to have that explanation from a sister who knew him.

I know that as chairman of the National Spiritual Assembly, ... we were a very young, inexperienced NSA of Canada and we had very definite opinions at times. John would ... patiently go around to each one and occasionally would hurry it up, and try to make us state ourselves clearly and distinctly. And only at the end would he give his opinion. He would never interject or try to influence anybody. But I think his very presence helped to make us aware of what we were building in administration. He was a young Bahá'í but wise.[16]

GLOSSARY

'Abdu'l-Bahá: (1844-1921) The eldest son of Bahá'u'lláh. Appointed by Him as the authorized interpreter of the Bahá'í teachings and as Head of the Faith after His passing.

Auxiliary Board Members: Individuals appointed to assist the Counsellors to advise, assist, and instruct Bahá'ís, Bahá'í communities, and Bahá'í institutions.

The Báb: (1819-1850) The Founder of the Bábí religion whose main purpose was to prepare the way for Bahá'u'lláh.

Bahá'í World Center: Situated in Haifa, Israel. From here the faith is administered internationally. It is also the location for several Bahá'í holy places, including the Shrines of the Báb and Bahá'u'lláh.

Bahá'u'lláh: (1817-1892) The Founder of the Bahá'í Faith. His central message is that humanity is one single race and that the day has come for its unification into one global society.

Bahíyyih Khánum, also The Greatest Holy Leaf: (1846-1932) Daughter of Bahá'u'lláh and sister of 'Abdu'l-Bahá.

Counsellors: Appointed by the Universal House of Justice and devoted to the functions of protection and propagation of the Faith.

Covenant: The Covenant in the Bahá'í Faith could be described as a spiritual contract binding God and humanity. Among its features, the clear designation of succession and authority within the Faith.

Declaration of the Báb: Commemoration of the day when the Báb first openly proclaimed that He was a Manifestation of God, May 23, 1844.

The Fast: During a 19-day period from around March 2 to 21 (the dates vary with the date of the spring equinox), Bahá'ís do not partake of food or drink during daylight hours. It is a time of spiritual and physical cleansing and rejuvenation.

THE GREATEST NAME: At its most basic, the title of Bahá'u'lláh (Arabic; English "The Glory of God") in various forms. As "Alláh-u-Abhá" ("God is Most Glorious"), it is sometimes used as a greeting between Bahá'ís.

HANDS OF THE CAUSE: Hands of the Cause were specially appointed by Bahá'u'lláh, 'Abdu'l-Bahá, and later by the Guardian; they were charged with the duties of protection and propagation of the Faith.

HAZIRATU'L-QUDS: "The Sacred Fold"; official title designating the headquarters of Bahá'í administrative activity in a particular country or region.

HOUSE OF WORSHIP: As the name suggests. There are currently seven Bahá'í Houses of Worship worldwide and an eighth under construction. In the future they will form the center of a nexus incorporating schools, hospitals, and homes for the aged.

LOCAL SPIRITUAL ASSEMBLY (LSA): an elected council that administers the affairs of the Faith on a local level. In the future it will be known as a local house of justice.

NATIONAL CONVENTION: An election held every year to elect the National Spiritual Assembly, the governing body of the country .

NATIONAL SPIRITUAL ASSEMBLY (NSA): an elected council that administers the affairs of the Faith at a national level.

NAW-RÚZ: The first day of the Bahá'í year, falling on the first day of spring.

NINETEEN-DAY FEAST: The principal regular gathering of Bahá'ís of a locality. The Feast takes place at the beginning of the month according to the Bahá'í religious calendar, and consists of three phases: devotional, consultative, and social.

OBLIGATORY PRAYERS: Three prayers revealed by Bahá'u'lláh. Bahá'ís are obligated to recite one of them daily. The choice of prayer is up to the individual believer on any given day.

PILGRIMAGE: Bahá'í pilgrimage involves travel to the Bahá'í Holy Sites in and near Haifa, Israel, where Bahá'u'lláh spent the last years of His life and is now buried.

PILGRIMS' NOTES: As the term suggests. Memoranda kept by pilgrims, frequently containing notes on conversations with 'Abdu'l-Bahá, Shoghi Effendi, or other prominent members of the Faith. Pilgrims' notes are not considered authoritative.

PIONEERS: Those who move to new locations to assist in the development of a Bahá'í community.

QIBLIH: "That which one faces; prayer-direction; point of adoration"; the focus to which the faithful turn in prayer. In Islám the Qiblih is the Ka'bah in Mecca; for Bahá'ís it is the Tomb of Bahá'u'lláh at Bahjí.

THE REMOVER OF DIFFICULTIES: A short prayer revealed by the Báb, to be said in times of need.

RIDVÁN: The Ridván Festival commemorates Bahá'u'lláh's declaration of His mission in the Garden of Ridván in Baghdad in 1863. The annual election of Local and National Spiritual Assemblies is held during this twelve-day period.

SHOGHI EFFENDI: (1897-1957) 'Abdu'l-Baha appointed His grandson Shoghi Effendi as Guardian of the Bahá'í Faith and interpreter of its teachings. His name and title are used interchangeably.

TABLET OF AHMAD: A tablet written in Arabic by Bahá'u'lláh in 1865 to a man named Ahmad, of the city Yazd. It was translated in 1924 by Shoghi Effendi, and is often used as a prayer by Bahá'ís during times of difficulty.

TABLET OF VISITATION: Either of two prayers sometimes recited to commemorate Bahá'u'lláh, the Báb, and 'Abdu'l-Bahá.

TEACHING: As suggested. In Bahá'í usage, collectively descriptive of efforts to propagate the Faith by example and by word.

TEN YEAR CRUSADE: (1953-1963) A plan of 10 years initiated by Shoghi Effendi for teaching the Bahá'í Faith. Many moved to "virgin" territories where no Bahá'ís yet lived. This plan resulted in the formation of many new National Spiritual Assemblies, and culminated in the election of the Universal House of Justice.

Travel teaching or Teaching trip: As the term suggests, a trip undertaken for the purpose of propagating the Faith.

Universal House of Justice: a nine-member body elected at five-year intervals to direct the spiritual and administrative affairs of the Bahá'í International Community.

ENDNOTES

INTRODUCTION

1. Universal House of Justice to the Bahá'ís of the World, "Announcing the convocation of 95 youth conferences around the world", 8 Feb. 2013. (the website of the Universal House of Justice. http://universalhouseofjustice.bahai.org/activities-bahai-community/.
2. Will C. van den Hoonaard, *Origins of the Bahá'í Community of Canada*. (Waterloo, ON: Wilfred Laurier Press, 1996), 303.

CHAPTER 1 • FROM OLD WORLD TO NEW

1. Emeric Sala, autobiography. Unpublished manuscript, pp. 1-2.
2. Sala, autobiography, p. 2.
3. Sala, autobiography, p. 2-3.
4. Sala, autobiography, p. 3.
5. Sala, autobiography, p. 4.
6. Sala, autobiography, pp. 5-7.

CHAPTER 2 • MONTREAL

1. Sala, autobiography, pp. 7-8.
2. Sala, autobiography, pp. 8-9.
3. Sala, autobiography, p. 9.
4. Sala, autobiography, p. 9.
5. Emeric Sala, *Some Reflections of My Early Days in the Faith in Canada*, pp. 1-2
6. Emeric Sala, autobiography, p. 10.
7. Emeric Sala and Rosemary Sala, interview by author, Guadalajara, Mexico, 1977.
8. Emeric Sala, interview by Will van den Hoonaard, 1990.
9. Emeric Sala, video interview by Rick Sala.
10. Emeric Sala, van den Hoonaard interview.

11. Ernest Harrison to Emeric Sala, 14 January 1928.
12. Shoghi Effendi to Emeric Sala, 7 March 1928.
13. Emeric and Rosemary Sala, interview by author.
14. Emeric and Rosemary Sala, interview by author.
15. Emeric and Rosemary Sala, interview by author.
16. Emeric and Rosemary Sala, interview by author.
17. van den Hoonaard, *Origins*, p. 105.
18. Sala, *Some Reflections*, pp. 6-7.
19. Violette Nakhjavani, *The Maxwells of Montreal*, vol. II (Oxford: George Ronald Publisher, 2012), p. 153.
20. Shoghi Effendi, *Messages to Canada*, 2nd ed. (Thornhill: Bahá'í Canada Publications, 1999), pp. 30-31.
21. Sala, *Some Reflections*, pp. 6-7.
22. Sala, *Some Reflections*, pp. 7-8.
23. Shoghi Effendi to Emeric Sala, 4 January 1932. In Canadian Bahá'í Archives.
24. van den Hoonaard, *Origins*, p. 79.
25. Emeric and Rosemary Sala, interview by author.
26. Rosemary Sala at Bosch Bahá'í School, 2 August 1977, Draft, p. 11.
27. Rosemary Sala: Albums at the Shrine.
28. May Maxwell to Emeric Sala, 10 May 1933. In Canadian Bahá'í Archives.
29. Emeric Sala, autobiography, p. 13.
30. Sala, autobiography, pp. 11-12.
31. Sala, autobiography, p. 12.
32. Rosemary Sala to Ilona Weinstein, 21 December 1977.
33. Sala, autobiography, p. 13.
34. Sala, autobiography, pp. 13-14.
35. Sala, autobiography, p. 14.
36. Cited by Shoghi Effendi in *The World Order of Bahá'u'lláh* (Wilmette, Illinois: Bahá'í Publishing Trust, 1991), p. 30.
37. Shoghi Effendi to Emeric Sala, 13 November 1933.
38. Shoghi Effendi to Emeric Sala, 13 November 1933.
39. Emeric Sala to Nina Robarts Tinnion, 21 December 1988. In Ninian Robarts Tinnion Papers.
40. Emeric Sala, autobiography, pp. 15-16.
41. May Maxwell to Emeric Sala, 9 June 1934. In Canadian Bahá'í Archives 154-014-01 1002/1/12.
42. May Maxwell to Emeric Sala, 9 June 1934. In Canadian Bahá'í Archives 154-014-01 1002/1/12.

43. van den Hoonaard, *Origins*, p. 214.
44. van den Hoonaard, *Origins*, p. 190.
45. van den Hoonaard, *Origins*, p. 307.
46. Abella, Irving, and Harold Troper, *None Is Too Many* (University of Toronto Press, 2012), vi.
47. Emeric Sala, autobiography, pp. 16-17.

CHAPTER 3 • THE MAXWELL FAMILY
1. Rosemary Sala Papers: Maxwell Memories, June 29, 1978.
2. Ibid.
3. Rosemary's papers, notes about May Maxwell, p. 5 (file on Maxwell Stories).
4. Rosemary Sala Papers: Maxwell Memories, June 29, 1978.
5. Emeric Sala, *Some Reflections*, pp 3-4.
6. Letter from May Maxwell to Emeric Sala, Aug. 26, 1931, in Bahá'í Archives of Canada.
7. Notes from Rosemary Sala, August 1975.
8. W. van den Hoonaard, *Origins*, p. 37. See also: Milk—A Matter of Life and Death. http://www.mccord-museum.qc.ca/en/keys/webtours/VQ_P3_6_EN.
9. W. van den Hoonaard, *Origins*, p. 88.
10. W. van den Hoonaard, *Origins*, p. 89.
11. W. van den Hoonaard, *Origins*, p. 37.
12. V. Nakhjavani, *The Maxwells*, vol. II, p. 273.
13. Notes from Rosemary Sala, August 1975.
14. V. Nakhjavani, *The Maxwells of Montreal*, vol. I (Oxford: George Ronald Publisher, 2011), pp. 8-9.
15. Notes from Rosemary Sala, August 1975, p. 4.
16. Emeric Sala, *Some Reflections*, p. 9.
17. Rosemary Sala Papers: Maxwell Memories, June 29, 1978.
18. Interview of Emeric Sala by Will van den Hoonaard, 1990.
19. Interview of Rosemary Sala by Evelyn Raynor (undated).
20. Rosemary Sala Papers : Maxwell Memories, June 29, 1978.
21. Letter from W.S. Maxwell to Dorothy Ward, May 9, 1940.
22. Letter from W.S. Maxwell to Rosemary Sala, March 8, 1947. In Canadian Bahá'í Archives 156-413-1.
23. Rosemary Sala Papers: Maxwell Memories, June 29, 1978.
24. Letter from Rosemary Sala to Amine DeMille, Mar.10, 1952.
25. Beaulac was a Bahá'í property north of Montreal, described in the next chapter.

26. Interview of the Salas by I. Weinstein, 1977, Guadalajara, Mexico, p. 14.
27. Interview of the Salas by I. Weinstein, 1977, Guadalajara, Mexico, p. 14.
28. Rosemary Sala Papers: Some incidents in the lives of May Maxwell and Rúhíyyih Khánum.
29. Rosemary Sala Papers: Some incidents in the lives of May Maxwell and Rúhíyyih Khánum.
30. Rosemary Sala Papers: Maxwell Memories, June 29, 1978.
31. Rosemary Sala Papers, Red Scribe notebook.
32. Rosemary Sala at Bosch Bahá'í School August 2, 1977 (DRAFT), p. 8
33. Ibid., p. 9.
34. Letter from Rosemary Sala to Rosemary Raynor, 11-9-74.
35. Ibid.
36. Ibid.
37. Rosemary Sala Papers: red and white 'Scribe' notebook.
38. Rosemary Sala, Travel Notes, in file South America Teaching trips.
39. Letter from Rúhíyyih Khánum to Emeric, March 22, 1946. In the author's possession.
40. Letter from Rosemary Sala to Dorothy Ward.
41. Shoghi Effendi, *Messages to Canada*, p. 179.

CHAPTER 4 • ST. LAMBERT

1. Interview of Moira, Margaret and Marjorie Lanning by Ilona Weinstein, 1998.
2. Interview of Emeric Sala and Rowland Estall by Michael Rochester, 1987.
3. V. Nakhjavani, *The Maxwells*, vol. 2, p. 302.
4. Letter from Rúhíyyih Khánum to the Salas, 22 November, 1937.
5. Emeric Sala, *Some Reflections*, p. 9.
6. Emeric Sala, unpublished autobiography, p. 17.
7. Jan Jasion, *Never Be Afraid To Dare: The Story of "General Jack"* (Oxford: George Ronald Publishers, 2001), p. 177.
8. Emeric Sala, unpublished autobiography, p. 17.
9. *World Order of Bahá'u'lláh*, p. 5.
10. Emeric Sala, "Shoghi Effendi's Question". In *The Vision of Shoghi Effendi*, pp. 189-193. See http://bahai-library.com/conferences/se.question.html for full talk.
11. Letter written on behalf of the Guardian to Emeric Sala, March 17th, 1938.
12. Rosemary Sala Papers: red and white 'Scribe' notebook.
13. Emeric Sala, unpublished autobiography, p. 18.
14. Interview of the Salas by I. Weinstein, 1977, Guadalajara, Mexico, p.17.

15. Letter from Rúhíyyih Khánum to the Salas, 10/11/39.
16. Letter from Elizabeth Cowles to Emeric, March 3, 1940.
17. Letter from Anne Savage to the Salas, March, 1940 (in file Special to family).
18. Letter from Emeric Sala to friends, March 25, 1940 (file marked Emeric, South America).
19. Letter from Emeric Sala (letter No. 3) April 27, 1940 (file marked Emeric, South America).
20. Letter from Emeric Sala (letter No. 4) June 29, 1940 (file marked Emeric, South America).
21. Letter from Rosemary, May 27, 1940.
22. From "List of Contacts During Our Stay in Caracas, Venezuela, March 15, 1940 to February 15, 1941".
23. Interview of the Salas by I. Weinstein, 1977, Guadalajara, Mexico, p. 22.
24. Ibid.
25. Ibid, p. 16.
26. Ibid, p. 18.
27. Letter from Rowland Estall to the Salas, Feb. 26, 1941. In Canadian Bahá'í Archives.
28. Interview of Emeric Sala and Rowland Estall by Michael Rochester.
29. Emeric Sala, *Some Reflections of My Early Days in the Faith in Canada*, p.10.
30. Emeric Sala, autobiography, p. 22.
31. Emeric's "Report to the family from Port Elizabeth, June 1, 1963".
32. Emeric Sala, autobiography, p. 15.
33. Emeric Sala, *This Earth One Country* (Boston: Bruce Humphries Inc., 1945), pp. 5-6.
34. Rick Sala, Family Video.
35. Letter from Emeric Sala to Ilona Weinstein, Nov. 4, 1973.
36. Letter from Edmund R. Brown to Bruce Humphries, October 18, 1944.
37. Letter from Emeric Sala to Ilona Weinstein, Nov. 4, 1973.
38. Letter from Mary E. Ketcham to Emeric Sala, May 4, 1949.
39. Letter from Bob Powers to Emeric Sala, June 15, 1947.
40. Emeric Sala, *This Earth One Country*, p. 74.
41. Letter from Anna L. Curtis to Emeric Sala, Island Workshop Press, May 4, 1950.
42. At http://babel.hathitrust.org/cgi/pt?id=mdp.39015049000832;view=1up;seq=40.
43. Letter from David M. Earl to Emeric Sala, June 17, 1950.
44. Letter from Dr. Ross Woodman to Ilona Weinstein, Oct. 7, 1994.
45. Letter from Marion Hofman to Emeric Sala, Jan.21, 1946.
46. Letter from W.S. Maxwell to Rosemary Sala, March 8, 1947. In Canadian Bahá'í Archives, 156-413-1.

47. Letter from Rúhíyyih Khánum to Emeric Sala, Feb. 26, 1947.
48. Letter from Shoghi Effendi to Emeric Sala, March 24, 1946.
49. *A Ten Year Crusade Diary for Southern Africa*, ed. L and E Johnson, Aug. 2, 1954.
50. Letter from Bahíyyih Ford to Emeric Sala, (undated), Montreal file.
51. Letter from Rosemary to Audrey Robarts, Mar. 5, 1976.
52. Draft of letter from Rosemary Sala to Rúhíyyih Khánum (undated) may be in file marked: to be re-copied... has flower border.
53. Dorothy Baker was a prominent American Bahá'í, then a member of the National Spiritual Assembly of the United States and Canada.
54. Emeric Sala, autobiography, pp.19-20.
55. From *Bahá'í World*, Volume 10. At http://bahai-library.com/docs/bw/usnsa_bahai_world_10.txt.
56. Rosemary Sala, Travel Notes, in file Central America.
57. Rosemary Sala, Travel Notes, in file South America.
58. Copy of letter from Emeric Sala to Shoghi Effendi, March 5, 1946.
59. Letter from Shoghi Effendi to Emeric Sala, March 24, 1946.
60. Letter written on behalf of the Guardian to Emeric Sala, Dec. 13, 1946.
61. Letter from Rosemary Sala to Ilona Weinstein, Jan. 22, 1978.
62. Ibid.
63. Rosemary Sala Papers : (file, Stories re Early Believers).
64. Emeric Sala, autobiography, p. 16.
65. Ibid., p.19.
66. Emeric Sala, *Two Worlds*, p. 28.
67. Interview of Emeric Sala by Will van den Hoonaard, 1990.
68. Emeric Sala, Report of Fifth Western Trip, Nov. 22-Dec. 8, 1946.
69. Ibid.
70. Emeric Sala, Draft report for the Canadian Bahá'í News Committee (1949).
71. Letter from John Robarts to Rosemary Sala, Jan. 6, 1944.
72. Letter from Rosemary to John and Audrey Robarts, Jan. 12, 1944, in John Robarts File.
73. Copy of letter from Rosemary Sala to Rúhíyyih Khánum, March, 26, 1944. In Canadian Bahá'í Archives.
74. Emeric Sala, autobiography, pp. 20- 21.
75. Canadian Bahá'í News, January, 1951, p. 12.
76. Interview of Rosemary Sala by Evelyn Raynor. [no date] Toronto, ON., pp. 16-17.
77. Letter from Ross Woodman to Ilona Weinstein, Oct. 7, 1994.
78. It was probably *Prescription for Living*, first published in 1950.

79. Letter from Rúhíyyih Khánum to Emeric Sala, Oct. 25, 1949.
80. Rosemary Sala, Pilgrim Notes – Dec. 1-9, 1952.
81. Letter from Rosemary Sala to Robert Mazibuko, Jan. 7, 1977.
82. Letter from Rosemary Sala to Jamie Bond and Palle Bishopff, Sept. 12, 1951.
83. Letter from Emeric Sala to Ilona Weinstein, 3/1/1990.
84. Letter from Rosemary Sala to Ilona Sala, Feb. 12, 1955.
85. Letter from Rosemary Sala to Amine DeMille, March 10, 1952.
86. Letter from Rosemary Sala to Amine DeMille, ca. spring, 1953.
87. Emeric Sala, autobiography, pp. 21-22.
88. Copy of letter from Rosemary Sala to Rúhíyyih Khánum, ca. May 28, 1952. 1002/1/21 Canadian Bahá'í Archives.
89. Bahá'u'lláh, *The Seven Valleys and the Four Valleys* (translated by Marzieh Gail; multiple editions), cited in Emeric Sala, *Two Worlds*, pp. 115-116.

CHAPTER 5 • AFRICA AND THE TEN YEAR CRUSADE

1. Shoghi Effendi, *Messages to the Bahá'í World 1950-1957*. (Wilmette, Illinois: Bahá'í Publishing Trust, 1971), pp. 152-153.
2. Rosemary and Emeric Sala's Pioneering Experiences during the Ten Year Crusade, p. 1.
3. National Spiritual Assembly of India to Emeric and Rosemary, Nov. 19, 1953.
4. Emeric Sala, letter to Mr. Jalal Nakhjavani, Nov. 26, 1953.
5. Emeric Sala, unpublished autobiography, p. 23.
6. Rosemary Sala Papers.
7. Richard St. Barbe Baker was a forester and early environmentalist who established The Men of the Trees.
8. Rosemary Sala, Pioneer Journey, pp. 1-2.
9. Rosemary Sala Papers: in AFRICA file.
10. Rosemary Sala, Stories Heard from Pioneers en Route to Africa.
11. A Pioneer Journey, p. 2.
12. Rosemary Sala, Stories Heard from Pioneers en Route to Africa.
13. A Pioneer Journey, pp. 2-3.
14. Postcard from Rosemary Sala to Dorothy Ward, June 29, 1954.
15. Letter from Rosemary Sala to John and Audrey Robarts, July 4, 1954.
16. A Pioneer Journey, p. 6.
17. Rosemary and Emeric Sala's Pioneering Experiences during the Ten Year Crusade.
18. Interview of the Salas by I. Weinstein, 1977, Guadalajara, Mexico.

19. Rosemary and Emeric Sala's Pioneering Experiences during the Ten Year Crusade.
20. Letter from Rosemary Sala to Hedda Rakovski, Sept.19, 1954.
21. *A Ten Year Crusade Diary for Southern Africa*, ed. L and E Johnson, Jan. 5, 1955.
22. Letter from Rosemary Sala to Ilona Sala, Feb. 12, 1955.
23. Letter from Rosemary Sala to Renee Sala, Jan. 24, 1955.
24. Emeric Sala, The Tip of the Moon, Samungu, 13-June-55.
25. Emeric Sala, unpublished autobiography, p. 24.
26. Rosemary and Emeric Sala's Pioneering Experiences during the Ten Year Crusade.
27. *A Ten Year Crusade Diary for Southern Africa*, ed. L and E Johnson, 11 Feb. 1955.
28. Postcard from Rosemary Sala to Lowell and Edith Johnson, March, 1955.
29. *A Ten Year Crusade Diary for Southern Africa*, ed. L and E Johnson, 16 Jan. 1955.
30. Ibid.
31. Andrew Mofokeng, *Tiger* (Baha'i Publishing Trust, South Africa, 2005), p. 84.
32. Ibid, pp. 84-85.
33. Ibid, p. 124.
34. Emeric Sala, 3,000 Miles Through Southern Africa, p. 1-2.
35. Letter from Shoghi Effendi to Emeric and Rosemary Sala, May 5, 1954.
36. *A Ten Year Crusade Diary for Southern Africa*, ed. L. and E. Johnson. Nov. 10, 1955.
37. Emeric Sala, 3,000 Miles Through Southern Africa, p. 2.
38. Emeric Sala, The Tip of the Moon, Samungu, 13 June 1955.
39. Emeric Sala, 3000 Miles Through Southern Africa, p. 3.
40. Emeric Sala, unpublished autobiography, p. 25.
41. Emeric Sala, The Tip of the Moon, Samungu, P.35-36.
42. http://www.bahai.org.za/cm/node/19.
43. Letter from Rosemary Sala to Dorothy Ward, May 15, ca. 1959.
44. Letter from Rosemary Sala to Robert Mazibuko, May 13, 1973.
45. *A Ten Year Crusade Diary for Southern Africa*, ed. L. and E. Johnson, 8 May 1956.
46. Letter from Rosemary Sala to Robert Mazibuko, 1974 (no month).
47. *A Ten Year Crusade Diary for Southern Africa*, ed. L. and E. Johnson, 8 May 1956.
48. Letter from Bahiyyeh Ford Winckler to the Salas, July 1, 1956.
49. Letter from Rosemary Sala to Lowell Johnson, June 28, 1956.
50. Letter from Rosemary Sala to Ilona Sala, Aug. 27, 1964.
51. In Rosemary Sala Papers.
52. Interview of Rosemary Sala by Louise Baker, 1977, Merida, Mexico.
53. Letter from Rosemary Sala to Ilona Sala, Dec. 17, 1957.
54. Letter from Rosemary Sala to Dorothy Ward, April 26 no year.
55. Letter from Rosemary Sala to Amine DeMille, Dorothy Wade and Louise Boudler, Nov. 2, 1960.

56. Hand-written on a newspaper clipping, June, 1964.
57. Robert Mazibuko, *This Side Up*, White Mountain Publications, p. 38.
58. Ibid, p. 39.
59. Letter from Robert Mazibuko to Ilona Weinstein, undated.
60. Robert Mazibuko, personal communication. (For a slightly different version of this story, see *This Side Up*, p. 69)
61. *A Ten Year Crusade Diary for Southern Africa*, ed. L. and E. Johnson, March 24, 1959.
62. Robert Mazibuko, personal communication; this is an early version of story later published in *This Side Up*, p. 71.
63. Draft of letter from Rosemary Sala to Shoghi Effendi, February 9, 1957.
64. *A Ten Year Crusade Diary for Southern Africa*, ed. L. and E. Johnson, 9 Feb. 1957.
65. *A Ten Year Crusade Diary for Southern Africa*, ed. L. and E. Johnson, 13 Dec. 1958.
66. According to Robert Mazibuko, the word is derived from "balasela" which is a verb that means "to stand out from others."
67. Ian Sogoni, transcript of remarks.
68. Letter from Emeric Sala to National Spiritual Assembly of Canada, 16 Nov., 1958.
69. *A Ten Year Crusade Diary for Southern Africa*, ed. L. and E. Johnson, 17 Feb. 1956.
70. *A Ten Year Crusade Diary for Southern Africa*, ed. L. and E. Johnson, 22 Feb. 1956.
71. Letter from Robert Mazibuko to Ilona Weinstein, undated.
72. Email from Robert Mazibuko to Ilona Weinstein, Feb. 25, 2002.
73. Robert Mazibuko, personal communication.
74. *A Ten Year Crusade Diary for Southern Africa*, ed. L. and E. Johnson, 31 May 1959.
75. Email from Robert Mazibuko to Ilona Weinstein Sept. 25, 2009.
76. Letter from Robert Mazibuko to Ilona Weinstein, undated.
77. Email from Robert Mazibuko to Ilona Weinstein, Dec. 2007.
78. Email from Robert Mazibuko to Ilona Weinstein, Feb. 24, 2002.
79. *A Ten Year Crusade Diary for Southern Africa*, ed. L. and E. Johnson, 25 Sept. 1956.
80. Letter from Robert Mazibuko to Ilona Weinstein, undated.
81. *A Ten Year Crusade Diary for Southern Africa*, ed. L. and E. Johnson, 4 Oct., 1960.
82. Ibid.
83. Ibid.
84. *A Ten Year Crusade Diary for Southern Africa*, ed. L. and E. Johnson, 23 Oct. 1960.
85. Ibid.
86. Letter from Emeric Sala to Ilona Sala, 2-1-1961.
87. Letter from Emeric Sala to Ilona Sala, Dec. 19, 1963.

89. Letter from Emeric and Rosemary Sala to John Robarts, Oct. 13, 1957, in John Robarts File.
90. Letter from John Robarts to the Salas, Oct. 26, 1957.

CHAPTER 6 • AFRICA—SHIFTING OF GEARS

1. The original text of this prayer is: "I cherish the hope that, from now on, the Beloved may bestow upon me all the strength and vigor that will enable me to pursue over a long and unbroken period of strenuous labor the supreme task of achieving, in collaboration with the friends in every land, the speedy triumph of the Cause of Bahá'u'lláh. This is the prayer I earnestly request all my fellow-brethren and sisters in the Faith to offer on my behalf." (Shoghi Effendi, *Bahá'í Administration*, pp. 51-52).
   The prayer book first published in the UK in 1941 included it at the very end of the book. That version removed the phrase "from now on" and substituted "Shoghi Effendi" for the word "me" in the first sentence.
2. See Shoghi Effendi, *Bahá'í Administration* (Wilmette, Illinois: Bahá'í Publishing Trust, 1974), p. 66 for the original of this supplication.
3. Letter from Rosemary Sala to Ilona Weinstein, Nov. 6 1977.
4. At top of page, in Rosemary's handwriting, Western Hemisphere Teaching Com. Nov-Dec.1959. From file, Bahá'í Conferences.
5. Letter from Rosemary Sala to Dorothy Ward, Dec. 13, 1959.
6. Letter from Rosemary Sala to Amine DeMille, Dorothy Wade and Louise Boudler, Nov. 2, 1960.
7. Letter from Rosemary Sala to Ted (Cardell?), April 26, 1962.
8. Emeric's Report to the Family, Port Elizabeth, June 1, 1963.
9. *A Ten Year Crusade Diary for Southern Africa*, ed. L and E Johnson, 25 July, 1961.
10. Emeric Sala, Some impressions of Seven Islands of the Indian Ocean, June 1962.
11. Emeric Sala, Some impressions of Seven Islands of the Indian Ocean, June 1962. (File, Africa, Emeric's reports).
12. Emeric Sala, Three Weeks Journey through Five Countries in West Africa.
13. Emeric Sala, unpublished autobiography, pp. 25-26.
14. Letter from Rosemary Sala to John and Audrey Robarts, Aug. 1, 1965. John Robarts Papers.
15. Letter from Rosemary Sala to Mrs. C. Lanning, June, 1967.
16. Letter from Rosemary Sala to Robert Mazibuko, June 28, 1975.
17. Letter from Rosemary Sala to Ilona Weinstein, Jan. 7, 1977.
18. Letter from Rosemary Sala to Janet and Forsyth Ward, ca. July, 1968.

19. Letter from Emeric Sala to John and Audrey Robarts, 3/11/ 1966. John Robarts Papers.
20. Emeric Sala, autobiography, p. 26.
21. Letter from Rosemary Sala to Janet and Forsyth Ward, ca. July, 1968.
22. Wiliam R. Masehla, Secretary, 15 August, 1968.
23. From Robert Mazibuko, October 12, 2009.
24. Emeric Sala, *Two Worlds*, p.40.
25. Interview of the Salas by I. Weinstein, 1977, Guadalajara, Mexico, p. 23
26. Email from Suzanne Schuurman to Ilona Weinstein, December 27, 2008.

CHAPTER 7 • MONTREAL—GUADALAJARA

1. Emeric Sala, autobiography, p. 27.
2. Emeric Sala, *Two Worlds*, p. 43.
3. Interview of Rosemary Sala by Evelyn Raynor. [no date] Toronto, Ontario, p. 12-13.
4. Letter from Rosemary Sala to the friends in South Africa, Dec.9, 1968.
5. Letter from Rosemary Sala to Robert Mazibuko, Feb. 4, 1969.
6. Letter from Rosemary Sala to Robert Mazibuko, Sept. 2, 1969.
7. Letter from Rosemary Sala to Doris Ballard, undated.
8. Letter from Rosemary Sala to Dorothy Wade, Sept. 14, 1969.
9. Emeric Sala, autobiography, p. 27.
10. Letter from Rosemary Sala to Ilona Sala, July 29, 1959.
11. Rosemary Sala Papers, in file: Asia.
12. Emeric Sala, *Two Worlds*, p. 51-54.
13. Rosemary Sala Papers, in file: Asia.
14. Letter from Rosemary Sala to Robert Mazibuko, Dec.7, 1969.
15. From Rosemary's notes, in file: Asia.
16. Letter from Rosemary Sala to Robert Mazibuko, Jan. 26, 1971.
17. Letter from Rosemary Sala to Dorothy Wade, 1971.
18. Letter from Rosemary Sala to Dorothy Wade, May 15, 1974.
19. Letter from Rosemary Sala to Robert Mazibuko, Sept. 2, 1969.
20. Email from Russell Kerr to Ilona Weinstein, August 27, 2009.
21. Letter from Rosemary Sala to friends in Africa, Montreal, St. Laurent, Outremont, etc., Dec. 1971.
22. The Colony Reporter, Guadalajara, Aug. 17, 1974.
23. Letter from Rosemary Sala to family and friends, Jan. 1972.
24. Letter from Emeric Sala to family, May 15, 1972.

25. Letter from Rosemary Sala to Ilona Weinstein, Nov. 14, 1972.
26. Words of the Guardian to Frau Consul Swartz (pilgrim's notes)
27. Letter from Rosemary Sala to Doris Ballard, undated (in Guadalajara file).
28. Letter from Rosemary Sala to Robert Mazibuko, Sept. 16, 1975.
29. Letter from Rosemary Sala to Amine DeMille, Oct. 13, 1975.
30. Stanwood Cobb, *Memories of 'Abdu'l-Bahá*. (Also in Honnold, Annamarie, *Vignettes from the Life of 'Abdu'l-Bahá*).
31. Emeric Sala, Report to International Goals Committee, May 13, 1976.
32. Ibid.
33. Letter from Emeric Sala to family, June 13, 1976.
34. The Universal House of Justice, Ridván Message, 2008.
35. Letter from Rosemary to Robert Mazibuko, no date.
36. 'Abdu'l-Bahá, *The Promulgation of Universal Peace*, (Wilmette, Illinois: Bahá'í Publishing Trust, 1982 ed.), p. 204.
37. Rosemary Sala Papers (in Maxwell Stories File).
38. Letter from Rosemary Sala to Ilona Weinstein, April 12, 1976.
39. Letter from Rosemary Sala to Ilona Weinstein, Aug. 28. 1979.
40. Letter from Rosemary Sala to Doris Ballard, Nov. 1, no year.
41. Letter to John and Audrey Robarts, Sept. 19, 1975.
42. Interview of Emeric Sala and Rowland Estall by Michael Rochester, 1987.
43. From Rosemary Sala's Papers.
44. Letter from Rosemary Sala to Louise Boudler, Erna Mattson, Priscilla Waugh, Alberta Dubin, July 9, 1977.
45. Letter from Rosemary Sala to Amine DeMille, April 17, 1977.
46. Card from Suzanne Tamas to Rosemary Sala, Feb. 26, 1977.
47. Letter from Rosemary Sala to Ilona Weinstein, Aug. 19 (no year).
48. 'Abdu'l-Bahá, *Tablets of 'Abdu'l-Bahá Abbás* (Bahá'í Publishing Committee, 1909 ed.), pp. 647-648.
49. Letter from Rosemary Sala to Renee Finlayson, Jan. 8, 1975.
50. Letter from Rosemary Sala to Leida Finlayson, Oct. 2, 1976.
51. Letter from Rosemary Sala to Angus and Bobbie Cowan (ca. 1976).
52. Letter from Rosemary Sala to Ilona Weinstein, Dec. 16, 1977.

CHAPTER 8 • THE BEAUTIFUL PROCESS OF DETACHING

1. Letter from Rosemary Sala to Lowell Johnson, March 8, 1979.
2. Letter from Rosemary Sala to friends in South Africa, May 17, 1979.

3. Letter from Rosemary Sala to Doris Ballard, April 5, 1979.
4. Letter from Gloria Faizi to Rosemary Sala, July 14, 1979.
5. Letter from Rosemary Sala to Doris Ballard, Oct. 17, 1979.
6. Letter from Doris Ballard to Rosemary Sala, Nov. 14, 1979.
7. Letter from Rosemary Sala to Doris Ballard, Nov. 27, 1979.
8. Letter from Rosemary Sala to Renee Finlayson, Jan. 10, 1980.
9. Letter from Rosemary Sala to Ilona Weinstein, Jan. 12, 1980.
10. Letter from Paul Sala to Ilona Weinstein, Feb. 11, 1980.
11. Letter from Ida Sala to Renee Finlayson, Jan. 28, 1980.
12. Emeric Sala, autobiography, p. 28.
13. Letter from Nina Robarts Tinnion to Emeric Sala, Feb. 4, 1980.
14. Emeric Sala, "About Rosemary's last days, Feb. 26, 1980".
15. Emeric Sala, Compilation of letters, 1980.
16. Letter from Nina Robarts Tinnion to Emeric Sala, March 20, 1980.
17. "In Memoriam". *The Bahá'í World*, vol. XVIII, p. 713.

CHAPTER 9 • FINAL JOURNEYS

1. Emeric Sala, autobiography, pp. 30-31.
2. Emeric Sala, autobiography, p. 32.
3. Emeric Sala's papers, 29 June, 1982.
4. Emeric Sala, autobiography, p. 32.
5. Letter from Emeric Sala to Ilona Weinstein, April 24, 1985.
6. Letter from Emeric Sala to Rúhíyyih Khánum, Aug. 26, 1990 (draft).
7. Letter from Robert Mazibuko to Ilona Weinstein, undated.
8. Letter from Emeric Sala to Gail and Jamie Bond, Nov. 23, 1953.

APPENDIX A

1. 'Abdu'l-Bahá, *The Promulgation of Universal Peace*, pp. 453–457.

APPENDIX B

1. Letter from May Maxwell to Anne Savage, August, 1912.
2. Rosemary Sala Papers (Early Montreal Bahá'ís file).
3. Letter from Rosemary Sala to Ilona Weinstein, 1973.
4. W. van den Hoonaard, *Origins*, p. 87.
5. Based on a video interview of Millie Rena Gordon by Ilona Weinstein, ca. 1991.
6. Rosemary Sala Papers, Red Scribe notebook.
7. Rosemary Sala Papers, Red Scribe notebook.
8. Letter from Rosemary Sala to Amine DeMille, April 17, 1977.
9. Rosemary Sala Papers (Bosch Bahá'í School file, p. 10).
10. Rosemary Sala at Bosch Bahá'í School August 2, 1977 (DRAFT), p. 11-12).
11. Letter from Rosemary Sala to Ilona Weinstein, June 13, 1975.
12. Interview of Rosemary Sala by Louise Baker, Mexico, Feb. 1977.
13. Letter from Rosemary Sala to Ilona Weinstein, Jan. 12, 1980.
14. Letter from Rosemary Sala to Amine DeMille, March 10, 1952.
15. Rosemary Sala Papers, Red Scribe notebook.
16. Interview of Rosemary Sala by Evelyn Raynor. [no date] Toronto, ON, p.16.

INDEX

1938 National Convention, 75–76'

'Abdu'l–Bahá: appointment of Hands of the Cause, 228; appoints Shoghi Effendi Guardian, 26, 73; biographical sketch, 238; exhortations, 127, 199; in Louis Gregory's healing, 114; and Lua Getsinger, 150; quoted, 38, 195–96, 199, 221–22; in Rosemary's dream, 27; visits Montreal, 28, 44–47, 56, 224–227, 229
Abu'l–Fadl, 45
Adler, Johanna (maternal grandmother of ES), 15
Adler, Marcus (maternal grandfather of ES), 15
African National Congress, 146
Ala'i, General Shuáu'lláh, 158
Allen, Dale, 131, 164
Allen, Kenton, 131, 164
Angelina (library helper), 143
Angkor Wat, 186
Antigua, 215
apartheid. *See* South Africa
anti-Semitism, 25, 41. *See also* Holocaust
Atlanta, Georgia, 154

The Báb: biographical sketch, 238; Shrine of, 50, 51, 53
Bahá'í Faith: administration of, 26, 161; and 1979 Islamic Revolution, 209; and political movements, 153–54, 171, 195, 197; and political non-involvement, 96, 130, 146, 151–54; in Africa, 137, 146, 164; in Canada, 104, 228; in Latin America, 93–101; in the United States, 154, 202; principles of, 222–23. *See also* race relations

The Bahá'í Faith: An Introduction (Faizi), 209
Bahá'í Houses of Worship, 159, 206, 217
Bahá'í World Congress, 162
Bahá'u'lláh: appointment of Hands of the Cause, 228; biographical sketch, 238; quoted, 118, 165, 193; translation of writings into Sesotho, 131–32
Bahá'u'lláh and the New Era (Esslemont), 24
Bahíyyih Khánum: in Mary Maxwell's dream, 57; Rosemary sees picture of, 230
Bailey, Norman, 137–38
Baker, Richard St. Barbe, 122–23, 171
Baker, Dorothy (*née* Beecher), 93, 95, 141, 229–30
Ballard, Doris, 209
Banani, Musa, 160
Basutoland, 166
Bates, Daisy, 202
Beecher, Henry C. (father of Dorothy Baker), 88
Belgrade (Yugoslavia; now Serbia), 38
Benatar, Sylvia, 138
Bennett, Irene, 124
Blake, Priscilla, 215
Bloom, Gertrude, 162
Bolgar, Natalie (aunt of ES) 39–40, 85
Bolivia, 100
Bolton, Celia, 165
Bolton, Ken, 165
Bond, Gail, 219
Bond, Jamie, 219
Brown, Bishop, 129
Brown, Mr. (publisher of *This Earth One Country*), 87–88
Brown, Ruth, 129, 134
Bucharest, Romania, 216–17
Bulgaria, 39

Calgary, Alberta, 104–105
Cambodia, 186
Canada: Bahá'í Faith incorporated, 147–48; National Spiritual Assembly, 108, 110–11, 119. *See also* individual names; individual locations
Cardiff, Wales, 122
Carcy, Agnes, 135
Carver, George Washington, 140–41
China, 184–86, 217
Cobb, Stanwood, 195–96, 201
Collins, Amelia, 231–32
Colombia, 100
Comoros Islands, 121, 164
Costa Rica, 96–97
Cowan, Angus, 205
Cowan Secondary School: library helpers, 143, 145; library project, 139–144, 146–147, 202; Sala Prize, 147
Cowles, Elizabeth, 24, 35, 78–79
Coy, Genevieve, 193, 194–95, 201
Czechoslovakia, 15, 37

Davis, Laura, 110
DeMille, Amine, 84, 202–204; involved in Cowan School Library project, 140–41

Effendi, Shoghi. *See* Shoghi Effendi
Elliot, Eddie, 226–27
Estall, Rowland: as youth, 29–33; during First Seven Year Plan (1937–1944), 82–84; elected to first Canadian NSA, 110; Emeric visits in Antigua, 215; and First Canadian Bahá'í Summer Conference (1941), 84; in Vancouver, 69
Europe: nationalism, 13–14; Salas flee, 85–86

Faizi, Gloria, 208–9
Ferraby, John, 148
Finlayson, Leida (great-niece of Salas), 205
Flournoy, Raymond, 212
Ford, Bahíyyih. *See* Winckler, Bahíyyih Ford
Fugard, Athol, 216

FUNDAEC (Foundation for the Application and Teaching of the Sciences), 100

Gabouri, Mr. (lawyer), 36–37
Gail, Marziah (Marzieh), 201
Gambia, 165
Gardner, Lloyd, 110
Getsinger, Lua, 150
Geyserville Bahá'í School, 83
Gillies, Catherine (mother of RS), 20, 40
Gillies, Helen (sister of RS), 20, 31
Gillies, Captain Malcolm (father of RS), 20, 37, 40, 117
Gillies, Margaret (sister of RS), 20, 80, 101
Ghadirian, Dr. Abdu'l-Missagh, 211–212
Glennie, Bourne, 137
Glennie, Sheila, 137
Gordon, Milly Rena, 154, 226–27
Gqola, Frederick, 146
Grant, Eva (niece of ES), 162
Grant, John (Eva's son), 162
Grant, Fred (Eva's husband), 162
Greatest Holy Leaf. *See* Bahíyyíh Khánum
Green Acre Bahá'í School, 31–32, 83, 113–115, 131, 193
Greenleaf, Elizabeth, 29, 34
Gregory, Louis, 114, 117, 230–31
Gregory, Louise, 38, 114, 230–31
Guadalajara, Mexico, 188–192
Guardian. *See* Shoghi Effendi
Guilaroff, Mrs. (Vera Raginsky's mother), 226–227

Hands of the Cause of God, 228–232
Haney, Marjorie, 159
Haney, Paul, 159
Harrison, Ernest, 25–26
Hofman, David, 32–33, 122
Hofman, Marion, 90, 122
Holocaust, 21, 85; affects Emeric's family, 38–39, 43, 85, 150, 162; victims, generally, 84–85
Hogg, Bruce, 104

Holley, Horace, 56, 75–76, 158, 193, 201
Honduras, 96
Hungary, 13, 37, 39, 86, 104, 218
  See also Sala, Emeric; individual names

Ioas, Leroy, 158, 231
Iranian (Islamic) Revolution (1979), 209
Ives, Howard Colby, 102
Ives, Mabel, 102

Jack, Marion, 38, 71, 77
Jasion, Jan, 71
Johannesburg, South Africa, 92, 129, 134, 137, 159
Johnson, Edith, 130, 146, 152–53
Johnson, Lowell, 130, 146, 152–53
Johnson, Malcolm (nephew of RS), 140
Jordan, Daniel, 122

Kampala, Uganda, 159–161
Kennedy, Dr. Rolland, 36–37
Kerr, Russell, 188
Kidder, Alice, 158, 207, 209
Kikuyu people, 122, 171
Kinshasa, Democratic Republic of the Congo, 164
Khadem, Dhrikru'llah, 158
Knobloch, Fanny, 135
Kraemer, Mr. (employment agent), 16–17
Kuna, Mr. (Emeric's employer), 22–23

Lanning sisters (St. Lambert Bahá'ís), 69
Laws, Beth, 132
Liedtke, Keith (son of Norma), 116–17
Liedtke, Klaus Harry (husband of Norma), 115–16, 218
Liedtke, Norma (*née* Sala; niece of ES), 115–117
Little Rock, Arkansas, 202
Louhelen Bahá'í School, 83, 131
Luthuli, Albert John Mvumbi (Zulu chief), 151–52

Macbean, Martha, 200
Martin, Douglas, 75
Masehla, William, 149
Matthews, Professor (South Africa), 152
Mau Mau Uprising, 122, 124
Mauritius, 163
Maxwell, May (*née* Bolles), 226; asks Shoghi Effendi to discuss Montreal community matters with Emeric, 69–70; biographical sketch, 44–50, 57–60; death, 52; and Emeric's conversion, 23–25; friendship with Salas, 33, 40; grave, 61, 99–100; in Montreal community, 29, 69; urges Emeric to go on pilgrimage, 69
Maxwell, Mary. *See* Rúhíyyih Khánum
Maxwell, William Sutherland, 44, 50–56, 117, 230
Mazibuko, Emeric Husayn Bonga, 151
Mazibuko, Robert: correspondence with Salas, 166–67, 181, 187–88; Cowan School library helper, 142–46; friendship with Salas, 170, 218; impression of Salas, 148–49, 150–51
McGill University, 153
McKay, Doris, 102
McKay, Willard, 102
Mexico: National Spiritual Assembly, 191; Salas arrive, 189; indigenous groups, 191
Mills, Montfort, 56, 117
Mofokeng, Andrew, 131–32
Mohapi, Chadwick, 166
Moncton, New Brunswick, 107
Monrovia, Liberia, 165
Montgomery, Leroy J., 89
Montalvo, Miss (El Salvador Bahá'í), 95
Montessori system, 48, 216
Moody, Dr. Susan, 208
Mottahedeh, Mildred, 198
Munirih Khánum, 76
Murday, Pouva, 163, 189
Musole, Joseph, 151–52

Nakhjavani, Ali, 124

Nakhjavani, Jalal, 120, 124
National Spiritual Assembly of the United States and Canada, 55, 62, 75–76,110
National Spiritual Assembly of South and West Africa. *See under* South Africa
"The Negro Problem: Its Significance, Strength, and Solution" (pamphlet), 89
Ndlovu, Maxwell, 131
Ngesi, Douglas (student at Cowan School), 140–41
Nicaragua, 96
Nur University, 100

Ober, Elizabeth (*née* Kidder), 158, 207
Ober, Harlan, 207
Ober, Grace (*née* Robarts), 76, 207, 224-26, 232
Olinga, Enoch, 159–60, 209
Oxford, England, 122
Panama, 191–92, 204
Pawlowska, Ola, 164
Petitt, Paul, 189
Port Elizabeth, 36, 132, 135–57, 169
Portugal, 196–97
Powers, Netta, 107–108

Qunta, Grace, 141, 151-52

race relations: in the Bahá'í Faith, 25; in Canada, 48, 226; in the United States, 154, 202. *See also* anti-Semitism; South Africa
Raginsky, Vera (*née* Guilaroff), 228
Rakovsky, Bert, 109
Rakovsky, Hedda, 199–200
Regina, Saskatchewan, 104–105
Reunion (Island), 163
Richardson, Doris, 110
Robarts, Audrey, 107, 120, 168, 233
Robarts, John, 84, 106–07, 158–59, 207; friendship with Salas, 201; member of National Spiritual Assembly of Canada, 110; named Hand of the Cause, 155–56; pioneering, 119–20, 168; personality, 233–34
Robarts, Nina, 121, 170, 211–12
Robarts, Patrick, 131
Romania, 13–14, 37, 71, 190; and Bahá'í Faith, 39, 101, 218
Romer, Annie, 102–103
Romer, Harry, 103
Root, Martha, 38, 81, 103
Ruhe, Dr. David, 192
Ruhe, Margaret, 192
Ruhi Institute, 100
Rúhíyyih Khánum, 32, 55–61, 72, 111, 158–61, 187; and Salas, 23–25, 28, 70, 216

Sala, Adolf (father of ES), 40, 42, 76, 85-86, 117
Sala, Blanca (sister of ES), 13, 34, 42, 115
Sala, Charlotte (mother of ES), 40, 42–43, 76, 84, 86
Sala, Emeric: birth and early life, 13–15; death, 218–19; dreams and premonitions, 168–69, 218; efforts to save family in Europe, 37–38, 39–42; emigrates to Canada, 15–23; 34–37; extended family, 15–16; 37–39; fluency in multiple languages, 199; spiritual observations, 118. *See also* Sala, Rosemary; Holocaust; South Africa; Venezuela; Mexico
—and Bahá'í Faith: 1938 National Convention, 75–65; 1944 Centenary, 92–93; encounters, 23–26; involved in Montreal Youth Group, 29–31; early friendship with Rosemary, 33–34; enrolls, 26–27; on National Spiritual Assembly of Canada, 110; pilgrimage, 70–75; plans to visit communities in Romania and Hungary, 39, 218; travel teaching in Latin America, 93–100
—books: *This Earth One Country,* 86–92; *Two Worlds* (unpublished), 194
—business ventures, in Montreal, 36; in Toronto, 103; in Zululand, 126–27, 134; in Port Elizabeth, 136, 149–50, 169; in China, 184

—name: first name and meaning, 151; original form of surname, 23
—personality, 35–36, 148–49, 190, dislike of ritual, 201; emphasis on character, 116; love of the outdoors, 183–84, 190; righteousness, 151–52; sense of humor, 132; talent for public speaking, 94, 131, 193, 199

Sala, Donya Vroclava Knox (second wife of ES), 215-18

Sala, Ernest (brother of ES), 13, 35, 41–42, 84, 86, 169, 218

Sala, Ida (*née* Kaplan; sister-in-law of ES), 42, 211

Sala, Nick (born Szalavitz, second cousin and brother-in-law of ES), 34, 115

Sala, Norma (niece of ES, daughter of Nick), 34, 115-17, 192, 218

Sala, Paul (brother of ES), 15, 84; aids relatives in postwar Europe, 86; becomes Bahá'í, 50; birth, 13; emigrates, 41–42; personality, 35

Sala, Renee (sister of author; niece of ES), 42, 128, 183, 209–10

Sala, Rosemary (*née* Gillies): birth and early life, 13, 20, 28; depression, 180–81; education and career, 27; pilgrimage, 112–113; visits the sick, 199–200. *See also* Sala, Emeric; South Africa; Venezuela; Mexico
—and Bahá'í Faith: encounters, 27; on National Spiritual Assembly of Canada, 110; on National Spiritual Assembly of South and West Africa, 166; serves on committee for care of Montreal Shrine, 187–88
—and Cowan School, 139–147, 202
—death, 210–14; message to Emeric, 215
—mystical nature, 111; dreams and premonitions, 116, 203, 212
—spiritual observations: on death, 117, 208; on overcoming temptation, 200–201; on life, 210
—personality: informed, 183; generosity, 167–68, 170; love of children, 204–205; love of plants and gardening, 69, 179, 189–90

Samandarí, Tarázu'lláh, 155, 158
Samandari, Ursula, 124
San Salvador, 95–96
Saskatoon, Saskatchewan, 105
Savage, Anne, 47, 79, 223–24
Schechter, Fred, 148
Schopflocher, Siegfried (Fred), 70, 228–229; and Beaulac School, 108; death, 119; elected to first National Spiritual Assembly of Canada, 110–11; friendship with Salas, 32, 36, 40–41; and teaching activities in Montreal, 30
Sears, William (Bill), 137
Segen, Al, 215
Segen, Edith, 215
Seven Year Plan (1937-1944), 77, 82–84
Shoghi Effendi: and Bahá'í theology, 91, 197–97; appointed Guardian, 26; appoints Hands of the Cause, 228; corresponds with Emeric, 26–27, 38 ; corresponds with Montreal youth group, 30–31; death, 157–59; designates Maxwell House as Shrine, 62; during Emeric's pilgrimage, 71–75; esteem for Horace Holley, 76; for Marion Jack, 77; initiates Seven Year Plan (1937), 77; initiates Ten Year Crusade (1953), 119; invites Sutherland Maxwell to work in Haifa, 52; marriage to Mary Maxwell, 55–59

See also Rúhíyyih <u>Kh</u>ánum; Seven Year Plan; specific individuals; specific places

Shook, Dr. Glen, 84, 201
Sierra Leone, 19
Silversides, Leslie, 105
Silversides, Mabel, 105
Skinner, Doris, 102
Spendlove, George, 23, 29, 31
Solt, Yvonne (cousin of ES), 84
South Africa: apartheid and race relations, 136–39, 141, 143–145, 153, 166; Bahá'í

community in, 148; National Spiritual Assembly, 148, 151–53, 166–70; Pass Laws (1952), 153; Salas investigated, 129-30, 136, 144–45; Sharpeville Massacre (March 21, 1960), 153; Suppression of Communism Act (1950), 136. *See also* individual names; individual places
Spain, 196–98
Sri Lanka, 165
St. Lambert, Quebec, 41, 69–70, 74–75
Steiner, Feri (cousin of ES), 162
Stories About 'Abdu'l-Bahá (Faizi), 209
Student Campaign for Nuclear Disarmament, 154
Suter, Bill, 108–9
Swaziland, 164
Szanto–Felbermann, Renee, 39

Takashiba, H., 105
Takashiba, Sunshine, 105
Tamas, Andy ("Tip"), 113–115, 204
Tamas, Susanne, 204
Tambo, Oliver, 152
This Side Up (Mazibuko), 142–46
Thompson, Juliet, 45, 225, 227
Tinnion, Nina Robarts, 211–12
Tirana (Albania), 39
Tumureanu, Josef, 216–17f
Turvey, Reginald, 137
Two Worlds (unpublished book by ES), 194

Uganda, 159
Umstadter, Eugene, 84
Umstadter, Lily (cousin of ES), 84
Universal House of Justice: election of, 161; Seat of, 206

Valko, Ilka (maternal aunt of ES), 14
Valko, Armin, 14
Vancouver, British Columbia, 104
Varkonyi, Erzsi (cousin of ES), 84–85
Varkonyi, Gyula, 85
Venezuela, 76–82

Vernon, British Columbia, 106
Verwoerd, Hendrik, Dr. (Minister of Native Affairs in South Africa), 132–33
Victoria, British Columbia, 104, 217

Ward, Dorothy, 52, 62
Weinstein, Ilona (*née* Sala; author; niece of ES & RS), 42–43, 69, 84–86, 113–116, 140, 153–155, 192
Weinstein, Marty (author's husband), 183
Wilhelm, Roy, 114
Winckler, Bahiyyih Ford, 92–93, 139
Woodman, Dr. Ross, 90, 110–11
Woolson, Gayle, 96
World War I, 13, 29, 39, 42,
World War II, 42–43, 53, 76–77, 84–86, 116

Xhosa, 146

Yazdí, Aziz, 124

Ziaiyyih Khanum (Diyá'iyyih K͟hánum), 59
Zulu people, Salas' impressions of, 127–29
Zululand (Kwazulu-Natal), 125–30, 132–33, 135

About the Author

Ilona Weinstein is the niece of Emeric and Rosemary Sala. She makes her home in Canada.